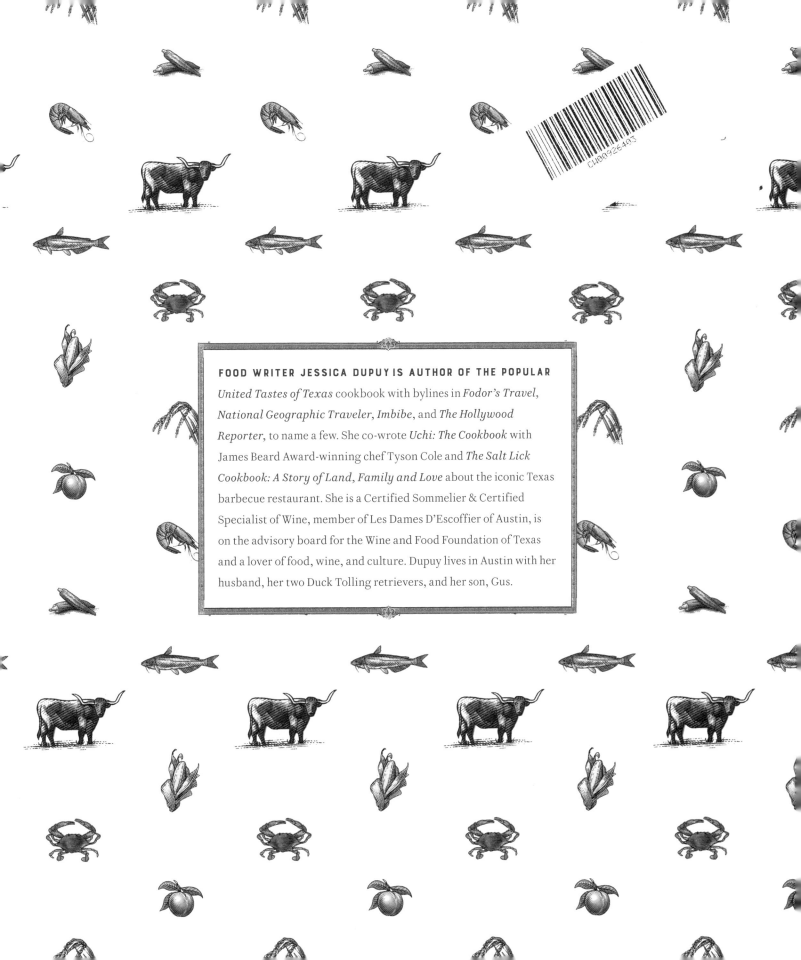

**FOOD WRITER JESSICA DUPUY IS AUTHOR OF THE POPULAR** *United Tastes of Texas* cookbook with bylines in *Fodor's Travel*, *National Geographic Traveler*, *Imbibe*, and *The Hollywood Reporter*, to name a few. She co-wrote *Uchi: The Cookbook* with James Beard Award-winning chef Tyson Cole and *The Salt Lick Cookbook: A Story of Land, Family and Love* about the iconic Texas barbecue restaurant. She is a Certified Sommelier & Certified Specialist of Wine, member of Les Dames D'Escoffier of Austin, is on the advisory board for the Wine and Food Foundation of Texas and a lover of food, wine, and culture. Dupuy lives in Austin with her husband, her two Duck Tolling retrievers, and her son, Gus.

Southern Living®

# UNITED TASTES

→→ *of the* ←←

# SOUTH

AUTHENTIC DISHES FROM APPALACHIA
TO THE BAYOU AND BEYOND

JESSICA DUPUY

Oxmoor
House®

©2018 Time Inc. Books, a division of Meredith Corporation
Published by Oxmoor House, an imprint of Time Inc. Books
225 Liberty Street, New York, NY 10281

**Executive Editor:** Katherine Cobbs

**Project Editor:** Melissa Brown

**Design Director:** Melissa Clark

**Photo Director:** Paden Reich

**Photographers:** Antonis Achilleos, Caitlin Bensel, Greg DuPree, Ben Gibson, Kelsey Hansen, Alison Miksch, Victor Protasio

**Food Stylists:** Mary Claire Britton, Torie Cox, Margaret Monroe Dickey, Emily Nabors Hall, Rishon Hanners, Karen Schroeder-Rankin, Tina Bell Stamos, Chelsea Zimmer

**Prop Stylists:** Cindy Barr, Kay E. Clarke, Missie Neville Crawford, Thom Driver, Mindi Shapiro Levine, Lindsey Lower, Claire Spollen

**Recipe Developers and Testers:** Robin Bashinsky, Adam Dolge, Mark Driskill, Paige Grandjean, Adam Hickman, Julia G. Levy, Pam Lolley, Ivy Odom, Kathleen Phillips, Marianne Williams, Deb Wise

**Associate Project & Production Manager:** Anna Riego Muñiz

**Assistant Production Manager:** Diane Rose Keener

**Copy Editors:** Donna Baldone, Rebecca Brennan

**Indexer:** Mary Ann Laurens

**Fellows:** Holly Ravazzolo, Hanna Yokeley

Trade Edition
ISBN-13: 978-0-8487-5585-0
Direct Mail Edition
ISBN-13: 978-0-8487-6086-1

Library of Congress Control Number: 2018949971

First Edition 2018
Printed in the United States of America
10 9 8 7 6 5 4 3 2 1

We welcome your comments and suggestions about Time Inc. Books.
Time Inc. Books
Attention: Book Editors
P.O. Box 62310
Tampa, Florida 33662-2310
(800) 765-6400

Time Inc. Books products may be purchased for business or promotional use. For information on bulk purchases, please contact Christi Crowley in the Special Sales Department at (845) 895-9858.

To my mom, who always has a
cup of sugar, and then some.

# CONTENTS

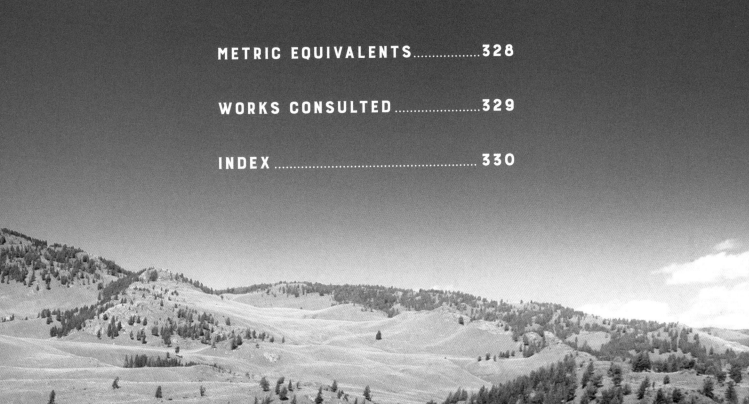

# Introduction

**THE CULINARY HERITAGE OF THE SOUTH IS A MULTICULTURAL MELTING POT.** The food of the South Carolina Lowcountry looks far different from what's on tables in the rolling hills of Kentucky or dished up in South Louisiana. And if you're not from Arkansas, the Rust Belt, the Southern Atlantic Coast, or Lake Pontchartrain, then you'll need more than a dictionary to find out what things like possum pie, leather britches, Frogmore stew, and court bouillon actually are. (Hint: None of them have anything to do with possums, leather, frogs, or a court of law.) But in a time when celebrity chefs throughout the country have looked to their own personal heritage to inspire their menus and people have looked to their own family histories to help inform their identities, it seemed like a good idea to take a deeper look at the regional dishes of the South—with its coastlines, bayous, hollers, and mountains—on a microlevel. After all, there's a lot more than just fried chicken and biscuits down here—though you will find a goodly sum of both as you cross state borders. If the eating part is more your thing than the cooking is, you'll appreciate the "Dining Detours" list at the start of each chapter, which highlights a handful of regional restaurants worth seeking out.

The entire region is a bit intimidating. Considering it includes a total of 15 states—Virginia, West Virginia, North Carolina, South Carolina, Georgia, Florida, Kentucky, Tennessee, Alabama, Mississippi, Louisiana, Texas, Arkansas, Oklahoma, and parts of Maryland—that stretch more than 1,000 miles from north to south and nearly 2,000 miles from east to west, there's quite a lot of ground to cover. These states are historically linked not only by Native Americans and the English, Scotch-Irish, French, Spanish, German, African, and Latin immigrants who settled throughout the area but also by the common experience of their alliances during the American Civil War.

To understand the South, it helps to break it into four distinct regions—Appalachia, Atlantic Coast, Gulf Coast and the Delta, and the Southwest. When you zoom in on the geographic differences and the history of how each was settled and developed, and uncover the many unique cultural traditions and cooking practices, you begin to understand why the South is one of the richest destinations on the American culinary landscape.

When I first started this book, I was strongly advised to begin my research with a few important guides, namely: *The Carolina Housewife* by Sarah Rutledge; *Southern Cooking* by Bill Neal; and *Southern Food: At Home, on the Road, in History* by John Egerton. I soon added a few other sources of inspiration including *Victuals* by Ronni Lundy, *Deep Run Roots* by Vivian Howard, and *The Potlikker Papers* by John T. Edge. While reading, I came to the conclusion that these works were complete, concise, and impressively authentic; offering much more than an inventory of recipes, they serve as a glimpse into the soul of the South.

In truth, I felt the weight of how to best represent the flavors of the South a bit daunting while reading these books. But I also found comfort. Because when it comes to Southern cooking, it's less about the ingredients and specific cooking steps—though those are certainly important—and more about time, patience, and the company with whom you're sharing these special dishes.

While periphery states such as Maryland, Oklahoma, and my home state of Texas are sometimes considered part of the region and sometimes not, depending on who you talk to, their undeniable connections to the South made it impossible to leave them out. Besides, if the old adage that you "catch more flies with honey than with vinegar" still holds true, it's best to be more inclusive than exclusive. After all, there's a little bit of the South in all of us. So slather some honey on your biscuits, grab a glass of sweet tea, and let's dig deep into the heart of Southern food.

**—JESSICA DUPUY**

# APPALACHIA

# Appalachia

**CONSIDERED THE "BACKBONE" OF THE SOUTH,** the hills of Appalachia were the wild frontier to America's earliest settlers. Land-seeking Germans brought farming methods, and the Scotch-Irish continued dairy farming, while freed slaves brought along cast-iron cookery. In addition, Czechs, Hungarians, and Jewish settlers also came. The Mountain South was settled in foothill communities in western parts of North Carolina, Virginia, West Virginia, throughout eastern Tennessee, and in the coalfields of eastern Kentucky, West Virginia, and southern Pennsylvania. In this area teeming with wildlife and edible plants, settlers learned about wild foods from the native Cherokees and built a cuisine based on farming, foraging, fishing, hunting, and trapping. Now considered five-star restaurant ingredients, earthy ramps, creek-fed watercress, morels, and river trout were as commonplace in spring as muscadines, wild boar, and sorghum syrup were in fall. This is a region of mostly meager means where mountain folk wasted nothing, cooked humble country food that was seasonal by necessity, and included beans and cornbread with almost every meal.

## DINING DETOURS

The Brown Hotel, Louisville, KY

Rhubarb, Asheville, NC

Bear Lake Reserve, Tuckasegee, NC

Arnold's Country Kitchen, Nashville, TN

Bolton's, Nashville, TN

Hattie B's Hot Chicken, Nashville, TN

Blackberry Farm, Walland, TN

Skeenies of West Virginia, Charleston, WV

Hutte Swiss Restaurant, Helvetia, WV

# CREAMY SAUSAGE GRAVY FOR BISCUITS

*Serves 6 to 8    Hands-on 20 minutes    Total 40 minutes*

1 (12-ounce) package ground pork
   sausage
1½ ounces (3 tablespoons) unsalted
   butter
¼ cup all-purpose flour

3 cups whole milk
1½ teaspoons kosher salt
½ teaspoon black pepper
1 dozen Buttermilk Biscuits (page 170)

**1.** Cook the sausage over medium-high, stirring often to crumble, until sausage is browned, about 6 to 8 minutes.

**2.** Using a slotted spoon, transfer the sausage to a plate lined with paper towels, reserving the drippings in skillet. Add the butter to the reserved drippings in the skillet, stirring until melted. Gradually add the flour, and cook, whisking constantly, until smooth, about 3 minutes. (For a darker gravy, cook the flour in the drippings to make a light brown or deep-colored roux.)

**3.** Gradually whisk in the milk, and cook, whisking often, until slightly thickened, about 8 to 10 minutes. Season with the salt and pepper, and stir in the cooked sausage. Reduce the heat to low, and simmer, whisking occasionally, until thickened, 12 to 15 minutes. If the gravy becomes too thick, stir in a little more milk. Serve with the hot biscuits.

*For some, biscuits aren't the same without a little butter and jam. For others, nothing but a plentiful ladle of creamy sausage gravy will do. In my book, you should never have to choose between the two. The key to gravy success is to watch the heat, add liquid slowly, and whisk often. This gravy is a winner spooned over most any style of biscuit.*

→→——←←
### SOUTHERN STAPLE
→→——←←

## Gravy

Gravy is essentially a spiritual sacrament in the South. Whether cream, red, brown, or even chocolate, some Southerners take gravy as seriously as they do religious holidays or college football. A happy union of flour, fat, and milk or water, for decades gravy has served as a resourceful way to add a little stick-to-your-ribs heft to a meal. Today, we often view a ladling of gravy over meat or biscuits as a bit of an indulgence, but in the South, it helped sustain generations of farmers and field-workers. Born of privation in what was once the poorest region in the nation from post-Civil War through the Depression, gravy was one of the principle ways to "make do" with what you had. It has since garnered such a stronghold in Southern cuisine that most Southerners wouldn't know how to "make do" without it.

*When it comes to farming, buckwheat has often been relied on as a type of insurance crop because of its good quality and short growing season. A kitchen pantry staple throughout Appalachia, it's a great ingredient for morning pancakes. Though gluten-free when used without wheat flour, buckwheat can have a bit of a bitter taste. This recipe includes flour and sorghum syrup to help cut the bitterness. Serve with maple syrup or Apple Butter (page 67).*

# BLUEBERRY BUCKWHEAT PANCAKES

*Serves 6     Hands-on 15 minutes     Total 30 minutes*

1 ¼ cups (about 5 ⅜ ounces) buckwheat flour

1 ¼ cups (about 5 ⅜ ounces) all-purpose flour

1 teaspoon table salt

1 tablespoon baking powder

2 cups whole milk

2 tablespoons sorghum syrup

1 cup fresh blueberries, mashed

4 ounces (½ cup) unsalted butter, melted, plus more for serving

2 large eggs, separated

Pure maple syrup or Apple Butter (page 67)

**1.** Stir together the flours, salt, and baking powder in a medium bowl. Whisk together the milk, syrup, blueberries, butter, and egg yolks in a separate medium bowl. Stir the milk mixture into the flour mixture. (Batter will be slightly thick.) Beat the egg whites in a separate bowl with a mixer on medium-high speed until stiff, 2 to 3 minutes. Carefully fold the egg whites into the batter.

**2.** Heat a large cast-iron skillet or griddle over medium. Pour the batter by ⅓ cupfuls into hot skillet, and cook until the top of the pancakes begins to bubble and edges begin to brown, 3 to 4 minutes. Turn the pancakes over, and cook other side until lightly browned, 2 to 3 minutes. Serve with the Apple Butter or additional melted butter and maple syrup.

**NOTE:** This also makes a great waffle batter.

VIRGINIA HAM
SALAD

# LOUISVILLE BENEDICTINE

*Makes 2 cups    Hands-on 10 minutes    Total 10 minutes*

1 large cucumber (about 12 ounces), peeled, seeded, and grated

10 ounces cream cheese

4 scallions, chopped (about ⅓ cup), plus more for garnish

1 garlic clove, minced (about 1 teaspoon)

8 bacon slices, cooked crisp and crumbled

1 teaspoon kosher salt

1 teaspoon black pepper

Process all the ingredients in a food processor until blended, about 30 seconds. Serve immediately, or chill in an airtight container up to 1 week. Let stand at room temperature 30 minutes before serving. Garnish with the chopped scallions, if desired.

*Benedictine, a common find at Louisville teas and lunches—not to be confused with the liqueur—is a step up from your average cucumber sandwich. Serve in the form of finger sandwiches, as a dip alongside thick crackers or toast, or as a condiment spread for grilled chicken sandwiches.*

# VIRGINIA HAM SALAD

*Serves 6    Hands-on 25 minutes    Total 1 hour*

2 tablespoons unsalted butter

1 pound leftover or thick-cut ham, trimmed and diced

½ cup finely chopped scallions (from 4 scallions)

½ cup finely chopped celery (from 2 stalks)

¾ cup finely chopped pickles (from 2 dill pickles)

⅓ cup mayonnaise

2 tablespoons Dijon mustard

¼ teaspoon black pepper

Assorted crackers

Melt the butter in a large skillet over medium-high. Add the ham, and cook, stirring often, until the edges become browned and caramelized, 7 to 8 minutes. Transfer to a medium bowl, and cool about 10 minutes. Add the scallions, celery, chopped pickles, mayonnaise, mustard, and pepper, stirring to combine. Chill at least 30 minutes before serving. Serve with the assorted crackers.

*There are a few times a year when a classic spiral-cut ham is in order for extended family gatherings. It's a rare occasion to have much ham left over, but if there is any, one of my favorite "next day" snacks is a tasty ham salad. I like to sauté cubed ham first before putting it all together. Served with crackers or in a sandwich, this salad is a perfect way to extend your holiday ham.*

*A form of English savory custard pudding, this dish is a staple at many Southern family or church gatherings, and it's often the first thing to run out. It achieves the perfect balance of sweetness from the corn and the savory ingredients.*

# CORN PUDDING

*Serves 8    Hands-on 15 minutes    Total 1 hour, 10 minutes*

Unsalted butter for greasing dish

1 ½ cups fresh corn kernels
  (from 3 ears)

¼ cup chopped scallions
  (from 2 scallions)

1 jalapeño chile, seeded and minced

1 ½ tablespoons granulated sugar

1 tablespoon fine plain yellow cornmeal

2 teaspoons kosher salt

1 cup whole milk

5 large eggs, beaten

4 ounces sharp Cheddar cheese,
  shredded (about 1 cup)

Preheat the oven to 350°F. Grease an 11- x 7-inch (2-quart) baking dish with butter. Stir together the corn, scallions, jalapeño, sugar, cornmeal, and salt in a medium bowl. Whisk together the milk, eggs, and cheese in a separate bowl until well blended. Stir the egg mixture into the corn mixture. Pour into the prepared baking dish, and bake in the preheated oven until fluffy and golden brown, about 45 minutes. Let stand about 10 minutes before serving.

⤜ ⤛

**SOUTHERN STAPLE**

⤜ ⤛

## Corn

Corn has been grown in the Americas for more than 3,000 years and remains a core ingredient throughout the United States, especially in the South. In the summer, fresh corn shines brightest in soups, relishes, salads, or straight off the cob, while cornmeal, a by-product of corn, comes in a variety of grinds from coarse to fine. The foundation ingredient in everything from hoecakes, spoon bread, tortillas, hush puppies, and muffins to pone, grits, tamales, and cornbread, cornmeal has sustained generations as part of every meal throughout the day. And, that's to say nothing of its use as a sweetener, binding agent, and in the production of bourbon and other spirits. Both white and yellow cornmeal are used throughout the region, but white cornmeal holds favor with most home cooks. On that note, they also prefer bacon grease to vegetable oil and typically eschew sugar in a recipe as the corn itself should be sweet enough.

*Simple and humble spoon bread is a savory, creamy cornbread that you...well... eat with a spoon. This puddinglike bread is thought to have some connection to a Native American recipe known as* Awendaw *and bears a resemblance to English savory puddings such as Yorkshire pudding. One helping of this indulgent, classic Southern side dish is sure to be followed by a second.*

# SOUTHERN SPOON BREAD

*Serves 8 to 10     Hands-on 15 minutes     Total 45 minutes*

5 ounces (10 tablespoons) unsalted
  butter
2 ½ cups water
1 teaspoon table salt
1 cup fine plain yellow cornmeal
½ cup whole milk
½ cup whole buttermilk

1 ounce Cheddar cheese, finely
  shredded (about ¼ cup)
½ teaspoon black pepper
¼ teaspoon cayenne pepper
3 large eggs, lightly beaten
½ teaspoon baking powder
½ teaspoon baking soda

**1.** Preheat the oven to 375°F. Grease an 8-inch square baking dish with 2 tablespoons of the butter.

**2.** Bring 2 ½ cups water and the salt to a boil in a medium saucepan over medium-high. Whisk in the cornmeal; cook, whisking vigorously, 1 minute. Reduce the heat to medium, and simmer, stirring occasionally with a wooden spoon, until just thickened, 3 to 4 minutes.

**3.** Meanwhile, combine the milk, buttermilk, and remaining ½ cup butter in a small saucepan, and bring to a simmer over high.

**4.** Stir the cheese, black pepper, and cayenne into the thickened cornmeal. Gradually add the warm milk mixture to the cornmeal mixture, and simmer, whisking occasionally, until slightly thickened, about 2 minutes.

**5.** Place the beaten eggs in a small bowl, and gradually stir in ⅔ cup of the warm cornmeal mixture. Add the egg mixture, baking powder, and baking soda to the rest of the cornmeal mixture, and stir vigorously until smooth, about 30 seconds. Pour into the prepared baking dish, and bake in the preheated oven until golden, 20 to 25 minutes.

# Travis Milton

## ROOTED IN APPALACHIA

For Chef Travis Milton, understanding the importance of heritage began when he was a young boy. He had the good fortune of knowing his paternal great-great-grandmother before she passed away when he was about 10 years old. And, though he may not have realized its significance at the time, he was able to witness a way of life through her.

"I was able to have insight into a way of life that a lot of people my age don't have access to in terms of the history of Appalachian food," says Milton. "Later, in my maternal great-grandmother's garden, we worked with heirloom vegetables that most people have really only read about and have all but been bred out of our food system."

Milton grew up in the restaurant industry. His great-grandparents owned a small restaurant in southwest Virginia, where his mom used to wait tables. Instead of preschool, Milton was often placed in a high chair in the kitchen to peel potatoes with a plastic butter knife to keep him occupied. It was a true family operation, one that initially turned Milton off as a teenager and young adult. Instead, he took a few different paths in his early career: working in radio, building race cars, and teaching English. But through it all, he cooked at home and eventually found his way into kitchens in the Northeast, challenging himself to learn more about the cutting edge of modern cuisine at places such as New York's wd-50.

And then he realized cooking was what he should have been doing all along. So, Milton went back to cook the food of his home.

"It took awhile for Appalachia to manifest itself in my cooking style, but once it clicked it really made sense that this is what I needed to do. I think to waste the food experiences I had would be a poor decision on my part," says Milton. "The love behind it and the sustaining nature of it really fits where my head and my heart are when it comes to cooking."

Milton points to leaders of Southern cuisine like Frank Stitt, Frank Lee, Sean Brock, and John Fleer who, as Milton puts it, paved the way for him to introduce the country to Appalachian food. He found work as the chef de cuisine at Richmond's Comfort restaurant, where he was given the opportunity to showcase the cooking of his heritage.

"It's not cutting-edge cuisine, but it's beautiful because it's honest and pure," says Milton. "There's this grandmotherly aspect to it, which I think is more accurate than saying it's 'humble,' because it's also soulful and has this authenticity that makes it more enchanting than something that is just simply humble."

Milton points to specific dishes such as leather britches to best represent the preservative nature of the Appalachian food culture. It's a dish with just a handful of ingredients, but it's the time required in preparation that makes it important. He recounts memories of sitting beneath an oak tree with his great-grandmother pulling and snapping beans for hours and then stringing them to dry.

"It was so boring, I'd try to find all sorts of ways to get out of it," says Milton. "But now I find it really therapeutic."

It might take four or five days before the beans are dry and ready to cook, but the process of drying them is what gives them their flavor.

"They take on this crazy pot-roast kind of flavor that is only possible if you have the patience to wait for all of those chemical reactions to take place during the drying," says Milton, who adds that the cooking is the easiest part. "If you cut any of the portions of time short, if you don't string your beans well, you're ruining the end product."

Compared to other parts of the South, Milton describes Appalachian cuisine as vegetable- and grain-dominant, with a trace of meat in the form of fats or flavor agents for cooking. "This is a food culture based largely on the land," says Milton. "Meat was a luxury, and when a hog was slaughtered for a family, every bit of it was used in cooking the vegetables grown in the garden."

For him, other classic Appalachian dishes include Apple Stack Cake, chocolate gravy, and sack sausage—an unusual sausage preparation involving air-drying and fermenting sausage. Adding to those are salt-rising bread, which has absolutely nothing to do with making the bread rise, and, one of his favorites, pickle beans, a lacto-fermented dish made of corn and beans fermented for weeks before cooking them up with bacon fat.

"And then there was cornbread; cornbread is served with everything," says Milton. "Without sugar. The corn we've grown in Appalachia was sweet enough for the bread. And when we wanted more sweetness, we would use butter sweetened with sorghum, which was our natural sweetener in the region."

The time and care required for such foods illustrates Milton's argument that Appalachian food is anything but simple. These are foods that sprang up from the many German, Czech, Irish, and Native American cultures that have long fostered a food heritage of fermented, dried, and preserved foods.

Milton now owns Shovel and Pick restaurant in Bristol, Virginia, Milton's at the Western Front in St. Paul, Virginia, and the soon-to-open (Spring 2019) Simply Grand. For him, going back to his roots has brought its own level of discovery as well. "There's this romantic notion about Appalachian food that has revealed to me something very intrinsic in the nature of its people as a whole," says Milton. "It's a culture rooted in creativity, ingenuity, and subsistence. Appalachia is the only part of the South that has four true seasons, and with that comes the need to preserve what you have in the summer to last you through the winter. You have to use everything without waste."

Milton often points to the creativity and ingenuity he witnessed through the example of his grandmother who used Red Hots candies in her apple butter because she couldn't afford real cinnamon. "It's things like that that reveal a resilience to this culture that's inspiring," he says. "What I'm doing is a continuance of that spirit."

# LEATHER BRITCHES/SHUCK BEANS

*By Travis Milton*

I have done some research and found no real rhyme or reason as to who calls them Shuck Beans and who calls them Leather Britches. I grew up knowing them as Shuck Beans and only came around to hearing the term Leather Britches as I got older and began to meet more and more cooks and chefs with ties to the region.

The process of making Shuck Beans seems rather simplistic upon initial thought, but once you start doing the work, it proves a bit laborious but well worth it. This "recipe" is more of a story than a recipe.

**The first step is choosing your pole bean.** My family had a couple preferences when it came to heirloom varieties. Typically, we used ones called Pink Tips, sometimes a Turkey Craw or Tobacco Worm, but usually it was a Greasy Bean. I realize that the number of folks familiar with the bean varieties that I just rattled off may not be in great abundance. These are old heirloom varieties that have been cherished and saved in the central part of the region for generations. It's a rarity that you would ever stumble across these varieties in a high-end grocery store, but they are a necessity when it comes to this dish. Luckily, there are many seed exchanges online, which brings me to the aforementioned first step: growing the beans. This can be a major hurdle for folks. I realize there are pitfalls for people that don't have much land to grow pole beans. My advice for people that don't have space or time to do this is to go to your local farmers' market and talk to the producers there. I have come across many farmers willing to plant seeds for customers, especially if they guarantee that the end result will be purchased.

**The second step is a two-parter: harvesting and processing.** Once the pods are full of beans, not like the haricots verts you can find at any chain grocer, they are ready to pick. Once harvested, there comes the long but almost meditative task of stringing them (and snapping them if you like). This was a part of the process that I utterly and completely abhorred when I was young. Once we got all the beans, my great-grandmother would make us all sit down under this huge oak tree in front of her house and string beans for hours on end, exactly the last thing a young teenager wants to do on a summer afternoon. Now, stringing beans is one of my favorite things to do.

After all the strings are removed, you have two options for drying. Take a needle and thread and string the beans like a popcorn garland for a Christmas tree and hang them from the ceiling. Or, snap the beans in half and lay them on a sheet in the summer sun. Take the sheets inside overnight to prevent the beans from falling prey to the early morning dew that occurs in the mountains and to make sure no critters come over for a bean snack. My family did the latter, although now I tend to utilize both methods simultaneously. I use the popcorn method for beans I dry in the restaurant due to lack of space, but it also affords me the ability to hang them over the wood fire hearths and grills, which speeds up the process as well as adds another layer of smoky flavor. Both methods are effective but do take a little time. And that depends on how full of moisture your beans are as well as atmospheric things like humidity levels in your house, etc., but it should take between one and two weeks.

Once dry, you can cook them! Just put your dried beans in a pot with a ham bone or a couple chunks of salt pork (if you strung them, remove the strings first!) and add enough water to go about two inches above them. Bring to a boil, and reduce to a simmer for 2 to 3 hours, adding water as needed if the level drops below the top of the beans. (I pull one out at the 2-hour mark and do the same every 30 minutes after that to test how done they are.) After 3 hours, cut off the heat and let them sit covered for a half hour. Then, adjust your seasoning and serve! There is a variation on this that my family used that I am fond of, but it requires yet another heirloom bean called October Shelly. These beans are typically removed from their pod, unlike the Greasy. We would add a handful of them to a pot of Shuck Beans after they had cooked for about an hour. October Shellys are very starchy, much like a Northern or a pinto bean, so their addition makes for a much creamier potlikker.

*Soup beans have long been a common fixture on the Appalachian table. As a significant part of protein in the regional diet, soup beans were a frequent food served over cornbread two or three days out of the week—often with a side of greens and fried potatoes. And, to further emphasize the preservation-minded nature of this region, the potlikker from these beans is often used as the broth for seasonal vegetables in a "next-day soup."*

# SOUP BEANS

*Serves 8   Hands-on 30 minutes   Total 12 hours, 40 minutes*

1 pound dried pinto beans
½ pound bacon slices (about 8 slices), chopped
1 ½ cups chopped white onions (from 2 onions)

2 garlic cloves (about 2 teaspoons)
2 teaspoons kosher salt
1 teaspoon black pepper

**1.** Rinse and sort the beans, discarding any stones, debris, or shriveled beans. Place the beans in a large bowl or saucepan, and add water to cover the beans by 3 inches; soak 8 hours or overnight. Drain the beans.

**2.** Cook the bacon in a large stockpot over medium-high, stirring occasionally, until the fat begins to render, about 7 minutes. Add the onion, and cook, stirring often, until tender, about 5 minutes. Add the garlic, salt, and pepper, and cook, stirring occasionally, until fragrant, about 1 minute. Add the beans, and stir well to combine. Add water to cover the beans by 2 inches. Cover and bring to a boil. Reduce the heat to medium-low, and simmer until the beans are soft and breaking, about 4 hours.

**3.** To serve just the beans, transfer about 1 cup cooked beans to a medium bowl, and mash with a potato masher. Return the mashed beans to the beans in the stockpot, stirring to thicken. If you want to use the bean cooking liquid for the "next-day soup," do not mash and add the beans. Before serving the beans, pour the bean mixture through a mesh strainer, reserving the cooking liquid in a separate bowl. Serve with cornbread and a side of chowchow or sauerkraut.

*Sour corn is a dish appreciated by Appalachian culture. It's one that requires time, but according to Chef Travis Milton, it's well worth the effort. The first part of the dish requires a two-week investment, and Milton points out that there are a lot of variables involved in fermenting and pickling, including the temperature of the room. In addition, the ambient bacteria can change the amount of time for all the necessary reactions to occur.*

# APPALACHIAN SOUR CORN

*Serves 16     Hands-on 30 minutes*
*Total 30 minutes, including 4 days brining*

24 ears fresh corn
  (such as Silver Queen)

¾ cup pickling salt
1 gallon water

**1.** Remove the husks and silks from the corn. Fill a large stockpot two-thirds full with water, and bring to a boil over high. Add the corn to the boiling water, in 2 batches if needed, and cook until tender, 2 to 3 minutes. Drain the corn in a colander, and transfer to a work surface; let stand until cool enough to handle, about 10 minutes. Cut the kernels from cobs, and transfer the kernels to a large ceramic crock or a nonreactive plastic container or bowl.

**2.** Stir together the pickling salt and 1 gallon water in a separate container until the salt dissolves. Place a couple of plates on top of the corn kernels in the crock, and pour in the salt water mixture. (The plates will keep the corn weighed down.)

**3.** Cover the crock with cheesecloth and secure with a piece of string. Brine in a cool, dry place until desired degree of sourness, at least 4 days or up to 2 weeks, checking the corn daily. During the first 2 to 3 days a film will develop on the top of the mixture. Skim it off with a clean spoon, and replace cheesecloth. The corn should taste briny, subtly sweet, and have a bit of sour, fermented flavor. Transfer the corn to 2 (2-quart) Mason jars, and add the brine to cover. Refrigerate until cold, about 1 hour. Store in refrigerator up to 1 week.

**4.** To serve, remove 1 quart corn from the container, draining off as much brine as possible. Place in a colander, and rinse well. Serve cold, at room temperature, or quickly sautéed in butter.

*No Southern meal is complete without a side of greens, whether it's collards, kale, or turnips. I like the saltiness that feta adds to this dish. The white beans add protein, making it a delicious meal on its own.*

# TURNIP GREENS AND BEANS

*Serves 8    Hands-on 20 minutes    Total 20 minutes*

3 (8 ½-ounce) bunches fresh
   turnip greens
3 tablespoons vegetable oil
1 medium-size yellow onion, thinly
   sliced (about 1 ½ cups)
3 garlic cloves, minced
   (about 1 tablespoon)
½ cup chicken broth

1 (15.5-ounce) can cannellini beans,
   drained and rinsed
¾ teaspoon kosher salt
¼ teaspoon black pepper
1 teaspoon fresh lemon juice
   (from 1 lemon)
2 ounces feta cheese, crumbled
   (about ½ cup)

**1.** Wash the greens, and let drain on a baking sheet lined with paper towels. Trim the stems from the leaves, and roughly chop the leaves. Fill a large stockpot with water (about 16 cups), and bring to a boil over high. Add the greens to the boiling water, and cook until bright green and almost tender, 1 to 2 minutes. Using a slotted spoon, remove the greens from water, and drain on paper towels; pat dry.

**2.** Heat the oil in a large, straight-sided skillet over medium-high. Add the onion, and cook, stirring often, until tender, 5 to 6 minutes. Add the garlic, and cook, stirring often, until fragrant, about 1 minute. Add the greens, chicken broth, beans, salt, and pepper; cook, stirring often, until the greens are tender, 5 to 7 minutes. Transfer the mixture to a plate; drizzle with the lemon juice, and sprinkle with the crumbled feta.

→→———←←

## SOUTHERN STAPLE

→→———←←

### Mess o' Greens

Turnip, collard, mustard, spinach, kale—it doesn't much matter which. When slow-cooked with a hunk of good seasoning meat such as a ham hock or pork back fat, a bowl of greens is a little slice of heaven. Though present throughout much of the world for centuries, their humble preparation was a soulful, nutrient-rich dish made by Native Americans and African slaves that found its way into Southern kitchens to become a permanent staple. In Appalachia, greens along with beans have long been served as a main course rather than a supportive side dish. Just be sure not to forget a hot slice of cornbread!

# SKILLET FRIED OKRA

*Serves 6    Hands-on 15 minutes    Total 15 minutes*

1 pound fresh okra
¾ cup plain yellow cornmeal
1 teaspoon black pepper
½ teaspoon cayenne pepper
2 teaspoons kosher salt
1 cup vegetable oil (or bacon drippings if you have them)

**1.** Slice the okra into ¼-inch rounds. Rinse and drain in a mesh strainer.

**2.** Combine the cornmeal, black pepper, cayenne pepper, and 1 teaspoon of the salt in a large bowl. Heat ½ cup of the oil in a 12-inch cast-iron skillet over medium-high. Drop handfuls of the okra slices into the cornmeal mixture, and toss to coat evenly. Transfer the okra to hot oil in batches; cook, stirring gently every minute or so, until the okra is tender and browned on all sides, 5 to 6 minutes. (Don't toss the few pieces that may have burned, they're the best ones.)

**3.** Add more oil as needed. Using a slotted spoon, transfer the cooked okra to a large sheet pan lined with paper towels to drain. Sprinkle with remaining 1 teaspoon salt.

*These tasty pods are a versatile vegetable. Stewed with tomatoes, simmered in a gumbo, pickled, charred on the backyard grill, or even steamed in their own special sliminess, okra has long enjoyed a place at the Southern table. But if you ask me, sliced and fried in a cast-iron skillet has always been the best way to watch these summer veggies fly into hungry mouths.*

*Slow-cooked green beans are a thing of beauty at the Southern table. Though they may be picked at the peak of freshness from the backyard garden, their ends are snipped before they're thrown into a pot with ham or bacon and simmered for a seemingly infinite amount of time. Modern-day cooks may praise the virtues of the nutrition packed in a raw green bean or those steamed for a hot minute or two, but when it comes to Southern green beans, the adage takes precedence: Good things come to those who wait.*

# KENTUCKY GREEN BEANS AND POTLIKKER

*Serves 8     Hands-on 15 minutes     Total 1 hour, 15 minutes*

2 pounds Kentucky Wonder fresh green beans, trimmed and snapped into 2-inch pieces

5 ounces slab bacon (or 5 bacon slices, rolled together and secured with a wooden pick)

2 tablespoons kosher salt

**1.** Place the beans in a heavy 6-quart stockpot. Nestle the bacon into the center of the beans, and add water to cover the beans; stir in the salt. Bring to a boil over medium-high; reduce heat to medium-low, cover, and simmer until the beans are tender, about 1 hour.

**2.** Serve warm with the potlikker, or serve with a slotted spoon, and reserve the potlikker for another use.

*A dish that pays respect to the Irish immigrants of the region, creamed potatoes come several ways. From fluffy mashed potatoes to this quartered red potato version with peas, the secret is really in the simple béchamel cream that brings a soulfulness to the plate. I always add a little lemon zest to brighten the flavors.*

# CREAMED POTATOES AND GREEN PEAS

*Serves 6 to 8    Hands-on 25 minutes    Total 25 minutes*

1 pound small red potatoes, quartered

2 cups frozen green peas

2 ounces (¼ cup) unsalted butter, cubed

2 scallions, sliced (about ¼ cup)

3 tablespoons all-purpose flour

1 ½ cups whole milk

2 teaspoons kosher salt

1 teaspoon black pepper

1 teaspoon lemon zest (from 1 lemon)

**1.** Place the potatoes in a large saucepan, and add water to cover. Bring to a boil over high; reduce the heat to medium, and simmer 10 minutes. Add the peas, and simmer 5 minutes.

**2.** Meanwhile, melt the butter in a large saucepan over medium. Add the scallions, and cook, stirring often, until tender, 3 to 4 minutes. Gradually stir in the flour until well blended. Gradually stir in the milk, and bring to a boil over medium-high. Reduce the heat to medium, and cook, stirring constantly, until the sauce is thickened, 3 to 4 minutes. Drain the potatoes and the peas, and toss with the sauce, salt, pepper, and lemon zest.

*Many in the Mountain South call sorghum "long sweetnin'" for its rich, lingering finish. Blending it with sweet potatoes is a match made in heaven. This classic casserole is a perfect addition to a holiday menu.*

## Sorghum

Sorghum is a cereal grain that grows tall like corn, and it's used for a lot more than just sweetening. First and foremost, in the United States, sorghum is used as livestock feed or turned into ethanol. It's a popular crop to grow within the drier regions of the country because it's drought resistant. Evidence suggests that sorghum made its way to America from Africa, where it has been grown for more than 4,000 years. Though most of the sorghum grown in the United States is in drylands areas throughout Kansas, Texas, Colorado, Oklahoma, and South Dakota, it has long been prized in the Mountain South. The sweet syrup yielded from boiling down the stalks of sorghum plants is served as a staple sweetener (sorghum molasses) in the South, particularly in Appalachia. Cheap and plentiful, the thick golden syrup was used in place of pricier sweeteners such as refined sugar. Those who grew up with it are partial to its deep, distinctive, earthy flavor. Whip a tablespoon or two of it into a few ounces of butter to serve alongside hot cornbread and a bowl of long-simmered greens.

# SORGHUM SYRUP SWEET POTATO CASSEROLE

*Serves 8 to 10      Hands-on 15 minutes      Total 1 hour, 15 minutes*

8 ounces (1 cup) unsalted butter, plus more for greasing dish

4 pounds sweet potatoes, peeled and cut into 1-inch chunks

¼ cup sorghum syrup

1 teaspoon black pepper

3 large eggs, beaten

2 teaspoons kosher salt

1 cup chopped pecans

½ cup packed dark brown sugar

¾ cup (about 3 ¼ ounces) all-purpose flour

**1.** Preheat the oven to 350°F. Grease a 13- x 9-inch baking dish with butter. Place the sweet potatoes in a large stockpot, and add water to cover. Bring to a boil over medium-high; reduce the heat to low, and simmer until the potatoes are tender, about 30 minutes. Drain the sweet potatoes, and place them in a large bowl. Add the sorghum syrup, pepper, eggs, ½ cup of the butter, and 1 ½ teaspoons of the salt, and mash with a potato masher until well blended.

**2.** Place the remaining ½ cup butter in a microwavable bowl. Microwave on HIGH until melted, about 1 minute. Stir together the pecans, brown sugar, flour, and remaining ½ teaspoon salt. Drizzle with the melted butter, and stir until just combined.

**3.** Pour the sweet potato mixture into prepared baking dish. Top with the pecan mixture, and bake in preheated oven until golden brown, about 30 minutes. Serve immediately.

# BABY BACK RIBS WITH SPICY CHEERWINE GLAZE

*Serves 6    Hands-on 2 hours    Total 5 hours*

**SPICY CHEERWINE GLAZE**

1 tablespoon vegetable oil

1 cup finely chopped yellow onion (from 1 onion)

1 tablespoon minced garlic (from 3 garlic cloves)

¾ cup cherry preserves

½ cup cherry-flavored soft drink (such as Cheerwine)

½ cup packed light brown sugar

½ cup unsulfured molasses

1 tablespoon Sriracha chili sauce

1 teaspoon hot pepper sauce (such as Tabasco)

**BABY BACK RIBS**

2 (2½-pound) slabs baby back pork ribs, trimmed

2 tablespoons kosher salt

1½ tablespoons black pepper

**1.** Prepare the Spicy Cheerwine Glaze: Heat the oil in a medium saucepan over medium until shimmering; add the onion, and cook, stirring often, until softened, about 4 to 5 minutes. Add the garlic, and cook, stirring often, until fragrant, about 1 minute. Add the preserves, soft drink, brown sugar, molasses, Sriracha, and hot pepper sauce, stirring to combine. Reduce the heat to low, and simmer, stirring often, until the liquid is reduced to 1½ cups, about 20 minutes. (Be careful not to scorch.)

**2.** Meanwhile, prepare the Baby Back Ribs: Sprinkle the ribs with the salt and pepper, and let stand at room temperature 20 minutes.

**3.** Prepare the charcoal fire in the smoker according to the manufacturer's instructions, bringing internal temperature to 250° to 275°F; maintain temperature for 15 to 20 minutes. Place the ribs, bone-side up, on the upper food grate, away from the charcoal; close the smoker. Smoke the ribs, covered with the smoker lid, until a meat thermometer inserted into the thickest portion registers 180°F, about 2 hours.

**4.** Remove ribs from the smoker, and baste on both sides with 3 to 4 tablespoons glaze. Wrap the ribs tightly in a double layer of heavy-duty aluminum foil, so you can reopen to baste; return the ribs to the smoker. Smoke, bone-side down, about 30 minutes. Carefully pull back the foil, and baste the meaty side of the ribs with 3 to 4 tablespoons of the glaze. Close the foil, and smoke until the meat begins to pull away from the bone, about 1 hour.

**5.** Remove the ribs from the smoker; let stand 10 to 15 minutes. Open the foil to allow the steam to escape. Drain and discard the liquid and foil. Cut the ribs between the bones to separate, and serve immediately with the remaining glaze.

*There's nothing wrong with ribs smoked in a coating of a simple meat rub; in fact, they're hard to beat. But when it comes to glazed ribs, there's something special about the cherry flavor of North Carolina's Cheerwine, a cherry-flavored soft drink, that makes the average rack of baby back ribs a weekend event—especially with the added kick of Sriracha. Don't worry, a lot of the heat dies down during the cooking process, but if you like it hot, add more to the sauce. Just be sure to warn those who'll be digging in.*

# CHICKEN AND DUMPLINGS

*Serves 6    Hands-on 30 minutes    Total 1 hour, 30 minutes*

*Hearty and comforting, this dish could easily be described as a more robust approach to chicken noodle soup. Depending on how your grandma served them, you know the dumplings are made either from rolled out dough cut into individual squares or the more abstract drop-biscuit dumpling. This recipe sort of straddles the line between the two. Be sure to leave enough space between the dumpling dough for them to rise a little bit.*

## CHICKEN

2 pounds boneless, skinless chicken breasts or thighs
1½ cups chopped carrots (from about 5 large carrots)
1½ cups chopped yellow onion (from 1 medium onion)
1½ cups chopped celery (from 4 celery stalks)
2 teaspoons kosher salt
2 teaspoons black pepper
2 tablespoons unsalted butter
2 teaspoons chopped fresh thyme
2 cups whole milk

## DUMPLINGS

1½ cups (about 6⅜ ounces) all-purpose flour
2 teaspoons baking powder
1 teaspoon kosher salt
¼ teaspoon baking soda
2 tablespoons cold unsalted butter, cut into cubes
⅔ cup whole buttermilk
1 teaspoon chopped fresh thyme

**1.** Prepare the Chicken: Place the chicken, carrots, onion, celery, and 1 teaspoon each of the salt and pepper in a large stockpot; add water to cover. Bring to a boil over high; reduce heat to medium-low, and simmer, skimming off any foam that rises, until the chicken is cooked through, 20 to 25 minutes. Transfer the chicken to a cutting board, reserving the broth in the stockpot. Let the chicken cool slightly, about 15 minutes. Pour the reserved broth through a mesh strainer into a medium bowl. Remove and reserve the vegetables. Reserve 2 cups of the broth. Shred the chicken.

**2.** Melt the butter in a large Dutch oven over medium. Add the reserved vegetables, shredded chicken, thyme, and remaining 1 teaspoon each salt and pepper; cook, stirring occasionally, until fragrant, about 3 minutes. Stir in the milk and reserved 2 cups broth; bring to a boil over medium-high. Reduce the heat to medium-low, and simmer until slightly thickened, about 10 minutes.

**3.** Meanwhile, prepare the Dumplings: Whisk together the flour, baking powder, salt, and baking soda in a medium bowl. Cut in the cubed butter with a pastry cutter until crumbly. Add the buttermilk and thyme, stirring until just combined. (Do not overwork the dough.) Turn the dough out onto a floured surface, and pat to a ¾-inch thickness. Cut the dough into 1-inch pieces.

**4.** Gently place the dough pieces ½ inch apart in a single layer on top of simmering chicken mixture. Cover and cook 20 minutes. Uncover and simmer until the dumplings are cooked through and tender, about 10 minutes.

# Sarah Steffan

## FALLING FOR THE FOOTHILLS

Sarah Steffan grew up on a farm milking goats, planting gardens, and cooking but never imagined her career would include much of the same. As a young teenager, she watched Julia Child and Chef Jamie Oliver on TV and then tinkered around her family kitchen trying to imitate their recipes. At the age of 15, she realized she could make a career out of it. Steffan went to culinary school in upstate New York at Paul Smith's College and studied in France at Le Cordon Bleu, where she did an internship in the Burgundy region of France, which she points to as one of the most seminal experiences of her life.

"I worked pastry for this little inn. Their restaurant was a converted mill that literally had a stream running right through the middle. Somehow it was also the job of the pastry chef to prep trout to order straight from the stream," says Steffan. "It was their house specialty, and when one was ordered, it didn't matter if I was in the middle of spinning ice cream, I'd have to get a trout, whack it on the head with a wooden spoon, and clean it for the chef. Then I'd go back to making desserts."

Steffan's career hit its stride with an internship at the Relais & Châteaux properties, The Point and Fearrington House Inn. She had fixed her eyes on the South, particularly the wilderness oasis of Blackberry Farm nestled at the foothills of the Smoky Mountains in Tennessee. For more than 75 years, the 4,200-acre property has operated an idyllic retreat for guests from near and far. Many come to enjoy a little luxury in the great outdoors as well as its internationally acclaimed culinary program, which has trademarked its style of food as Foothills Cuisine.

"I'd heard so much about how intentional and thoughtful their culinary program was under Cassidee Dabney. I was determined to work there," says Steffan. Her wish came true in 2015 when she became executive chef for The Dogwood.

Though armed with a broad knowledge of culinary skills and techniques, Steffan admits she had a pretty steep learning curve when it came to Appalachian food.

"I literally knew nothing about this whole genre of food," she says. "It was actually a really cool place to be because I was able to learn and discover and let everything soak in without any preconceptions. It was really an inspiring time, and witnessing the soul and thoughtfulness the whole culinary team pours into the food here has been really humbling."

At The Dogwood, Steffan is charged with building a menu that reflects the ingredient-driven nature of Appalachian cooking with a familiar, homestyle feel.

"I've loved that there is a real sense of place with the food of this region," says Steffan. "Anytime I put a dish on the menu, we talk through the idea, always asking about the purpose of the dish and how it represents the region."

With an extensive seasonal garden, forager, cheesemaker, and butcher at her disposal, Steffan has spent the past three years finding a balance between respecting the traditional foodways and weaving in creativity and fresh inspiration.

"We serve beans and cornbread in some form pretty much year-round," says Steffan. "But I lighten it up in the summer with maybe a bright bean salad tossed with cornbread croutons. Or, I'll whip up an herb-and-spice mix from our garden to roast a lamb or chicken. As we move into a new season, I'm always looking at ways to preserve what we have in abundance to last us through the coming months."

With a diverse clientele that visits Blackberry Farm from all over the world, Steffan is aware that many of the guests dining at her tables may be experiencing Southern or Appalachian food for the first time so she doesn't let any detail escape her. Whether it's infusing cordials with lavender or elderflower buds from the garden or making a quick pickle from the season's ramps, the flavor of the foothills directs her path.

"It's what I love most about what I do," she says. "This region has stolen my heart and it's my job to pass that on to our guests."

*At Blackberry Farm in Walland, Tennessee, Chef Sarah Steffan looks to the seasonal ingredients from the surrounding Appalachian region.*

# DOGWOOD CHICKEN WITH ROASTED ROOTS IN GARLIC BROTH

*Serves 4    Hands-on 35 minutes*
*Total 10 hours, 35 minutes, including 8 hours chilling*

**CHICKEN**

1 gallon cold water

3 cups sorghum syrup

1½ cups kosher salt

1 (4-pound) whole organic chicken

½ cup dried culinary lavender and
  rosemary, ground into a powder

¼ cup olive oil

1 cup chicken stock

1½ ounces (3 tablespoons) unsalted
  butter

**ROASTED ROOTS IN GARLIC BROTH**

1 large rutabaga (about 10 ounces)

2 medium turnips (about 6 ounces each)

1 large celery root (about 8 ounces)

3 tablespoons olive oil

1 teaspoon kosher salt

½ teaspoon black pepper

1½ cups chicken stock

3 thyme sprigs

1 teaspoon crushed red pepper

2 garlic cloves, shaved thin

4 ounces (½ cup) salted butter

**1.** Prepare the Chicken: Stir together the water, sorghum, and salt in a large bowl until the salt dissolves. Add the chicken; cover and chill 8 hours or overnight.

**2.** Remove the chicken from the water mixture, discarding liquid. Let the chicken stand at room temperature 1 hour before cooking.

**3.** Preheat the oven to 400°F. Tie the ends of the legs together with kitchen string; tuck the wing tips under. Place the chicken on a rack in a large roasting pan. Stir together the ground herbs and the oil in a small bowl. Loosen the skin from chicken without totally detaching the skin; rub the herb mixture under and on the skin, thoroughly coating the chicken with the mixture. Add the stock and the butter to the bottom of the roasting pan. Roast the chicken in the preheated oven until a meat thermometer inserted into the thickest part of the thigh registers 160°F, about 1 hour, basting the chicken with the drippings every 20 minutes. Tent with aluminum foil if the skin gets too dark. Let rest 20 to 30 minutes before carving.

**4.** Prepare the Roasted Roots in Garlic Broth: Preheat a second oven to 400°F, or arrange a second rack to accommodate a cast-iron skillet under the rack where the chicken is roasting in the first oven. Peel and coarsely chop the rutabaga, turnips, and celery root.

*continued on next page*

(Shape isn't important, but vegetable pieces need to be uniform in size.) Toss the vegetables with the oil in a large bowl, and stir in the salt and the pepper. Transfer the vegetables to a large cast-iron skillet, and roast in the preheated oven, stirring occasionally, until just tender, 20 to 30 minutes. Remove and set aside.

**5.** Meanwhile, simmer the stock, thyme, crushed red pepper, and garlic in a small saucepan over medium-high until reduced by about half, 10 to 12 minutes. Whisk in the butter, 1 tablespoon at a time, and continue to cook, stirring occasionally, until the stock mixture coats the back of a spoon. Drizzle 3 tablespoons of the stock mixture over the roasted vegetables and return to the oven until the vegetables are hot, 5 to 8 minutes. Serve the vegetables with the roasted chicken and the remaining stock mixture.

# ROASTED SQUASH WITH BROWNED BUTTER-HAZELNUT DRESSING

*Serves 6     Hands-on 25 minutes     Total 45 minutes*

*Corn and a wide variety of heirloom beans and peas have long been a staple at the Appalachian dinner table. Another commonly found vegetable: squash. This homey version of roasted acorn squash from Blackberry Farm chef Sarah Steffan is a perfect accompaniment with the Thanksgiving turkey.*

3 (1-pound) acorn squash, cut in half and seeded
1 tablespoon olive oil
2 garlic cloves, minced
2 fresh rosemary sprigs, leaves removed and chopped (about 1½ teaspoons)
1 teaspoon sea salt

4 ounces (½ cup) unsalted butter
1 cup hazelnuts, lightly toasted
2 shallots, thinly sliced (about ⅔ cup)
1 tablespoon fresh lemon juice (from 1 lemon)
1 teaspoon dark brown sugar
¼ teaspoon crushed Aleppo chile or crushed red pepper

**1.** Preheat the oven to 400°F. Coat cut sides of the squash with the oil; sprinkle with the garlic, rosemary, and ½ teaspoon of the salt. Place on an ungreased baking sheet, cut sides up, and bake in the preheated oven until tender, 30 to 35 minutes.

**2.** Meanwhile, melt the butter in a medium skillet over medium; cook, stirring occasionally, until the butter starts to turn golden brown and has a nutty aroma, 13 to 15 minutes. Remove the skillet from the heat. Pulse the hazelnuts in a food processor until coarsely chopped, 2 to 4 times. Stir the hazelnuts, sliced shallots, lemon juice, brown sugar, Aleppo chile, and remaining ½ teaspoon salt into the browned butter. Pour over the roasted squash, and serve immediately.

DOGWOOD CHICKEN WITH ROASTED ROOTS IN GARLIC BROTH, PG 43

ROASTED SQUASH WITH BROWNED BUTTER-HAZELNUT DRESSING

*The lore behind the name "red-eye" gravy stems from a story in which President Andrew Jackson in the early nineteenth century asked his cook— who had been drunk from drinking too much whiskey the night before—to bring him some country ham with gravy as red as his eyes. The gravy is made typically with the addition of coffee, which makes it deep in color. Allegedly, when served over ham, the dish looks like a red eye peering out from the plate. Not your average flour-based gravy, this one uses the fat from the meat, maple syrup, and coffee to get its telltale red-eye name.*

# COUNTRY HAM WITH RED-EYE GRAVY

*Serves 4    Hands-on 10 minutes    Total 10 minutes*

2 (10-ounce) country ham slices or ham steaks (about ¼ inch thick), untrimmed

2 teaspoons vegetable oil

½ cup fresh hot coffee

2 tablespoons pure maple syrup

½ teaspoon kosher salt

½ teaspoon black pepper

Hot cooked Basic Grits (page 132) or Buttermilk Biscuits (page 170)

Trim the fat from the ham slices, and cook the fat in a large cast-iron skillet over medium until melted, about 4 minutes. Add the vegetable oil and the ham, and cook until browned, 2 to 3 minutes on each side. Remove the ham, reserving drippings in skillet. Stir in the coffee, syrup, salt, and pepper, and cook until slightly thickened. Return the ham to skillet; cover and cook 2 to 3 minutes. Serve the ham topped with gravy alongside hot cooked grits or biscuits.

## The Cast-Iron Skillet

If you ask me, no Southern kitchen is complete without one. But simply owning one isn't enough. It should be well seasoned and used often. Frying, roasting, baking—all can be achieved with a cast-iron skillet. But you better know how to treat it. Before using a new one, it should be washed in hot water (no soap), dried immediately and rubbed—inside and out—with vegetable oil. Place it in a 250°F oven for an hour. After that, clean it only with hot water and kosher salt for any necessary scouring. Always dry it and "cure" by rubbing it with vegetable oil on the inside and placing it over low heat on the stove top for at least 30 minutes, then allowing it to cool before putting it away.

*Though not officially a Southern creation, Hamburger Steak made its way to this part of the country with the German immigrants in the mid-eighteenth century. A humble dish made of ground beef, at the time likely the scraps from better beef cuttings, lumped into a patty and panfried. The South warmly embraced it and smothered it with variations of brown pan gravy.*

# HAMBURGER STEAK WITH SWEET ONION GRAVY

*Serves 4    Hands-on 20 minutes    Total 20 minutes*

2 large yellow onions

1 pound lean ground chuck

1 jalapeño chile, seeded and chopped (about 3 tablespoons)

3 garlic cloves, minced (about 1 tablespoon)

1 teaspoon Worcestershire sauce

1 ½ teaspoons kosher salt

½ teaspoon black pepper

1 ½ ounces (3 tablespoons) unsalted butter

2 tablespoons all-purpose flour

1 teaspoon chopped fresh thyme

2 cups beef broth

**1.** Chop 1 onion to equal ¼ cup; thinly slice the remaining onion to equal 1 ½ cups. Set aside the slices. Using your hands, combine the beef, jalapeño, garlic, Worcestershire sauce, salt, black pepper, and ¼ cup chopped onion in a medium bowl. Shape the mixture into 4 patties.

**2.** Heat a large skillet over medium-high. Cook the patties until seared and a nice crust forms, 3 to 4 minutes per side. Transfer the burgers to a plate, reserving 2 tablespoons drippings in skillet.

**3.** Add the butter to the reserved drippings in the skillet, and return to medium-high. Add 1 ½ cups sliced onion, and cook, stirring occasionally, until the onion is tender and golden, about 4 minutes. Sprinkle in the flour and thyme; cook, stirring constantly, until the sauce becomes brown, 2 to 3 minutes. Slowly pour in the broth, stirring well to incorporate.

**4.** Reduce heat to medium, and bring the mixture to a simmer; return the burgers to the skillet. Simmer until the gravy has thickened and the hamburgers are cooked through, about 5 minutes. Serve the hamburger steaks topped with a spoonful of the gravy.

*If there's a big stew for every region, Kentucky Burgoo would be the one for Appalachia. Typically made using a variety of game meat ranging from venison to squirrel, this Kentucky classic has origins that predate the Civil War. While there are an infinite number of variations in recipes, the common threads include a variety of meats, tomatoes, corn, potatoes, beans, and a texture that's thick enough to stand a wooden spoon. This stick-to-your-ribs dish is even better as leftovers.*

# KENTUCKY BURGOO

*Serves 24    Hands-on 35 minutes    Total 2 hours, 45 minutes*

2 ounces (¼ cup) unsalted butter

2 cups chopped yellow onions
    (from 2 onions)

2 cups chopped carrots
    (from 6 carrots)

2 cups chopped green bell peppers
    (from 2 bell peppers)

3 garlic cloves, minced
    (about 1 tablespoon)

1 (3- to 4-pound) whole rotisserie
    chicken or Beer Can Smoked
    Chicken (page 268), skinned,
    boned, and shredded (about 4 cups)

1 pound beef stew meat

1 pound of your favorite pulled pork
    or Slow-Cooker Pulled Pork
    (page 57)

4 cups chicken broth or Soup Beans
    potlikker (page 28)

4 cups beef broth

4 pounds red potatoes, diced

2 cups shredded cabbage (from
    1 head)

3 (14.5-ounce) cans diced tomatoes,
    undrained

3 cups frozen or fresh corn kernels
    (from 6 ears)

1 (15.5-ounce) can cannellini beans,
    drained and rinsed

2 (6-ounce) cans tomato paste

¼ cup Worcestershire sauce

2 teaspoons kosher salt

2 teaspoons black pepper

Melt the butter in a very large stockpot over medium-high. Add the onions, and cook, stirring often, until tender, 3 to 4 minutes. Add the carrots and bell peppers, and cook, stirring often, until tender, 3 to 4 minutes. Add the garlic, and cook until fragrant, 1 minute. Stir in the chicken, beef, and pork. Add the chicken broth, beef broth, potatoes, cabbage, tomatoes, corn, beans, tomato paste, Worcestershire sauce, salt, and black pepper, and stir until blended. Bring to a boil; reduce heat to low, and simmer until the meats and the vegetables are tender, 2 to 3 hours.

→→——◄◄

## SOUTHERN STAPLE

→→——◄◄

### Wooden Spoons

I once read that "If you ain't cookin' with a wooden spoon, you ain't cookin'." It was like a revelation. While I have plenty of rubber, metal, and plastic spoons, I've always been drawn to the wooden variety. Something about them seems to be the most appropriate, as if the food itself is calling for it to be the instrument of marrying flavors. For the Southern cook, the wooden spoon is the best tool for scraping up the extra bits of flavor that get stuck at the bottom of pots and pans. The sturdy structure adds strength for stirring thicker stews and batters. Most important, it represents cooking with care. And as they say, "Cooking without care is not cooking, it's work."

*No trip to Louisville is complete without a visit to the historic Brown Hotel for a Hot Brown. A little more than your average turkey sandwich, this open-face savory treat is a great way to use leftover roasted turkey. Baked with a decadent Mornay sauce makes it indulgent. Though you can now find various versions of it throughout Louisville today, this is an adaptation of the original.*

# CLASSIC HOT BROWN

*Serves 8     Hands-on 15 minutes     Total 40 minutes*

4 ounces (½ cup) unsalted butter

½ cup (about 2 ⅛ ounces) all-purpose flour

2 cups whole milk

1 large egg, lightly beaten

3 ounces Parmesan cheese, shredded (about ¾ cup)

1 cup heavy cream

¼ teaspoon ground nutmeg

1 teaspoon kosher salt

¾ teaspoon black pepper

8 thick French bread slices

Cooking spray

2 pounds thickly sliced roasted turkey

3 ripe tomatoes, sliced (about 1 ½ cups)

16 bacon slices, crisply cooked

1 teaspoon chopped fresh thyme

**1.** Melt the butter in a medium saucepan over medium. Quickly whisk in the flour, and cook, whisking constantly, until the mixture is light brown, about 3 minutes. Gradually whisk in the milk until smooth. Bring to a boil, whisking constantly, and cook until thickened, about 1 minute. Whisk about ¼ cup of the hot milk mixture into the beaten egg in a small bowl, whisking constantly; whisk the egg mixture into the hot milk mixture in the saucepan, and cook 2 minutes, whisking constantly. Remove from heat, and whisk in ½ cup of the Parmesan until melted. Whisk in the cream, nutmeg, and ½ teaspoon each of the salt and pepper. Remove from the heat, and cover to keep warm.

**2.** Preheat the broiler with oven rack 6 to 8 inches from heat. Place the French bread slices on a lightly greased baking sheet, and spray the bread lightly with cooking spray. Place under broiler until the bread slices are lightly toasted, 30 seconds to 1 minute. Remove from oven, and top evenly with the turkey and the tomato slices; sprinkle the sandwiches with remaining ½ teaspoon salt and ¼ teaspoon pepper. Broil on baking sheet until the turkey and the tomato slices are warmed through and edges of bread slices are lightly browned, 1 to 2 minutes. Remove from oven, and spoon desired amount of the sauce over top of the sandwiches; sprinkle evenly with remaining ¼ cup Parmesan cheese. Broil until lightly browned, about 3 minutes.

**3.** Arrange 2 bacon slices in a cross shape on top of each sandwich. Top with the chopped fresh thyme; serve immediately with additional sauce.

CREAMY
COLESLAW,
PG 61

SLOW-COOKER
PULLED PORK

SKILLET FRIED
OKRA, PG 33

*There's no question that the addition of smoke from an outdoor pit brings a little magic to the average pork butt. This recipe makes no effort to compare itself to smoked pork, but if you're faced with feeding fifteen or more people at the last minute—say for a pickup tailgate party—this is a delicious and cost-effective way to do it.*

# SLOW-COOKER PULLED PORK

*Serves 15 to 18     Hands-on 10 minutes     Total 8 hours, 30 minutes*

1 (8-pound) bone-in pork shoulder (Boston butt) (Choose one with a long, flat, skinny bone on one side)
1 tablespoon plus 2 teaspoons kosher salt
1 tablespoon plus 1 teaspoon black pepper
1 (16-ounce) can cola soft drink
1 cup water
3 garlic cloves
3 celery stalks
1 medium-size white onion, halved
3 cups barbecue sauce
1 cup dill pickle chips
1 cup finely chopped white onion (from 1 onion)
Buns or white bread

**1.** Place the pork, fat cap up, in a 6-quart slow cooker. Sprinkle with 1 tablespoon each of the salt and pepper. Pour the cola over the pork. Add 1 cup water. (You may not need all the water; pork should be almost covered.) Add the garlic, celery, and onion halves. Cover and cook on HIGH until a meat thermometer inserted in pork registers 195°F, 8 to 9 hours.

**2.** Remove the garlic, celery, and onion; discard. Trim the fat cap; discard. Use tongs and a serving fork to pull pork into chunks; place in a large bowl. Wipe the cooker clean. Reduce the slow cooker temperature to WARM.

**3.** Stir together the pulled pork, 2 cups of the barbecue sauce, and the remaining 2 teaspoons salt and 1 teaspoon pepper in slow cooker until combined. Cover and keep warm until ready to serve. Serve with the dill pickles, chopped onion, buns, and remaining 1 cup barbecue sauce.

## SOUTHERN STAPLE

## Southern Soft Drinks

Though the modern-day American soda industry is a $25 billion juggernaut, it's worth noting that the nation's most iconic brands all began in the South. Many began as pharmaceutical elixirs to help remedy stomach- and headaches. (It's probably the reason your mother served you ginger ale when you were sick.) In the early 1880s, a young Charles Alderton designed an elixir formula that he later perfected in 1885 in Waco, Texas, to become Dr Pepper. Soon after, local pharmacist John S. Pemberton designed a syrup using coca leaf and the cola nut in Atlanta. He sold the formula, which was named Coca-Cola, to a pharmacist named Asa G. Candler, who formed The Coca-Cola Company, and the nation's leading soft drink was born. But Dr Pepper and Coca-Cola aren't the only Southern-born sodas. By the early twentieth century, there were many, many more:

**Pepsi-Cola**, 1898,
New Bern, North Carolina

**Barq's Root Beer**, 1898,
Biloxi, Mississippi

**Buffalo Rock Ginger Ale**, 1901,
Birmingham, Alabama

**RC Cola**, 1905,
Columbus, Georgia

SOUTH CAROLINA
COLESLAW, PG 60

# COLESLAW

## FOR ONE AND ALL

In the South, slaw isn't just an afterthought. It's as important as the barbecue it typically sits alongside. And while there are any number of variations on the cabbage-rich dish, there are a few dividing lines when it comes to the following: vinegar versus mayonnaise, shredded cabbage versus chopped, and with barbecue sauce versus without. In any case, it's not just used as a side but also as a condiment in barbecue sandwiches. Pick from these regional favorites, and you're sure to find your match.

CREAMY COLESLAW,
PG 61

WESTERN NORTH
CAROLINA COLESLAW,
PG 60

TEXAS COLESLAW,
PG 61

# WESTERN NORTH CAROLINA COLESLAW

*Serves 8 to 10    Hands-on 10 minutes*
*Total 3 hours, 10 minutes, including 3 hours chilling*

*What sets Western North Carolina Coleslaw apart is its red hue from the tomato and barbecue sauce ingredients. It's a slaw commonly served around Piedmont, and it's delicious on a pulled pork sandwich.*

2 (10-ounce) packages angel hair cabbage
1 cup shredded carrot (about 5 carrots)
1 ½ cups apple cider vinegar
⅓ cup packed light brown sugar
3 tablespoons tomato paste
1 tablespoon kosher salt
1 teaspoon crushed red pepper
1 teaspoon black pepper

Place the cabbage and the carrot in a large bowl. Whisk together the vinegar, brown sugar, tomato paste, salt, red pepper, and black pepper in a separate bowl until blended. Pour the vinegar mixture over the cabbage mixture, and toss to coat thoroughly. Cover and refrigerate at least 3 hours, or preferably overnight, before serving.

# SOUTH CAROLINA COLESLAW

*Serves 8 to 10    Hands-on 5 minutes    Total 5 minutes*

*The key ingredient in South Carolina Coleslaw is mustard—both Dijon and dry bring a little more punch to the finished product.*

2 (10-ounce) packages angel hair cabbage
1 cup shredded carrots (from 2 carrots)
½ cup apple cider vinegar
¼ cup granulated sugar
¼ cup vegetable oil
2 tablespoons Dijon mustard
1 teaspoon dry mustard
1 teaspoon celery seeds
1 teaspoon kosher salt
½ teaspoon black pepper

Combine the cabbage and the carrots in a large bowl. Whisk together the vinegar, sugar, oil, Dijon mustard, dry mustard, celery seeds, salt, and pepper in a small bowl. Pour the dressing over the cabbage mixture; toss to coat, and serve immediately.

# CREAMY COLESLAW

*Serves 8 to 10    Hands-on 10 minutes*
*Total 1 hour, 10 minutes, including chilling*

2 (10-ounce) packages angel hair
   cabbage
1 cup shredded carrots
   (from 2 carrots)
½ cup mayonnaise
¼ cup granulated sugar

1 tablespoon Dijon mustard
1 tablespoon fresh lemon juice
   (from 1 lemon)
1 tablespoon white vinegar
½ teaspoon kosher salt
⅛ teaspoon black pepper

*In addition to regional variations, the classic creamy coleslaw is something you'll find with a fair bit of consistency from state to state.*

Combine the cabbage and carrots in a large bowl. Whisk together the mayonnaise, sugar, mustard, lemon juice, vinegar, salt, and pepper in a small bowl; drizzle the mayonnaise mixture over the cabbage mixture, and toss to coat. Cover and chill 1 hour or up to overnight before serving.

# TEXAS COLESLAW

*Serves 8    Hands-on 10 minutes    Total 10 minutes*

2 (10-ounce) packages angel hair
   cabbage
1 cup shredded carrot
   (from 1 large carrot)
1 cup shredded red cabbage
1 cup chopped fresh cilantro
2 tablespoons finely chopped white
   onion (from 1 onion)

1 jalapeño chile, diced
   (about 3 tablespoons)
1 tablespoon white vinegar
½ cup mayonnaise
2 tablespoons lime juice (from 1 lime)
1 teaspoon table salt

*In Texas, you'll find slaws ranging from creamy to vinegary, but one defining characteristic is the addition of jalapeño and cilantro. That combo pairs well with barbecue as well as seafood-centric Tex-Mex dishes as well.*

Combine the cabbage, carrot, red cabbage, and cilantro in a large bowl. Whisk together the onion, jalapeño, vinegar, mayonnaise, lime juice, and salt in a medium bowl. Pour the dressing over the cabbage mixture; toss to coat, and serve immediately.

# SMOTHERED PORK CHOPS

*Serves 4     Hands-on 30 minutes     Total 30 minutes*

*In its simplest form, this warm and comforting dish brings together two of the South's most treasured ingredients: pork and gravy. Gravy can take many different forms, including the white and fluffy kind adorned with breakfast sausage and the deep coffee-colored variety served with a thick-cut slice of ham and called red-eye. In this case, the humble panfried pork chop is lovingly smothered in more of a creamy mushroom gravy. Serve these chops over rice or with a side of mashed potatoes—just be sure to cover them with a heavy hand of the good stuff.*

1 teaspoon kosher salt

1 teaspoon black pepper

1 cup (about 4 ¼ ounces) all-purpose flour, plus 1 ½ tablespoons

2 large eggs, beaten

1 cup whole milk

1 cup unseasoned dry breadcrumbs

4 boneless 1-inch-thick pork chops (about 7 ounces each)

1 tablespoon unsalted butter

¼ cup olive oil

1 cup chopped yellow onion (from 1 small onion)

8 ounces sliced fresh cremini mushrooms

2 tablespoons minced garlic (from 6 garlic cloves)

¼ cup Dijon mustard

½ cup dry white wine

1 cup chicken broth

½ cup heavy cream

1 tablespoon chopped fresh rosemary

1 tablespoon chopped fresh thyme

**1.** Combine the salt, pepper, and 1 cup of the flour in a shallow baking dish. Whisk together the eggs and milk in a small bowl. Spread the breadcrumbs in a separate shallow baking dish or pie plate. Lightly dredge the pork chops in the flour mixture on both sides. Dip the chops in the egg mixture on both sides, and then coat with the breadcrumbs on both sides.

**2.** Heat the butter and the olive oil in a large cast-iron skillet over medium-high. Add the chops, and cook until golden brown or until a meat thermometer inserted into the thickest portion of chop registers 135°F, about 5 to 6 minutes per side. Transfer chops to a wire rack; keep warm in 180°F (or as low as your oven will go) oven.

**3.** Reserve 2 tablespoons oil in skillet, and discard any remaining oil. Heat the oil in skillet over medium-high; add the onion and mushrooms, and cook, stirring often, until the onion is soft and translucent and the mushrooms are browned, about 7 to 8 minutes. Add the garlic, and cook, stirring often, until fragrant, about 1 minute. Add remaining 1 ½ tablespoons flour, and stir to coat the mushrooms and onion. Reduce heat to medium. Stir in the Dijon and wine, and simmer, stirring often, until thickened and the liquid is reduced by about half. Add the broth, and simmer, stirring occasionally, until thickened, about 4 to 5 minutes. Stir in the cream, and simmer, stirring occasionally, until thickened, about 2 to 3 minutes more. Stir in the rosemary and thyme. Spoon about ¾ cup gravy over the top of each pork chop, and serve immediately.

TURNIP GREENS
AND BEANS,
PG 32

*Coursing through the clear mountain waters of the Smoky Mountains rivers, you'll find rainbow, brown, and brook trout are plentiful and all but waiting for fly-fishing enthusiasts to present the perfect cast. Of course, most anglers adhere to the gentlemanly catch-and-release policy. But, if saving a catch or two for dinner, this simple panfried recipe is a delicious go-to way to serve up your fresh catch. Serve with cornbread and Turnip Greens and Beans (page 32).*

# CORNMEAL-DUSTED PANFRIED TROUT

*Serves 4     Hands-on 15 minutes     Total 15 minutes*

4 (6-ounce) skin-on trout fillets or 2 whole trout, cleaned, scaled, butterflied, and pin bones removed

1 ½ teaspoons kosher salt

½ teaspoon black pepper

½ cup (about 2 ⅞ ounces) fine plain yellow cornmeal

¼ cup (about 1 ounce) all-purpose flour

½ teaspoon cayenne pepper

1 tablespoon chopped fresh flat-leaf parsley

2 teaspoons chopped fresh thyme

1 teaspoon lemon zest (from 1 lemon)

¼ cup canola oil

1 tablespoon unsalted butter

Lemon wedges

**1.** Preheat the oven to 200°F. Sprinkle the fish with ½ teaspoon of the salt and the black pepper. Combine the cornmeal, flour, cayenne, parsley, thyme, zest, and remaining 1 teaspoon salt. Dip the flesh side of the trout in the cornmeal mixture, pressing and dusting by hand to adhere.

**2.** Heat 2 tablespoons of the oil in a large nonstick skillet over medium-high. Add 2 fillets, flesh side down, and cook 1 minute. Add ½ tablespoon of the butter to skillet, and cook until the skin begins to curl on the edges, 1 to 2 minutes. Turn the fish over, and cook, skin side down, until golden brown, about 1 minute. Transfer the fish from the skillet to a rimmed baking sheet, and keep warm in the preheated oven. Repeat the process with the remaining oil, fish, and butter. Serve hot with the lemon wedges.

# APPLE STACK CAKE

*Serves 12 to 14    Hands-on 45 minutes*
*Total 25 hours, 45 minutes, including 24 hours chilling*

*A true hallmark of Appalachian culture, the Apple Stack Cake has long been a symbol of the importance of community. As the story goes, at special gatherings such as barn dances or church suppers, families would each prepare a layer of this spiced cake to donate to the shindig, stacking the cake with each new attendee. Whether fact or fiction, a stack cake is a labor of love and an exercise in patience. Some recipes use dried apples while others, such as this one, opt for homemade apple butter. This Apple Butter recipe will make at least an additional pint that can be used for other purposes.*

4 ounces (½ cup) unsalted butter, softened
½ cup granulated sugar
½ cup whole buttermilk
⅓ cup unsulfured molasses
1 large egg
1 teaspoon vanilla extract
3 ½ cups (about 14 ¼ ounces) all-purpose flour, plus more for work surface
1 teaspoon ground ginger
½ teaspoon baking soda
½ teaspoon table salt
½ teaspoon ground cinnamon
¼ teaspoon ground nutmeg
Apple Butter (recipe follows)
Powdered sugar

**1.** Preheat the oven to 350°F. Spray 6 (9-inch) round cake pans with cooking spray. (You can bake the cake layers in batches of 2 or 3, depending on how many cake pans you have.) Line bottoms of pans with parchment paper, and spray parchment with cooking spray.

**2.** Beat the butter and the sugar in a large bowl with a mixer on medium speed until creamy, about 2 to 3 minutes. Add the buttermilk, molasses, egg, and vanilla, beating well. Stir together the flour, ginger, baking soda, salt, cinnamon, and nutmeg in a medium bowl.

**3.** Gradually add the flour mixture to the butter mixture, beating on low speed just until blended after each addition. (Mixture will be more like cookie dough than cake batter.) Shape the dough into a log on a lightly floured surface; cut into 6 equal portions. Place 1 portion in each prepared pan, and use fingers to gently press the dough from center to edges of pans.

**4.** Bake in the preheated oven until lightly browned, 10 to 12 minutes. Cool in the pans on wire racks 5 to 10 minutes; remove from the pans, and cool completely on wire racks, about 30 minutes. Place 1 cake layer on a serving plate or cake stand; spread with about 1 cup Apple Butter. Repeat the procedure with the remaining layers and Apple Butter, stacking each on the previous layer and ending with a cake layer. Cover and chill the cake 24 hours. Remove the cake from the refrigerator 30 minutes before serving. Garnish with the powdered sugar, if desired.

**NOTE:** The cake layers will be thin, almost resembling large gingerbread cookies.

# APPLE BUTTER

*Makes about 6 cups    Hands-on 30 minutes    Total 7 hours, 30 minutes*

12 medium apples (such as McIntosh or
    Golden Delicious), peeled, cored, and
    sliced (about 4 ¾ pounds)
2 ½ cups granulated sugar
2 teaspoons ground cinnamon

1 teaspoon ground nutmeg
½ teaspoon ground allspice
½ teaspoon ground cloves
¼ teaspoon table salt

Stir together all the ingredients in a 6-quart slow cooker. Cover and cook on HIGH
4 hours. Uncover and stir. Cook, uncovered, until the apples are tender and most of
the liquid has evaporated, 2 to 2 ½ hours. Stir and let cool at least 1 hour before using,
or transfer to an airtight container, and chill 8 hours or overnight.

*This cake is dedicated to those who believe that butter makes everything better. In the case of this cake, it's the God's honest truth. It's also one of the easiest desserts you can whip up on short notice. If you don't have any bourbon lying around, you can omit it from the sugary butter glaze, but we're willing to bet you do.*

# KENTUCKY BOURBON BUTTER CAKE

*Serves 10 to 12    Hands-on 20 minutes    Total 1 hour, 30 minutes*

**CAKE**

8 ounces (1 cup) unsalted butter, softened, plus more for greasing pan

3 cups (about 12 ¾ ounces) all-purpose flour, plus more for dusting

2 cups granulated sugar

4 large eggs

1 tablespoon vanilla extract

1 teaspoon kosher salt

1 teaspoon baking powder

½ teaspoon baking soda

1 cup whole buttermilk

**GLAZE**

¾ cup granulated sugar

2 ⅔ ounces (⅓ cup) unsalted butter

3 tablespoons bourbon

1 tablespoon water

2 teaspoons vanilla extract

**1.** Prepare the Cake: Preheat the oven to 350°F. Grease a 10-inch (10-cup) Bundt pan with butter, and dust the pan with flour. Combine the sugar and 1 cup butter in bowl of a heavy-duty stand mixer fitted with paddle attachment; beat on medium-high speed until light and fluffy, 3 to 4 minutes. Add eggs, 1 at a time, beating on medium speed until blended after each addition. Add the vanilla, and beat until blended. Place 3 cups flour in a large bowl, and whisk in the salt, baking powder, and baking soda. Gradually add flour mixture to butter mixture in 3 parts, alternately with buttermilk, beginning and ending with flour mixture. Beat on low speed just until blended after each addition.

**2.** Pour the batter into the prepared pan, and bake in the preheated oven until a wooden pick inserted in the center of cake comes out clean, 55 minutes to 1 hour. Cool the cake in the pan on a wire rack 30 minutes.

**3.** Meanwhile, prepare the Glaze: Combine all Glaze ingredients in a small saucepan, and cook over medium, stirring often, until melted and smooth, about 5 to 6 minutes. (Do not boil.)

**4.** Using a skewer or a straw, poke holes all over the cake in the pan. Slowly pour half of the Glaze over cake, letting it drip into the holes. Invert the cake onto a serving plate, and drizzle with remaining Glaze.

*There's a long-standing debate on whether buttermilk pie and chess pie are the same thing. Just take a look at any Southern recipe collection box from the past few generations and you'll see what I mean. The main difference between the two is chess pie often includes cornmeal and omits buttermilk. Either way, it's a simple pie to throw together, especially when fruit isn't in season, which is why you typically find it around Thanksgiving. This recipe raises the ante on richness with a chocolate ganache bottom and a splash of brandy.*

# BLACKBOTTOM BUTTERMILK PIE

*Serves 8    Hands-on 30 minutes    Total 2 hours*

Chilled dough from Crust (page 114)
1¼ cups semisweet chocolate chips
   (8 ounces )
¼ cup (2 ounces) brandy
⅓ cup heavy cream
4 ounces (½ cup) unsalted butter,
   melted

1½ cups granulated sugar
3 large eggs, lightly beaten
1 teaspoon vanilla extract
3 tablespoons all-purpose flour
¼ teaspoon table salt
1 cup whole buttermilk

**1.** Preheat the oven to 350°F. Roll the dough into a 12-inch circle on a lightly floured surface. Fit into a 9-inch pie pan; crimp edges. Chill until ready to fill.

**2.** Place the chocolate chips and 2 tablespoons of the brandy in a small bowl. Bring the cream to a simmer in a small saucepan over medium-high, stirring often. Remove from the heat, and pour over the chocolate; let stand 1 minute. Whisk gently until smooth. Pour into the prepared piecrust, and spread evenly. Freeze until firm, about 10 minutes.

**3.** Beat the butter and sugar in a large bowl with a mixer on medium speed until well blended, about 1 minute. Beat in the eggs, vanilla, and remaining 2 tablespoons brandy. Whisk together the flour and the salt in a small bowl; add the flour mixture to the egg mixture alternately with the buttermilk, beating until smooth after each addition. Pour over the chocolate layer in the piecrust, and bake in preheated oven until golden brown and a wooden pick inserted in center comes out clean, 1 hour to 1 hour and 10 minutes, covering loosely with aluminum foil after 50 minutes to prevent overbrowning. Cool on a wire rack 1 hour before serving.

*To me, the word cobbler always elicits images of the sunny days of summer. Perhaps because the primary fruits I remember enjoying in a cobbler were always peaches and blackberries, each of which flood the farmers' markets in the sultry summer months. But really, I'll use any ripe and flavorful fruit, such as the dewberries that grow wild in my backyard.*

# BLACKBERRY COBBLER

*Serves 6    Hands-on 20 minutes    Total 1 hour, 10 minutes*

Butter for greasing skillet

1½ pounds fresh or frozen thawed blackberries

¼ cup packed light brown sugar

2 tablespoons cornstarch

1 tablespoon vanilla extract

2 teaspoons fresh lemon juice (from 1 lemon)

½ teaspoon ground cinnamon

1¼ cups granulated sugar

1 cup (about 4¼ ounces) all-purpose flour

1 teaspoon baking powder

1 cup whole milk

2 ounces (¼ cup) unsalted butter, melted

1 large egg, lightly beaten

Vanilla ice cream, for serving

**1.** Preheat the oven to 375°F. Grease a 10-inch cast-iron skillet with butter. Stir together the blackberries, brown sugar, cornstarch, vanilla, lemon juice, cinnamon, and ¼ cup of the granulated sugar in a medium bowl; pour into prepared skillet.

**2.** Combine the flour, baking powder, and remaining 1 cup sugar in a medium bowl. Whisk in the milk, melted butter, and egg; pour over the berry mixture in skillet. Bake in preheated oven 15 minutes. Reduce oven temperature to 350°F, and bake until deep golden brown and berry juices thicken, 40 to 45 minutes. (Tent with aluminum foil if edges become too brown.) Let stand 10 minutes before serving. Serve with ice cream.

## SOUTHERN STAPLE

## The Sonker

Originally from Surry County, North Carolina, the sonker is a regional dessert that falls somewhere between a potpie and a cobbler. It was often made to stretch seasonal fruits, such as blackberries, peaches, raspberries, huckleberries, and apples. You'll even find them made with sweet potatoes. Prepared similarly to a cobbler, the sonker typically has a cake-like batter or pie dough placed on top of fruit in a baking dish and baked until the crust is golden brown and the sweet fruit is bubbling beneath. While a scoop of vanilla ice cream is a perfectly fine accompaniment, the traditional topping is a special glaze made of cream, sugar or molasses, and a few drops of vanilla extract. It's usually poured over the sonker in the dish.

# Sheri Castle

## FIVE TRUTHS ABOUT CHOCOLATE GRAVY, ACCORDING TO THE GRAVY WHISPERER

Sheri Castle has long been a food writer and storyteller with a penchant for championing Southern foodways—particularly for Appalachia. But among those who know her well, Castle has garnered a prolific reputation as the Gravy Whisperer. That's because when it comes to any sauce containing flour, fat, and liquid to accompany any number of classic Southern dishes, Castle is a wizard. And when it comes to the unlikely Appalachian delicacy of chocolate gravy, she is a tireless evangelist.

"To be honest, the two words together really don't make any sense," says Castle. "Which is probably why it was never really well known, even in its heyday. For most people, chocolate and gravy are not supposed to be together. But once they have a chance to taste it, they realize how truly wrong they are."

Castle aimed to remedy that beginning with her 2011 book *The New Southern Garden Cookbook*. It includes a recipe for chocolate gravy with biscuits that had very little to do with a garden at all, save for the strawberries served on top. But to Castle the story of chocolate gravy deserved some much-needed attention.

### 1) WHY IT'S GRAVY

Despite its curious name, this sweet has earned its name as a true gravy by nature of its cooking method.

"The reason it's called gravy is because it's widely accepted in the South that any sauce—whether sweet or savory—that includes a roux in some form and was made in a skillet is known as a gravy," says Castle. "There's even evidence that the original icing for red velvet cake was called a gravy icing because it was flour-based and made in a skillet."

### 2) CHOCOLATE GRAVY BELONGS TO APPALACHIA

Through Castle's extensive research, there isn't documentation of one specific person inventing chocolate gravy, but there is evidence that points to its origins somewhere in the Appalachian Mountains with mention of it in East Tennessee as well as in the Ozark Mountains.

"The beauty of it shows the resourcefulness of mountain farm cooks because most people had access to dairy ingredients and the other ingredients were relatively available," says Castle.

### 3) THE FIVE MAIN INGREDIENTS

According to Castle, tweaks and additions to the standard chocolate gravy recipe may have been made over the years, but in its simplest form, the velvety sauce is made with five ingredients: milk, flour, butter, cocoa, and sugar.

"And it's always refined sugar," says Castle. "Never molasses, sorghum, or brown sugar. Part of what made it special was the use of refined sugar, which, in harder economic times, was considered a luxury."

This combination of homestead products such as butter and milk, combined with simple shelf-stable commodities—cocoa, flour, and sugar—from the local country store made it an accessible treat for many Appalachian families. In some circumstances, people would use water instead of milk, and if butter wasn't available, it wasn't uncommon for home cooks to use a little bacon grease instead.

### 4) CHOCOLATE GRAVY WAS MEANT FOR BISCUITS

Considering it's essentially a chocolate fudge sauce, there are many ways it can be served—like over scoops of ice cream. But traditionally, chocolate gravy has one true companion. "It's biscuits," says Castle. "Not cornbread, not white bread—biscuits. And, it's always served for breakfast.

### 5) THE SWEET TREAT FOR THE COMMON MAN

It's worth noting that chocolate gravy and biscuits wasn't an everyday dish. It was usually for celebrations or special occasions. The simplicity of the dish made it accessible to everyone.

Though her specific recipe is well guarded, Castle's version falls somewhere between being thicker than fudge sauce and thinner than chocolate pudding. Stick to the five main ingredients and keep these consistency goals in mind, and you'll be on your way to serving a true Appalachian treasure.

*Ask most anyone in Appalachia about their regional foods and chocolate gravy is bound to come up. A simple chocolate sauce, its composition with flour and milk in a skillet is what makes it a gravy. According to the region's affectionately dubbed "Gravy Whisperer," food writer Sheri Castle, this is a sweet treat that is defined by its use of refined sugar, a precious commodity that was typically used for a special occasion. Though delicious on anything from a bowl of ice cream to a pint of fresh strawberries, this recipe, inspired by Castle's, is most traditionally served over biscuits.*

# CHOCOLATE GRAVY

*Serves 10    Hands-on 15 minutes    Total 15 minutes*

¼ cup unsweetened cocoa

3 tablespoons all-purpose flour

¾ cup granulated sugar

2 tablespoons unsalted butter

2 cups whole milk

2 teaspoons vanilla extract

Pinch of kosher salt

**1.** Whisk together the cocoa, flour, and sugar in a medium bowl, removing all lumps.

**2.** Melt the butter in a large cast-iron skillet over medium. Gradually whisk in the cocoa mixture until well combined and thick. Gradually whisk in the milk, whisking vigorously until the mixture is well blended. Bring to a boil, whisking constantly; boil, whisking constantly, until thickened, about 1 minute. Remove from heat, and whisk in the vanilla and the salt. Serve immediately.

## The Strawberry: The Favorite State Fruit

There's no question that the strawberry is a favorite fruit among many. Packed with vitamins C and A, iron, antioxidants, and fiber, the little sixty-calorie berry is a powerful bite of nutrition. The little berry is so well loved that it's been designated an official state fruit of Louisiana, North Carolina, and Oklahoma. Louisiana was the first to christen the berry in 1980, followed by North Carolina in 2001, which also included the blueberry as a co-state fruit. Oklahoma was the more recent adopter in 2005, crowning it in honor of Stilwell, Oklahoma's annual strawberry festival, which has been running since 1948.

*There's just something about the sound of an ice-cream machine churning away in the corner of the kitchen that signals the arrival of a special summer treat. Roasted strawberries are a delicious addition to just about any breakfast bread or dessert, and they're the superb ingredient to swirl into this rich ice cream. The cream cheese and buttermilk give this frozen delight a bit of a tang. Make this a main attraction by dressing it up as a strawberry shortcake sundae with Appalachian-style chocolate gravy. It's a great way to use biscuits left over from breakfast.*

# ROASTED STRAWBERRY ICE-CREAM SHORTCAKE WITH CHOCOLATE GRAVY

*Serves 10     Hands-on 30 minutes     Total 5 hours, 30 minutes*

2 cups fresh strawberries, hulled and cut into ½-inch-thick slices
1½ cups plus 2 tablespoons granulated sugar
3 tablespoons fresh lemon juice (from 2 lemons)
2 tablespoons cornstarch
⅛ teaspoon table salt

2½ cups whole milk
4 tablespoons strawberry cream cheese spread
½ cup whole buttermilk
10 Buttermilk Biscuits (page 170)
2 tablespoons unsalted butter, softened
Chocolate Gravy (page 75), warmed

**1.** Preheat the oven to 350°F. Spread the strawberries in a single layer on a rimmed baking sheet; sprinkle with ½ cup of the sugar. Roast in preheated oven until just soft, about 10 minutes. Remove from oven, and cool 10 minutes. Transfer the berries and the pan juices to a blender or food processor, and add the lemon juice; process until pureed. Reserve ½ cup puree for ice cream; cover and chill remaining ½ cup puree for topping.

**2.** Whisk together the cornstarch, salt, and 1 cup of sugar in a medium saucepan; gradually whisk in the milk. Bring to a boil over medium, whisking constantly. Boil, whisking constantly, 1 minute. Remove from heat, and whisk in the cream cheese, buttermilk, and reserved ½ cup puree until smooth. Place pan immediately in a large bowl of ice to cool quickly.

**3.** Place plastic wrap directly on surface of cooled mixture, and place pan and ice bath in refrigerator. Let chill at least 30 minutes, adding more ice, if necessary.

**4.** Pour the chilled milk mixture into frozen freezer bowl of a 2-quart electric

ice-cream maker, and proceed according to manufacturer's instructions. Transfer the ice cream to an airtight freezer-safe container, and place a piece of plastic wrap or parchment paper directly on surface of the ice cream to prevent ice crystals. Freeze in coldest part of freezer until firm, at least 4 hours.

**5.** When ready to serve, preheat broiler with oven rack 5 to 6 inches from heat. Split the biscuits in half, and place on a small baking sheet. Spread the butter on cut sides of the biscuits, and sprinkle with remaining 2 tablespoons sugar. Broil until lightly toasted, 1 to 2 minutes.

**6.** Place 2 biscuit halves in the bottom of each of 10 bowls. Place ice cream scoops on top. Drizzle with the Chocolate Gravy and chilled strawberry puree; serve immediately.

*The earliest reference to a cola cake recipe appears in 1950s cookbooks. In 1952, the* Charleston Gazette *published a recipe for having won third place in a contest for most "unusual" dishes. This version follows the same idea of the old sheet cake, requiring the frosting to be poured immediately over the cake as soon as it's removed from the oven. Instead of regular cola, I love the sweet cherry flavor this North Carolina-produced soft drink brings to the cake.*

# CHEERWINE CHOCOLATE CAKE

*Serves 8 to 10     Hands-on 15 minutes     Total 1 hour, 45 minutes*

**CAKE**

Vegetable shortening for greasing pan

2 cups (about 8 ½ ounces) all-purpose flour, plus more for dusting

2 cups granulated sugar

1 teaspoon baking soda

½ teaspoon table salt

1 (12-ounce) bottle Cheerwine

8 ounces (1 cup) unsalted butter, cut into cubes

¼ cup unsweetened cocoa

2 large eggs

½ cup whole buttermilk

1 teaspoon vanilla extract

**GLAZE**

1 (1-ounce) unsweetened chocolate baking square

1 ½ ounces (3 tablespoons) unsalted butter

1 ½ cups powdered sugar

1 tablespoon whole milk

2 tablespoons Cheerwine

**1.** Prepare the Cake: Preheat the oven to 350°F. Grease and flour a 13- x 9-inch baking pan. Place 2 cups flour in a large bowl. Whisk in the granulated sugar, baking soda, and salt.

**2.** Combine the soft drink, butter, and cocoa in a medium saucepan. Bring to a boil over medium-high, whisking constantly, until smooth. Remove from heat, and pour into the flour mixture, whisking until blended.

**3.** Whisk together the eggs, buttermilk, and vanilla in a small bowl. Add to the flour mixture, whisking until blended. Pour into prepared pan, and bake in the preheated oven until a wooden pick inserted in center comes out clean, about 28 to 30 minutes.

**4.** Prepare the Glaze: About 5 minutes before the cake is finished baking, melt the chocolate and butter in a small saucepan over medium-low, stirring constantly, until smooth. Whisk in the powdered sugar alternately with the milk and soft drink, whisking rapidly until smooth and silky. Pour over the hot cake in the pan; cool completely in the pan, about 1 hour.

ATLANTIC SOUTH

# Atlantic South

**ALMOST 500 YEARS AGO,** Europeans from Portugal, Spain, France, and England began settling along the southern Atlantic Coast, stretching from the Chesapeake Bay southward to Georgia and its dozen barrier islands. These new arrivals were the lucky beneficiaries of foods from the Atlantic with its many estuaries and brackish bays with oyster beds and an abundance of shrimp, mussels, clams, and fish. Up and down the coast the available ingredients and food traditions of African slaves and Native Americans merged with the unique traditions of the various European immigrants to create something wholly new and rooted in the New World. From Gullah-Geechee and Lowcountry cuisine to Creole and Cajun cookery, there are a handful of distinctive cuisines and dishes firmly rooted in place.

## DINING DETOURS

JCT. Kitchen & Bar, Atlanta, GA

Revival, Decatur, GA

Elizabeth on 37th, Savannah, GA

Mrs. Wilkes Dining Room, Savannah, GA

The Grey, Savannah, GA

The Dabney, Washington, DC

Chef & the Farmer, Kinston, NC

Boiler Room Oyster Bar, Kinston, NC

Poole's Diner, Raleigh, NC

Hominy Grill, Charleston, SC

Husk, Charleston, SC

Rodney Scott's BBQ, Charleston, SC

*If you're looking to change up your average Saturday pancake breakfast, these Johnnycakes—with a touch of sugar—are a great alternative. I love the texture the cornmeal brings to these fluffy little flat cakes. This recipe borrows from a family pancake recipe that includes baking powder as a leavening agent. You can omit the baking powder to yield a more dense, crisp version of cornbread, which is more often referred to as a hoecake, and serve it with savory dishes such as creamed corn or braised greens.*

# BREAKFAST JOHNNYCAKES

*Serves 4     Hands-on 30 minutes     Total 30 minutes*

1 cup (about 4 ¼ ounces) all-purpose flour

1 cup (about 5 ¾ ounces) fine plain yellow cornmeal

3 tablespoons granulated sugar

1 tablespoon baking powder

1 teaspoon table salt

2 large eggs, lightly beaten

1 cup whole milk

⅓ cup (2 ⅔ ounces) salted butter, melted

1 teaspoon vanilla extract

Vegetable oil or melted butter for greasing skillet

Pure maple syrup

Fresh fruit

**1.** Preheat the oven to 200°F. Whisk together the flour, cornmeal, sugar, baking powder, and salt in a medium bowl. Whisk together the eggs, milk, melted butter, and vanilla in a large bowl; add the flour mixture, and stir until well blended. (The batter will be slightly thick, like pancake batter.)

**2.** Heat a large cast-iron or nonstick skillet over medium-high. Brush the skillet with 1 to 2 teaspoons oil or melted butter. Pour the batter by ¼ cupfuls into the hot skillet, spreading into a 4-inch circle and leaving a few inches between each johnnycake. Cook until the centers become bubbly and edges begin to brown, 1 to 2 minutes. Turn the johnnycakes over, and cook until golden, about 1 minute. Transfer to a plate, cover with aluminum foil, and keep warm in the preheated oven. Serve with the syrup and the fresh fruit.

# COUNTRY CORNBREAD

*Serves 8     Hands-on 15 minutes     Total 55 minutes*

*There are any number of ways to make cornbread, but if you ask me, they can often be a little too savory or a little too sweet. This offshoot of an old Junior League recipe has always served me well, offering the best balancing between the two. I prefer coarse cornmeal to add a little bit of texture.*

Unsalted butter for greasing pan
1 cup (about 4 ¼ ounces) stone-ground plain yellow cornmeal
½ cup (about 2 ⅛ ounces) all-purpose flour
1 tablespoon baking powder
1 teaspoon kosher salt
½ teaspoon baking soda
1 cup whole buttermilk
¼ cup vegetable oil
½ cup canned cream-style corn *(such as Del Monte Fresh Cut Cream Style Golden Sweet Corn)*
1 large egg

**1.** Preheat the oven to 450°F. Grease an 8-inch square pan with butter, and place the pan in the preheated oven until hot, about 5 minutes.

**2.** Meanwhile, whisk together the cornmeal, flour, baking powder, salt, and baking soda in a medium bowl. Whisk together the buttermilk, oil, corn, and egg in a separate bowl until well blended. Add the buttermilk mixture to the cornmeal mixture, stirring until blended. Pour the batter into the hot pan, and bake until it is golden brown and a wooden pick inserted in center comes out clean, about 18 minutes. Cool in the pan on a wire rack 15 minutes. Cut into 2-inch squares, and serve warm, or cool completely in the pan on a wire rack, about 45 minutes.

---

# SPICY OLIVE-CHEESE PUFFS

*Serves 12     Hands-on 30 minutes     Total 55 minutes*

*When it comes to Southern cocktail parties, you're likely to find a dish of cheese straws and cocktail olives set out among the finger foods. This recipe brings the two together with a bit of a spicy kick.*

8 ounces sharp Cheddar cheese, shredded (about 2 cups)
½ cup (4 ounces) unsalted butter, softened
1 cup (about 4 ¼ ounces) all-purpose flour
1 teaspoon paprika
½ teaspoon table salt
½ teaspoon cayenne pepper
¾ cup small pimiento-stuffed green olives, drained

Preheat the oven to 400°F. Combine the cheese and butter in a food processor; pulse until blended, about 8 times. Add the flour, paprika, salt, and cayenne; pulse until the dough comes together, about 10 times. Press 1 rounded teaspoon of the dough around 1 olive, surrounding it completely. Repeat with the remaining dough and olives. Place 2 inches apart on a parchment paper-lined baking sheet. Bake in preheated oven until slightly golden brown on the bottom, about 13 minutes.

SPICY
OLIVE-CHEESE
PUFFS

*For those who have a soft spot for the classic cheese straw, these wafers will soon steal your heart. Packed with all the savory cheese flavor you could want, the key ingredient that gives this little cracker its playful texture is crisp rice cereal. I like to serve these with the Spicy Olive-Cheese Puffs (page 86) as dinner party appetizers.*

# CRISPY CHEESE WAFERS

*Makes about 6 dozen    Hands-on 25 minutes    Total 55 minutes*

1 cup (8 ounces) unsalted butter, softened

8 ounces sharp Cheddar cheese, shredded (about 2 cups)

2 cups (about 8 ½ ounces) all-purpose flour

1 teaspoon cayenne pepper

½ teaspoon table salt

2 cups crisp rice cereal *(such as Rice Krispies)*

Preheat the oven to 350°F. Beat the butter with a mixer on medium speed until smooth. Add the cheese, and beat until fully incorporated. Stir together the flour, cayenne pepper, and salt in a small bowl, and gradually add to the cheese mixture, beating until well blended after each addition. Stir in the cereal by hand. Using a 1-tablespoon cookie scoop, form the cheese mixture into 1-inch balls, and place on ungreased baking sheets. Flatten each slightly with fingers. Bake in preheated oven until lightly browned on edges, 12 to 14 minutes. Cool on baking sheet 2 minutes; remove from baking sheet to wire racks, and cool completely, about 20 minutes.

*A classic dish for the Southerner's entertaining table, the deviled egg, which is served in various ways all over the world, is nothing more than a hard-cooked egg with the yolk dressed up with any number of condiments. From yellow mustard and dill relish to truffle oil and fish roe, you can take a deviled egg down any flavorful road you please. Just don't forget to bring them to the table for any and every occasion.*

# DEVILED EGGS

*Serves 8 to 12    Hands-on 15 minutes    Total 1 hour*

12 large eggs
½ cup mayonnaise
¼ cup spicy brown mustard
3 bacon slices, cooked and crumbled

2 teaspoons chopped fresh chives,
  plus more for garnish
¼ teaspoon cayenne pepper
  (optional)

**1.** Bring a large saucepan of water to a boil over medium-high. Gently place the eggs in water using a large slotted spoon; boil 8 minutes. Transfer the eggs from water to a clean dish towel using slotted spoon, and let cool 20 to 30 minutes. Gently remove the eggshells, being careful not to nick the egg whites.

**2.** Carefully cut the eggs in half lengthwise using a sharp knife, and scoop the yolks into a bowl. Place the egg white halves on a plate.

**3.** Add the mayonnaise, mustard, bacon, chives, and, if desired, cayenne to yolks; whisk until well blended. (For a creamier texture, you can beat the yolk mixture with an electric mixer on low speed for a few minutes.) Spoon the mixture into the egg white halves, or spoon the mixture into a piping bag, and pipe into the egg white halves. Garnish with additional chopped chives, if desired, and chill until ready to serve.

# PORK RIND ROOSTERS

*Serves 12     Hands-on 15 minutes     Total 1 hour, 15 minutes*

*If you've spent any time at a coastal oyster bar in North Carolina, you likely already know what a rooster is. If you haven't, the first thing to know is that an actual rooster has nothing to do with it. According to Chef Vivian Howard, this traditional bar snack is usually requested among friends over a pitcher of beer. Though they may be ordered as more of a friendly dare—the horseradish and jalapeño can pack quite a punch—they tend to make you crave more.*

¼ cup minced pickled jalapeño chile
¼ cup prepared horseradish
2 tablespoons mayonnaise
1 large fresh jalapeño chile, cut into rounds
3 tablespoons fresh lemon juice (from 1 lemon)

24 fried pork rinds (each about the size of a saltine cracker)
24 fresh shucked oysters, drained
¼ cup cocktail sauce

**1.** Stir together the pickled jalapeño, horseradish, and mayonnaise in a small bowl, and chill 1 hour to allow flavors to come together. Combine the jalapeño rounds and lemon juice in a separate small bowl, and let stand at room temperature 1 hour. Just before serving, drain the jalapeño rounds, reserving the lemon juice and jalapeño rounds separately. Stir 1 tablespoon of the reserved lemon juice into the pickled jalapeño mixture.

**2.** To serve, spoon a heaping teaspoon of the pickled jalapeño mixture on each pork rind. Top each with 1 oyster, 1 teaspoon cocktail sauce, and a reserved fresh jalapeño round; serve immediately.

**NOTE:** If you don't have pork rinds, you can easily use a standard saltine cracker.

### SOUTHERN STAPLE

## Chitterlings or Chitlins?

As with many cultures around the world, using everything from a slaughtered animal is common; from your standard cuts of meat such as ribs and tenderloins to organ meat, ears, hooves, and in the case of chitlins, intestines. Chitterlings is the more formal name, but most people in the South call them chitlins, and they're most commonly used from pork. Chitterlings were peasant food in medieval England and remained a staple of the diet of low-income families right up until the late nineteenth century. That tradition was brought to America in Colonial times, and as slavery proliferated through the South, most slave owners gave the scraps of meat to slaves as sustenance. Chitlins were typically cooked outdoors, cleaned, sliced up, and boiled in pots. They're often served drained, doused with hot pepper sauce or apple cider vinegar, but they can also be battered and fried.

PORK RIND ROOSTERS

BOILED PEANUTS.
PG 94

*Some of the best boiled peanuts are enjoyed green just after the harvest. They can usually be found between May and November. But you can also use dried raw peanuts as well. Boiled peanuts came to fame in South Carolina, but their addictive quality spread throughout the South. You can often find warm stockpots of them in gas stations including spicy Cajun-flavored variations as well.*

# BOILED PEANUTS

*Serves 10    Hands-on 30 minutes    Total 5 hours, 30 minutes*

6 quarts water

½ cup kosher salt

1 pound raw peanuts

Fill a large stockpot with 6 quarts water. Add the salt, stirring to dissolve. Bring to a boil over medium-high. Add the peanuts, and place 1 to 2 dinner plates over the peanuts to weigh them down under the water. Reduce the heat to medium-low; cover and simmer until the peanuts in the shell are tender and salty, 5 to 6 hours. (It's a good idea to taste the peanuts every so often to check for doneness.) Remove from the heat, and serve immediately, or let the peanuts cool in the cooking liquid, and transfer both peanuts and cooking liquid to an airtight container. Store in the refrigerator up to 1 week. Serve the peanuts hot, at room temperature, or chilled.

**NOTE:** The cooking for a fresh, green peanut is significantly less than for raw peanuts—only about one to two hours.

## SOUTHERN STAPLE

## Peanuts

Originally a South American legume brought to Europe by Spanish missionaries and later to Asia, Africa, and then to North America, the peanut proved to be a vital ingredient for the African slave diet. Packed with protein and easy to grow, the peanut later became a major cash crop in the South with Georgia, Alabama, Virginia, and Florida leading overall production. Southern botanist George Washington Carver is credited with propagating them as a domestic crop based on his research at Alabama's Tuskegee Institute in the early twentieth century.

*Traditional Southern peanut soup is a creamy, nourishing soup brought to light by George Washington Carver during his agricultural studies on peanuts at Tuskegee Institute in Alabama in the early 1900s. (It is also often referred to as Tuskegee Soup.) Some variations include other vegetables and the substitution of cream for broth, but the basic elements of the soup include chicken stock and peanut butter, both easy to find and inexpensive throughout the South. This version marries the eastern Thai influences to better accentuate the exotic side of the peanut flavor.*

# SPICY THAI PEANUT SOUP

*Serves 6    Hands-on 30 minutes    Total 1 hour, 30 minutes*

2 tablespoons peanut oil

½ cup yellow onion, chopped (from 1 onion)

1 small jalapeño chile, chopped (about 2 tablespoons)

2 garlic cloves, crushed (about 2 teaspoons)

2 tablespoons red curry paste

1 tablespoon chopped fresh ginger

1 (2-inch) lemongrass stalk, halved

16 ounces sweet potatoes, peeled and chopped

2 cups refrigerated coconut milk beverage (*such as So Delicious*)

2 cups chicken broth

⅓ cup creamy peanut butter

2 tablespoons fresh lime juice (from 1 lime)

1 teaspoon kosher salt

3 tablespoons chopped fresh cilantro

½ cup roasted salted peanuts, chopped

6 lime wedges

Sriracha chili sauce (optional)

**1.** Heat the oil in a medium saucepan over medium until shimmering. Add the onion and jalapeño, and cook, stirring occasionally, until tender, 4 to 5 minutes. Add the garlic, curry paste, ginger, and lemongrass; cook, stirring often, until fragrant, about 1 minute. Stir in the chopped sweet potato, coconut milk beverage, chicken broth, and peanut butter until well blended. Bring the sweet potato mixture to a boil; cover, reduce heat to medium-low, and simmer until flavors incorporate, about 25 minutes. Remove from heat, uncover, and cool 15 minutes.

**2.** Pour the sweet potato mixture into a blender in two batches. Remove the center piece of the blender lid to allow steam to escape; secure the lid on the blender. Place a clean towel over the opening in the lid to avoid splatters, and process until smooth, about 1 minute. Return the soup to the saucepan, and stir in the lime juice and the salt. Heat over medium-low until heated through. Sprinkle each serving with the chopped cilantro and the roasted peanuts; serve with a lime wedge and, if desired, Sriracha.

*It's just a simple fact that if it's fried, it's probably a Southern recipe. Even if it's the humble garden tomato. The truth is, vegetables are fried in all sorts of cuisines. The fried green tomato has been co-opted by the region as authentically Southern. It's one of my favorite ways to use up green cherry tomatoes from my garden to make bite-size morsels. This version introduces the light and crispy texture of Japanese tempura, and be sure to use very cold beer or sparkling water to keep it light.*

# TEMPURA FRIED GREEN TOMATO WEDGES

*Serves 6     Hands-on 1 hour, 50 minutes     Total 1 hour, 50 minutes*

6 to 8 green tomatoes (3 ½ pounds) or
  2 pints green cherry tomatoes
Vegetable oil
1 cup (about 4 ¼ ounces) all-purpose
  flour
½ cup cornstarch
½ teaspoon table salt

¼ teaspoon cayenne pepper
1 large egg, lightly beaten
1 cup ice-cold beer or club soda
Mississippi Comeback Sauce
  (page 226) or Creole Rémoulade
  (page 189)

**1.** Preheat the oven to 200°F. Rinse the tomatoes, and pat dry. If using large green tomatoes, cut each into 6 wedges. (Leave cherry tomatoes whole.) Pour the oil to a depth of 1 ½ inches in a large, deep cast-iron skillet, and heat over medium-high to 360°F.

**2.** Place ½ cup of the flour in a small bowl. Combine the cornstarch, salt, cayenne pepper, and remaining ½ cup flour in a medium bowl. Add the egg and beer to the cornstarch mixture, and gently stir until mixture is just blended. (Mixture will be lumpy—do not overmix.)

**3.** Working with 3 or 4 tomato wedges (or 5 or 6 cherry tomatoes) at a time, dip in the flour, and coat well. Place in the batter, and coat well. Immediately place in the hot oil, and fry, turning regularly, until all sides are golden brown, 3 to 4 minutes. Remove with a metal slotted spoon or spider, and place on a plate lined with paper towels to drain. Transfer to a rimmed baking sheet, and keep warm in preheated oven. Repeat procedure with remaining tomatoes and batter. Serve immediately with the Mississippi Comeback Sauce or Creole Rémoulade.

→>——<←
## SOUTHERN STAPLE
→>——<←

## Meat & Three

A true Southern original, the meat-and-three concept popped up all around cities in the region in the 1920s as a cafeteria-style luncheonette that catered to working people. For a flat fee, customers could select from one of a handful of meat options such as fried chicken, meat loaf, or smothered pork chops, along with three side dishes—greens, potatoes any which way, black-eyed peas, and even that oddest of Southern vegetables: mac 'n' cheese. Most are usually served with a slice of cornbread and sweet tea. Conceived to serve a quick and easy lunch for a reasonable price, the many eateries still championing this style of service have managed to carry on a tradition of Southern foodways.

# BARBECUE SAUCE

Southern food historian John Egerton once said that there are more barbecue factions scattered throughout the South "than there are denominations in the far-flung Judeo-Christian establishment." And he was right. Friends become foes, geographical regions are divided, families cast inheritors out of their wills, and veritable lines are drawn in the sand over the hairsplitting details of what makes truly good barbecue. By extension, barbecue sauce is no less important. Depending on which region you call home, the style of sauce you prefer is a defining characteristic of your barbecue heritage—unless of course, you hail from a place like Central Texas, which eschews the sauce altogether.

MEMPHIS BARBECUE
SAUCE, PG 100

ALABAMA WHITE
BARBECUE SAUCE,
PG 100

EAST CAROLINA
BARBECUE SAUCE,
PG 102

SOUTH CAROLINA
BARBECUE SAUCE,
PG 103

TEXAS BARBECUE
SAUCE, PG 101

NORTH CAROLINA
BARBECUE SAUCE,
PG 102

# MEMPHIS BARBECUE SAUCE

*Makes 2 cups    Hands-on 10 minutes*
*Total 1 day, 10 minutes, including 1 day chilling*

A thicker, sweeter sauce, the
Memphis barbecue sauce relies
more on tomato and brown sugar to
give it a rich flavor. It's perfect for
mixing into a pulled pork sandwich
or basting on baby back ribs.

1 tablespoon unsalted butter, melted
1 small yellow onion, minced
  (about ⅓ cup)
2 garlic cloves, minced (about
  2 teaspoons)
1 (6-ounce) can tomato paste
¾ cup apple cider vinegar

¼ cup packed dark brown sugar
3 tablespoons unsulfured molasses
2 tablespoons Worcestershire sauce
2 tablespoons yellow mustard
1 teaspoon kosher salt
1 teaspoon black pepper

Melt the butter in a medium saucepan over medium-high. Add the onion and
garlic, and cook, stirring often, until tender, 3 to 4 minutes. Transfer the mixture
to a blender, and add the tomato paste, vinegar, sugar, molasses, Worcestershire
sauce, mustard, salt, and pepper; process until blended and smooth, about
1 minute. Chill in an airtight container at least 24 hours before using. Store in
refrigerator up to 2 weeks.

# ALABAMA WHITE BARBECUE SAUCE

*Makes 1½ cups    Hands-on 10 minutes*
*Total 1 day, 10 minutes, including 1 day chilling*

This white 'cue sauce owes its
fame to Big Bob Gibson Bar-B-Q in
Decatur, Alabama. While most other
barbecue sauce consists of vinegar
and/or tomato, this sauce gets its
tangy character from mayonnaise.
This isn't the actual Big Bob recipe,
but it's inspired by its tart, peppery
prowess. It's delicious on grilled
chicken but also as a dipping sauce
for anything from fried green
tomatoes to hush puppies.

1 cup mayonnaise
¼ cup apple cider vinegar
1 garlic clove, minced
1 tablespoon black pepper
1 tablespoon spicy brown mustard

1 teaspoon kosher salt
2 teaspoons prepared horseradish
1 teaspoon fresh lemon juice (from
  1 lemon)

Whisk together all the ingredients until well blended. Chill in an airtight
container at least 24 hours before using. Store in refrigerator up to 1 week.

*Texas sauce also has a bit of tomato and brown sugar, but the addition of chile pepper makes it bold enough to use with smoked brisket—assuming you're brave enough to serve sauce with brisket at all.*

# TEXAS BARBECUE SAUCE

*Makes 2 cups     Hands-on 20 minutes*
*Total 1 day, 25 minutes, including 1 day chilling*

2 tablespoons salted butter

1 small yellow onion, minced (about ⅓ cup)

2 garlic cloves, minced (about 2 teaspoons)

3 jalapeño chiles, seeded and minced (about ⅓ cup)

2 canned chipotle chiles in adobo sauce (from 1 [7-ounce] can), coarsely chopped

2 (6-ounce) cans tomato paste

2 tablespoons unsulfured molasses

½ cup packed dark brown sugar

1 tablespoon apple cider vinegar

¼ cup Worcestershire sauce

2 tablespoons fresh lemon or lime juice (from 1 lemon or lime)

2 teaspoons kosher salt

1 teaspoon ground cumin

½ teaspoon black pepper

Melt the butter in a medium saucepan over medium-high. Add the onion, garlic, and jalapeño, and cook, stirring often, until softened, 3 to 4 minutes. Stir in the chipotle chiles, tomato paste, molasses, brown sugar, vinegar, Worcestershire sauce, lemon juice, salt, cumin, and black pepper; reduce heat to low, and simmer, stirring often, 10 minutes. Transfer the mixture to a blender, and remove center piece of blender lid to allow steam to escape; secure lid on blender. Place a clean towel over opening in lid to avoid splatters, and process until smooth, about 1 minute. Chill in an airtight container at least 24 hours before using. Store in refrigerator up to 1 week.

## Southern Barbecue

When it comes to regional barbecue, there are a number of competing elements that stir up controversy. Among the chief debates are whether to use pork or beef, a rub versus a sauce, or pecan, oak, hickory, or mesquite wood. Other questions abound: Do you use an off-set, vertical, box, pellet, or porcelain egg for smoking? Should smoked meat be finished in the oven? Do you wrap with foil or butcher paper towards the end of a smoke? If you haven't made up your mind yet on any of the above, tread lightly, you have future relationships at stake. The main thing virtually everyone agrees on is that barbecue requires fire, smoke, hardwood, and a whole lot of time and patience. If you haven't got these, you haven't got barbecue.

# NORTH CAROLINA BARBECUE SAUCE

*Makes 2½ cups    Hands-on 10 minutes*
*Total 1 day, 1 hour, 10 minutes, including 1 day chilling*

*This thinner, vinegar-based sauce is a classic North Carolina-style sauce common in the Piedmont region between the Atlantic Coast and the Appalachian Mountains. Use it to baste pork or chicken about twenty minutes before pulling it off the grill or smoker and to help soften the sharpness of the vinegar.*

1½ cups apple cider vinegar
½ cup ketchup
½ cup water

1 tablespoon granulated sugar
1 teaspoon kosher salt
½ teaspoon crushed red pepper

Whisk together all the ingredients in a medium saucepan, and bring to a simmer over medium, stirring often. Reduce the heat to medium-low, and simmer, stirring occasionally, 8 to 10 minutes. Remove from the heat, and let cool to room temperature, about 1 hour. Chill in an airtight container at least 24 hours before using. Store in refrigerator up to 1 week

# EAST CAROLINA BARBECUE SAUCE

*Makes 2 cups    Hands-on 10 minutes*
*Total 1 day, 10 minutes, including 1 day chilling*

*In the eastern parts of North Carolina and South Carolina, the most classic form of barbecue sauce is also its simplest. This is the basis on which 'cue masters like Rodney Scott have built their reputations. Likely originating with African slaves, this sauce was mopped onto the meat during cooking, allowing the vinegar to help break down and flavor the meat. Cooked into the meat is ideal, though some with an acquired taste like to put it on their pulled pork when served.*

2 cups apple cider vinegar
1 tablespoon light brown sugar
½ teaspoon cayenne pepper
1 tablespoon crushed red pepper, or
  more to taste

½ teaspoon kosher salt
½ teaspoon black pepper

Whisk together all the ingredients in a medium bowl until the sugar has dissolved. Chill in an airtight container at least 24 hours before using. Store in the refrigerator up to 2 months.

# SOUTH CAROLINA BARBECUE SAUCE

*Makes 1 ¾ cups     Hands-on 10 minutes*
*Total 1 day, 10 minutes, including 1 day chilling*

¾ cup yellow mustard

¼ cup honey

¼ cup apple cider vinegar

2 tablespoons ketchup

1 tablespoon dark brown sugar

2 teaspoons Worcestershire sauce

1 teaspoon hot sauce

Whisk together all the ingredients in a small bowl. Chill in an airtight container at least 24 hours before serving. Store in refrigerator up to 2 weeks.

*In mid-South Carolina, from Columbia to the coast around Charleston, barbecue sauce is mustard-based and takes on a decidedly yellow color. Slightly tangy, yet slightly sweet, it offers a great accent to pulled pork or slathered on ribs.*

# Rodney Scott

## HOW RODNEY SCOTT GOES WHOLE HOG

Rodney Scott doesn't blink an eye at cooking thirty hogs a week. It's his cooking tradition. Before he opened Charleston's Rodney Scott's BBQ in 2017, he got his start in the small town of Hemingway, about ninety miles north. Here, his family runs Scott's Variety Store selling sundry grocery items as well as whole hog barbecue.

"The decision to focus on whole hog cooking was really pretty easy," says Scott. "It's been a tradition in my family for generations after harvest season, for Thanksgiving and Christmas. It was the best way to feed the whole family, and it's what I know how to do best." Apparently he does. Rodney just won a James Beard Award for Best Chef: Southeast.

The process is all about hot coals from wood. To prepare a whole hog, he first prepares the coals, which takes at least an hour. To feed an average of 120 people, he counts on at least twelve hours for a 145-pound hog, which means that for lunch, the fire is lit at around 11 p.m. the night before, plus waiting at least an hour for the coals to be ready to begin cooking the hog. You'll need about a cord of wood to keep those coals coming. (That's enough wood to fill the bed of a full-sized pickup truck.) Scott uses oak and hickory together, but the world's your oyster if you want to try other hardwoods such as pecan or aged mesquite. (Green mesquite imparts acrid flavors.)

Scott's fire is separate from the pit. Once the coals are ready, he moves them to the pit to begin cooking the hog and continues to tend the fire to produce coals for the entire cooking process.

### HOW TO PREPARE THE HOG

Prior to cooking, Scott removes the feet and the head of the hog. From there, he splits the hams and shoulders, and butterflies the hog down the middle. The hog is then laid out, belly-side-down, on a metal grate over the coals. The hog is left to cook for twelve hours, while he feeds the heat with fresh coals regularly. Scott doesn't use anything—rub or sauce—until the end of the cooking process.

### WHEN IS IT DONE?

Scott doesn't use any scientific tools to determine when his hogs are done. Instead, he relies on sight, feel, and a lot of intuition.

"You'll start to see the skin separate from the meat," says Scott. "The fat has rendered through the meat and you should be able to pull a ham bone right out." That's when Scott flips the hog to cook the skin a little.

### WHAT'S THE SECRET SAUCE?

Once the hog is flipped, this is when he begins to add flavor. You can add a little salt, pepper, or other spices. Scott likes to mop the hog down with a special sauce.

### WHAT'S IN HIS SAUCE?

Good question. For most pitmasters—famous or not—sauce and rub are highly secretive concoctions. Scott is no exception. Though he prefers to keep specifics to himself, you'd be in the ballpark with a blend of iodized salt, pepper, crushed red pepper, and cayenne sprinkled over the hog once it has been flipped.

Mop the hog with ample amounts of apple cider or white distilled vinegar and a vinegar-pepper sauce made with a little vinegar, ketchup, and crushed red pepper.

"The vinegar helps give the meat tenderness, and the acid brightens its flavor, or as an old guy from my hometown used to say, it gives it a little 'twang'," says Scott, who adds that letting the sauce cook with the meat as it finishes softens the vinegar's pungency and keeps it from being too overpowering.

Within an hour of flipping the hog and mopping it with sauce, you can begin serving it, just as Scott does, by pulling portions of meat right from the pit and serving it with sauce and all the fixin's.

### WHAT'S THE BEST PART TO EAT?

"I like to grab just below the shoulder and right above the rib cage," says Scott. "Some of that turns out to be pork belly and then some is just shoulder and belly; it's just tenderized perfectly at that part and it's delicious."

*With barbecue—be it pork, beef, or chicken—it's understandable that the protein takes center stage. But just as no great theater production is complete without its supporting cast, no barbecue meal is great if the side dishes are more of an afterthought. At Rodney Scott's BBQ in Charleston, the sides are just as good as the whole hog that they often accompany, and this potato salad is no exception.*

# RODNEY SCOTT'S POTATO SALAD

*Serves 14     Hands-on 20 minutes     Total 1 hour, 30 minutes*

5 pounds russet potatoes, peeled and quartered (8 to 10 medium potatoes)

4 teaspoons kosher salt

1 ½ cups mayonnaise

1 ¼ cups finely chopped celery (from 3 stalks)

¾ cup finely chopped red onion (from 1 onion)

⅓ cup sweet pickle relish

⅓ cup chopped fresh flat-leaf parsley

¼ cup yellow mustard

¼ teaspoon cayenne pepper

¾ teaspoon black pepper

5 hard-cooked large eggs, peeled

**1.** Place the potatoes in a large stockpot; add 2 teaspoons of the salt and cold water to cover. Bring to a boil over medium-high, and boil until the potatoes are tender, 20 to 25 minutes.

**2.** Meanwhile, stir together the mayonnaise, celery, red onion, relish, parsley, mustard, cayenne, black pepper, and remaining 2 teaspoons salt.

**3.** Remove the potatoes from the heat, and drain. Cool 30 minutes. Using your hands, crumble the potatoes into a large bowl. Crumble the hard-cooked eggs over the potatoes. Add the mayonnaise mixture, and stir well. Serve at room temperature, or cover and chill until ready to serve.

Collards are the official state vegetable of South Carolina, and Georgia has multiple city festivals devoted to this lowly green. The collard green isn't native to the Americas—there's evidence it was grown by the ancient Greeks and Romans—but far be it from me to strip the South of this hallowed broad-leaf vegetable as one of its own. While a raw collard green is packed with a super helping of nutrients, they're traditionally leeched out in the slow cooking process, which traditionally includes a large hunk of pork, leaving a savory portion of deliciousness and potlikker—and this recipe offers no exception.

## Poke Sallet

A common North American weed that has been foraged in the South since Native Americans roamed the land, poke sallet has long been cooked down like mustard or collard greens. *Never mind the fact that it could kill you.* That's right, the dark leafy plant is considered poisonous and its roots and berries can be deadly in even the smallest portions. Those raised on poke sallet know to use only the leaves of young plants. These are then boiled two to three times with the potlikker discarded each time. After that, it's typically thrown on a skillet with a little bacon grease and green or white onions and sautéed for a side dish at supper. Prepare at your own risk.

# WILTED COLLARD GREENS

*Serves 6 to 8     Hands-on 15 minutes     Total 1 hour, 10 minutes*

1 teaspoon vegetable oil
3 bacon slices, diced
1 ½ cups diced yellow onion (from 1 onion)
2 pounds fresh collard greens, trimmed, washed, and roughly chopped (about 6 cups)

1 cup chicken broth
2 teaspoons kosher salt
1 teaspoon granulated sugar
1 teaspoon black pepper
1 (10-ounce) smoked ham hock

Heat the oil in a large heavy stockpot over medium-high. Add the bacon, and cook, stirring often, until crisp, 7 to 10 minutes. Add the onion, and cook, stirring often, until translucent, about 5 to 6 minutes. Add the collard greens, and cook, stirring constantly, until the greens begin to wilt, about 1 to 2 minutes. Stir in the broth, salt, sugar, and pepper, and place the ham hock in the center of the greens in the pot. Reduce the heat to medium-low; cover and simmer 30 minutes. Remove the ham hock, and let stand until cool enough to handle, about 10 minutes. Remove and discard the bones and fat from the ham hock; roughly chop the meat, and stir into the collard green mixture. Cook the greens, stirring occasionally, until tender, 15 to 20 minutes. Serve warm.

*Also known as "Carolina Peas and Rice," something about this dish makes me want to say, "Glory be to the black-eyed pea!" Often served on New Year's Day to bring luck in the year ahead, Hoppin' John is a celebration of the humble field pea that deserves an appearance on the table more than once a year.*

# HOPPIN' JOHN

*Serves 10 to 12     Hands-on 25 minutes     Total 1 hour, 15 minutes*

PEAS

1 pound smoked sausage, diced

1 cup diced yellow onion (from 1 onion)

1 cup diced carrots (from 3 carrots)

1 cup diced celery (from 3 stalks)

2 garlic cloves, minced (about
    2 teaspoons)

1 jalapeño chile, seeded (if less heat is
    desired) and diced (about
    3 tablespoons)

1 pound dried black-eyed peas, soaked
    overnight and drained, or fresh
    black-eyed peas

6 cups chicken stock

1 bay leaf

4 thyme sprigs

1½ tablespoons kosher salt

1 teaspoon black pepper

RICE

4 cups water

2 cups long-grain white rice
    (*such as Carolina Gold Rice*)

2 teaspoons kosher salt

1 cup fresh corn kernels (from 2 ears)

2 tablespoons unsalted butter

1 teaspoon black pepper

2 tablespoons apple cider vinegar

**1.** Prepare the Peas: Cook the sausage in a Dutch oven over medium-low, stirring occasionally, until heated through, 6 to 8 minutes. Transfer the sausage to a plate lined with paper towels to drain, reserving the drippings in the Dutch oven.

**2.** Add the onion, carrots, celery, garlic, and jalapeño to drippings in the Dutch oven, and cook, stirring often, until softened, about 5 to 7 minutes. Return the sausage to the Dutch oven, and stir in the black-eyed peas, chicken stock, bay leaf, thyme sprigs, salt, and pepper. Bring to a simmer over high, and reduce heat to medium. Simmer until the peas are tender, about 45 minutes. Discard the bay leaf and the thyme sprigs, and drain any excess liquid.

**3.** Prepare the Rice: Bring 4 cups water, rice, and salt to a boil in a medium saucepan over high. Cover, reduce heat to medium, and simmer until water has completely evaporated, about 20 minutes. Stir in the corn, butter, and pepper.

**4.** Combine the black-eyed pea mixture and the rice in a large serving bowl. Stir in the vinegar. Serve hot as a main course or side dish.

*A definitive dish of the Georgia Coast, this version of a pilau likely found its origin from Spanish immigrants who arrived in the Savannah area, bringing with them Mediterranean cuisine. This dish blends vegetables, spices, and herbs into a one-pot rice bake that is made even more alluring with the addition of bacon. The best result is when the rice forms a crispy crust at the bottom of the dish beneath an aromatic bed of plump, savory goodness.*

# GEORGIA RED RICE

*Serves 6 to 8     Hands-on 25 minutes     Total 1 hour, 10 minutes*

Unsalted butter for greasing baking dish
6 bacon slices
1 cup diced yellow onion (from 1 onion)
1 cup diced celery (from 3 stalks)
1 cup diced green bell pepper
   (from 1 bell pepper)
2 cups uncooked long-grain white rice
1 (14.5-ounce) can diced tomatoes,
   undrained

2 teaspoons kosher salt
2 teaspoons black pepper
2 cups water
¼ cup chopped fresh flat-leaf parsley
Lemon wedges (optional)
Hot sauce (*such as Tabasco*) (optional)

Preheat the oven to 350°F. Grease a 13- x 9-inch (3-quart) baking dish with butter. Cook the bacon in a large heavy skillet over medium, turning often, until crisp, about 10 minutes. Transfer the bacon to a plate lined with paper towels to drain, reserving drippings in skillet. Crumble the bacon. Cook the onion, celery, and bell pepper in the reserved drippings in skillet until just tender, 6 to 8 minutes. Stir in the rice, tomatoes, bacon, salt, pepper, and 2 cups water. Bring to a boil over medium-high. Reduce the heat to low, and simmer 5 minutes. Transfer to the prepared baking dish. Cover tightly with aluminum foil, and bake in the preheated oven until the rice is tender, about 45 minutes. (Check the rice after 30 minutes to see if you need to add a little water to keep the rice moist.) Fluff the rice with a fork, and sprinkle with the chopped parsley; serve with the lemon wedges and the hot sauce, if desired.

*Some people look forward to tomato season in anticipation of bright summer salads and flavorful pasta and rice dishes. Personally, I crave tomato pie. While savory pies have a long-standing history that traces their roots to all parts of Europe, there's something resolutely Southern about tomato pie. A healthy addition of fresh basil adds beautiful brightness. There's absolutely no shame in using a store-bought piecrust—the flavors for this dish are all packed in the filling.*

# TOMATO PIE

*Serves 8    Hands-on 20 minutes    Total 1 hour, 45 minutes*

Chilled dough from Crust (page 114)
All-purpose flour for work surface
3 to 4 ripe tomatoes (1½ pounds), thinly sliced
1 teaspoon kosher salt
½ teaspoon black pepper
1 tablespoon unsalted butter
½ cup finely chopped sweet onion (from 1 onion)

4 ounces Cheddar cheese, shredded (about 1 cup)
2 ounces Parmesan cheese, shredded (about ½ cup)
1 teaspoon chopped fresh thyme
8 large basil leaves
2 large eggs
1 cup mayonnaise

**1.** Preheat the oven to 425°F. Roll the dough into a 12-inch circle on a lightly floured surface. Fit into a 9-inch pie pan; crimp edges. Line the dough with aluminum foil, and fill with pie weights or dried beans. Bake in the preheated oven until the crust is set and edges are light golden, about 15 minutes. Remove the weights and foil, and bake 5 more minutes. Transfer to a wire rack. Reduce the oven temperature to 350°F. Cool the piecrust completely, about 30 minutes.

**2.** Meanwhile, sprinkle the tomato slices with salt and pepper, and arrange in a single layer on baking sheets lined with paper towels; let stand 30 minutes.

**3.** Melt the butter in a medium skillet over medium-high. Add the onion, and cook until tender, 4 to 5 minutes. Remove from the heat, and cool 10 minutes.

**4.** Combine the Cheddar, Parmesan, and thyme in a small bowl. Sprinkle half of the cheese mixture on bottom of cooled crust. Layer the tomatoes over the cheese in the crust, overlapping slices slightly; sprinkle with the onion. Arrange the basil leaves in a starburst pattern in center of the pie. Sprinkle with the remaining cheese mixture. Whisk the eggs in a medium bowl, and slowly whisk in the mayonnaise; pour the egg mixture over the pie. Carefully transfer the pie to oven, and bake at 350°F until golden brown, about 45 minutes, shielding edges of crust with foil after 30 to 35 minutes to prevent overbrowning. Cool on a wire rack at least 15 minutes before serving.

VIDALIA
ONION TART,
PG 114

TOMATO PIE

When it comes to sweet, tender onions, there's no better place to look than Vidalia, Georgia, where the onion of the same name has been cultivated since the early 1930s. This hybrid is characterized by its sweet, rather than hot, flavor best accented by the creaminess of a classic French onion tart and a kiss of savoriness from crispy bacon.

# VIDALIA ONION TART

*Serves 6 to 8    Hands-on 30 minutes    Total 2 hours, 25 minutes*

CRUST

3 cups (about 12 ¾ ounces) all-purpose flour, plus more for work surface

1 cup (8 ounces) cold unsalted butter

1 teaspoon kosher salt

8 to 10 tablespoons ice water

TART

5 bacon slices

3 large Vidalia onions, thinly sliced (about 2 pounds)

¼ cup dry white wine

4 large eggs

¾ cup heavy cream

1 teaspoon kosher salt

½ teaspoon black pepper

¼ teaspoon ground nutmeg

**1.** Prepare the Crust: Combine the flour, butter, and salt in a food processor bowl fitted with plastic blade; pulse until the butter is about the size of small peas, 8 to 10 times. Gradually drizzle in the ice water, 1 tablespoon at a time, pulsing until dough forms a loose ball, 10 to 12 times. (You may not need all the water.) Turn the dough out onto a lightly floured surface. Shape the dough into a 1-inch-thick disk. Wrap with plastic wrap, and chill 30 minutes.

**2.** Preheat the oven to 375°F. Grease a 12-inch tart pan with cooking spray. Remove the dough from refrigerator; place on a floured surface. Using a rolling pin, roll out the dough to ¼-inch thickness. Place the dough in prepared tart pan, and gently press dough into pan. Refrigerate 10 minutes. Line the dough with parchment paper, and fill with pie weights or dried beans. Bake until lightly browned, 20 to 25 minutes. Remove weights and parchment, and bake until bottom of crust is browned, about 15 minutes. Transfer the piecrust to a wire rack. Reduce oven temperature to 350°F. Cool slightly before filling, about 30 minutes.

**3.** Meanwhile, prepare the Tart: Cook the bacon in a large high-sided 12-inch sauté pan or skillet over medium-high, turning as needed, until the bacon is crispy; transfer bacon to a plate lined with paper towels to drain, reserving 3 to 4 tablespoons drippings in pan and discarding remaining drippings. Crumble the bacon. Cook the onions in reserved drippings over medium, stirring often, until the onions have softened but are not browned, 12 to 15 minutes. Stir in the wine, and simmer until the wine has almost completely evaporated, 4 to 5 minutes. Remove from heat.

**4.** Whisk together the eggs and the cream in a medium bowl until blended. Add the salt, pepper, and nutmeg, and stir until blended. Stir in the onion mixture. Transfer the onion mixture into the cooled crust, and bake at 350°F until golden brown and a wooden pick inserted in center of the tart comes out clean, about 40 minutes. Let stand 10 minutes before serving.

———◆———

*There's nothing quite as good or as simple as sautéing sweet summer squash in a skillet with a little butter and salt. But when you want to cook something like it that's a little more substantial for a crowd, this rice casserole is a perfect way to enjoy an abundance of squash and zucchini from the garden.*

# SUMMER SQUASH-RICE GRATIN

*Serves 10     Hands-on 30 minutes     Total 1 hour, 30 minutes*

½ cup panko (Japanese-style breadcrumbs)

4 ounces Parmesan cheese, finely shredded (about 1 cup)

2 tablespoons olive oil

1 cup chopped yellow onion (from 1 onion)

2 garlic cloves, minced

3 tablespoons all-purpose flour

3 cups coarsely chopped yellow squash (from 3 squash)

3 cups coarsely chopped zucchini (from 2 zucchini)

2 cups whole milk

2 teaspoons chopped fresh thyme

1 teaspoon kosher salt

½ teaspoon black pepper

¼ teaspoon cayenne pepper

2 cups cooked long-grain white rice

6 ounces Cheddar and/or Monterey Jack cheese, shredded (about 1 ½ cups)

**1.** Preheat the oven to 350°F. Combine the panko and ½ cup of the Parmesan in a small bowl. Grease a 13- x 9-inch baking dish with cooking spray.

**2.** Heat the oil in a large skillet over medium. Add the onion, and cook, stirring often, until tender, 5 to 7 minutes. Add the garlic, and cook, stirring often, until fragrant, about 30 seconds. Stir in the flour until combined. (Mixture will be dry.) Stir in the yellow squash and the zucchini. Add the milk, thyme, salt, black pepper, and cayenne, stirring until well blended. Cook, stirring constantly, over medium-high until thickened, 6 to 8 minutes. Remove from heat, and stir in the rice, Cheddar, and remaining ½ cup Parmesan. Pour the mixture into prepared baking dish, and sprinkle evenly with the panko mixture. Bake in the preheated oven until golden brown and the squash is tender, about 45 minutes. Let stand 10 minutes before serving.

*Depending on who you ask, Brunswick Stew originated in either Georgia or Virginia, both of which have a city and a county with the name, and both claim to be the official home of this hearty one-pot meal. Also unclear is exactly which meats should be used to make it, or whether it should be served on its own, with rice, or with sliced white bread. The truth is, this is a hunter's stew—the kind made from whatever was available to put in a pot to be cooked over an open fire. You'll find evidence of any and everything from venison, beef, pork, chicken, rabbit, and even squirrel and possum. To keep from arousing too much concern, I usually keep it simple with chicken and pork but have been known to include venison or rabbit when I have it on hand. Serve it however it suits your fancy.*

# BRUNSWICK STEW

Serves 8    Hands-on 20 minutes    Total 1 hour, 50 minutes

2 tablespoons canola oil

1½ cups chopped yellow onion
(from 1 medium onion)

1 cup chopped celery (from 3 stalks)

1 cup chopped green bell pepper
(from 1 medium bell pepper)

1 (6-ounce) can tomato paste

1 cup frozen sliced okra

4 cups chopped peeled new potatoes
(from 8 potatoes)

1 pound of your favorite pulled pork or
Slow-Cooker Pulled Pork (page 57)

1 (2-pound) whole rotisserie chicken,
skinned, boned, and shredded
(about 3 cups)

1 (14.5-ounce) can diced tomatoes,
undrained

1 cup fresh corn kernels (about 2 ears)

1 (15.5-ounce) can butter beans or
cannellini beans, drained and rinsed

3 cups chicken broth

2 teaspoons Worcestershire sauce

1 tablespoon kosher salt

1½ teaspoons black pepper

Cooked white rice (optional)

Heat the oil in a large Dutch oven over medium-high. Add the onion, celery, and bell pepper; cook, stirring occasionally, until softened, about 6 minutes. Add the tomato paste; cook, stirring constantly, until slightly caramelized, about 2 minutes. Stir in the okra, potatoes, pork, chicken, tomatoes, corn, butter beans, chicken broth, Worcestershire sauce, salt, and pepper. Bring to a boil; reduce heat to medium-low. Simmer, stirring occasionally, until the potatoes are tender, about 1½ hours. Serve with a mound of cooked white rice, if desired.

*There are similar cultural dishes to pirlau. From Spanish paella and Middle Eastern pilaf to East Indian pilau, Cajun jambalaya, and even Lowcountry chicken bog, the common thread for this dish is its composition as a general rice porridge cooked with vegetables and either chicken, seafood, or game. The only thing that's less certain is exactly how it's pronounced. Most people generally agree that "per-loo" is acceptable, but "per-low," "pra-loo," and "per-la" have all been tossed out there as well. Your safest bet is to follow my grandfather's favorite advice, "Don't ask questions, just eat it."*

## Lowcountry Gullah

The Gullahs, or Geechees, are descendants of slaves who lived and still live in the coastal plains and on the bordering sea islands along the coast of the southeastern United States. Their communities are scattered along the 400-mile strip from the St. Johns River in Florida to the Cape Fear River in North Carolina. (Gullah tends to be the preferred name in North Carolina and South Carolina; Geechee in Georgia and Florida.) Along with a unique Creole language shared among this micro-culture, the Gullahs represent a whole way of cooking that blends island, African, and Southern traditions based on the resources of the Atlantic Coast.

# LOWCOUNTRY CHICKEN-AND-HAM PIRLAU

*Serves 8    Hands-on 20 minutes    Total 40 minutes*

2 tablespoons unsalted butter
1 cup chopped yellow onion (from 1 small onion)
1 large red bell pepper, chopped (about 1 cup)
1 jalapeño chile, seeded and chopped (about 3 tablespoons)
2 celery stalks, chopped (about ½ cup)
1 cup diced ham or crumbled bacon (about 5 ounces)
1 garlic clove, minced (about 1 teaspoon)
2 cups uncooked long-grain white rice
2 cups chicken broth

1 cup dry white wine
1 (14.5-ounce) can diced tomatoes, undrained
1 bay leaf
2 ½ teaspoons kosher salt
½ teaspoon black pepper
2 cups diced roasted chicken (about 9 ounces)
1 cup cubed country ham steak (about 5 ounces)
1 teaspoon chopped fresh thyme
¼ cup chopped fresh parsley
1 teaspoon lemon zest (from 1 lemon)

Melt the butter in a large deep skillet or Dutch oven over medium-high. Add the onion; cook, stirring, until slightly tender, about 4 minutes. Add the bell pepper, jalapeño, celery, and diced ham; cook, stirring, until the bell pepper is tender, about 4 minutes. Add the garlic, and cook, stirring constantly, 1 minute. Add the rice; cook, stirring often, until lightly toasted, about 1 minute. Stir in the chicken broth, white wine, tomatoes, bay leaf, salt, and pepper, and bring to a simmer. Reduce heat to medium-low. Cover and cook until the rice is tender and liquid is absorbed, about 18 minutes. Stir in the chicken, country ham, thyme, parsley, and lemon zest; cook, stirring, until the meat is heated through, about 2 minutes. Discard the bay leaf. Serve on a large platter.

*At its core, a chicken bog is essentially a one-pot dish reminiscent of many Caribbean meat and rice dishes in which a chicken is boiled in a pot, then rice is added to the pot to cook until the grains absorb the water. A dish typically well known around the South Carolina Lowcountry, this is a variation that doesn't require the boiling of a whole chicken, but I promise you won't miss a thing.*

# CHICKEN BOG

*Serves 8    Hands-on 20 minutes    Total 40 minutes*

6 tablespoons (3 ounces) unsalted butter

1 cup chopped yellow onion (from 1 small onion)

1 cup chopped carrot (from 3 large carrots)

2 garlic cloves, minced (about 2 teaspoons)

2 cups uncooked long-grain white rice

2 ½ teaspoons kosher salt

1 teaspoon black pepper

4 cups chicken stock

1 (2-pound) rotisserie chicken, skinned, boned, and diced (about 4 cups)

1 cup fresh corn kernels (from 2 ears)

1 tablespoon chopped fresh thyme

3 tablespoons fresh lemon juice (from 1 lemon)

¼ cup grated Parmesan cheese

⅓ cup chopped fresh flat-leaf parsley

Melt 4 tablespoons of the butter in a large Dutch oven over medium-high. Add the onion and the carrots; cook, stirring often, until slightly softened, 4 to 5 minutes. Add the garlic, and cook, stirring constantly, 1 minute. Add the rice, and cook, stirring often, until lightly toasted, 2 to 3 minutes. Stir in the salt, pepper, and chicken stock, and bring to a boil. Cover, reduce heat to medium-low, and cook until the rice is tender and the liquid is absorbed, 18 to 20 minutes. Reduce heat to medium-low, and stir in the chicken, corn, and thyme, and cook until heated through, about 3 minutes. Stir in the lemon juice, Parmesan cheese, parsley, and remaining 2 tablespoons butter. Serve warm.

## SOUTHERN STAPLE

## Lowcountry Defined

It's not uncommon to hear the term "Lowcountry" as a blanket term for the Southeast. But this coastal area of saltwater marsh and Spanish moss-draped live oaks is more specifically defined along the South Carolina and Georgia coastlines that are broadly bookended by Charleston and Savannah. Once a center for slave-based rice farming, the region today is more commonly associated with its historic cities, cultural heritage, and flavorful dishes such as she-crab soup, Frogmore stew, and Hoppin' John.

# COUNTRY CAPTAIN

*Serves 4    Hands-on 30 minutes    Total 1 hour*

*Comforting and exotic, and perhaps a little confusing considering the blend of spices stirred into this soulful dish. But make no mistake, the Country Captain is indeed a Southern staple. And one that celebrates the ports of entry at Charleston and Savannah where not only did African cuisine make its way to the United States, but Indian and other Eastern cuisines as well.*

1¼ cups chicken broth
½ cup golden raisins
1 tablespoon curry powder
1 tablespoon garam masala
2 teaspoons kosher salt, plus more
   to taste
1 teaspoon black pepper, plus more
   to taste
4 bacon slices
2 pounds boneless, skinless chicken
   thighs (8 thighs)
1 dried guajillo chile

1 cup sliced carrot (about 1 medium)
½ cup chopped yellow bell pepper
½ cup chopped red bell pepper
½ cup chopped yellow onion
2 garlic cloves, minced (about
   2 teaspoons)
3 tablespoons tomato paste
1 cup dry white wine
1 tablespoon minced fresh ginger
4 cups hot cooked basmati rice
⅓ cup slivered almonds, toasted

**1.** Preheat the oven to 350°F. Heat the broth in a small saucepan over medium-high until just boiling. Remove from heat, and add the raisins. Let stand 15 minutes.

**2.** Combine the curry powder, garam masala, 1 teaspoon of the salt, and ½ teaspoon of the black pepper in a small bowl.

**3.** Cook the bacon in a large enameled cast-iron Dutch oven over medium, turning occasionally, until crisp, about 6 minutes. Transfer the bacon to a plate lined with paper towels, reserving 2 tablespoons drippings in the Dutch oven and discarding remaining drippings. Crumble the bacon.

**4.** Sprinkle the chicken thighs with remaining 1 teaspoon salt and ½ teaspoon black pepper. Cook, in batches, in reserved hot drippings in Dutch oven over medium-high until well browned, about 5 minutes per side. Remove the chicken to a plate, reserving drippings in the Dutch oven.

**5.** Add the guajillo chile to the reserved drippings in the Dutch oven, and cook until lightly toasted, about 30 seconds per side. Add the carrot, yellow and red bell peppers, onion, and garlic; cook, stirring occasionally, until softened, 5 to 6 minutes. Add the tomato paste, wine, ginger, curry powder mixture, and raisin-broth mixture, stirring well. Reduce heat to medium-low, and simmer, stirring occasionally, until the sauce begins to thicken, 5 to 6 minutes.

**6.** Place the chicken thighs in the sauce. Cover; bake in the preheated oven 15 minutes. Uncover; bake until the sauce has thickened, about 15 more minutes.

**7.** Remove and discard the chile. Season to taste with additional salt and pepper. Serve the chicken and the sauce over the basmati rice in shallow bowls, and top with the almonds and the crumbled bacon.

*When this one-pot meal is in the works, it usually means company is coming and rolling up your sleeves is in order. For me, the four main components of this dish—sausage, corn, potatoes, and shrimp—all show better with a little smoke from the grill. So, I scrapped the boiling pot and fired up the backyard grill.*

# GRILLED FROGMORE STEW

*Serves 8      Hands-on 25 minutes      Total 45 minutes*

2 pounds small red potatoes, sliced
    into ½-inch-thick wedges
¼ cup Old Bay seasoning
¼ cup olive oil
5 ears fresh corn, husked and cut
    into thirds

3 pounds large, unpeeled raw shrimp
2 pounds smoked sausage links
Hot sauce, cocktail sauce, and tartar
    sauce

**1.** Preheat the oven to 350°F. Preheat a charcoal or gas grill to medium-high (400° to 450°F). Combine the potato wedges and 4 teaspoons each of the Old Bay seasoning and olive oil in a 1-gallon ziplock plastic bag. Seal the bag, and rub ingredients together until the potatoes are well coated. Transfer the potatoes to a large bowl, and set aside. Reserve the ziplock bag.

**2.** Using a large nonstick grill basket, grill the potato wedges, uncovered, turning until browned on both sides, 10 to 15 minutes. Transfer to a baking sheet, and bake in the preheated oven until tender, about 20 minutes. Remove the potatoes, and reduce the oven temperature to 200°F.

**3.** While the potatoes bake, add the corn and 4 teaspoons each of the Old Bay seasoning and oil to the reserved ziplock bag; repeat the coating process. Place the corn in a medium-size bowl, and set aside.

**4.** Add the shrimp and remaining 4 teaspoons each of seasoning and oil to the bag; repeat the coating process. (Note: It's important to coat the shrimp last while using the same bag.) Remove the shrimp from the bag, and place in a bowl.

**5.** Grill the sausage, uncovered, until they begin to char lightly, 5 minutes per side. Transfer to a plate, and cover with aluminum foil. Place in 200°F oven to keep warm.

**6.** Grill corn on grill, uncovered, turning occasionally, until lightly charred on all sides, 10 to 15 minutes. Place on a baking sheet with the potatoes in the oven.

**7.** Using the nonstick grill basket or metal skewers, grill the shrimp, uncovered, until opaque and lightly charred, about 2 minutes per side.

**8.** Transfer the potatoes, corn, sausage, and shrimp to a large platter. Serve with the hot sauce, cocktail sauce, and tartar sauce.

## Ben Moïse

Known more for his tenure as a South Carolina game warden, Ben Moïse has garnered a reputation as a consummate Southern storyteller. In his book, *Ramblings of a Lowcountry Game Warden,* you gain insight into the harrowing tales of alligator wrestling, dove burgling, and fishing fiascos. But as a commentator on all things Southern, Moïse is a master. As he tells it, "Most people who have never had this dish think it's a boiling cauldron with eye of newt and toe of frog, but I'm pleased to tell you that there ain't a frog in it." According to Moïse, the recipe did not exist prior to about 1965 as a named recipe. It's called Frogmore Stew because a shrimper lived in a little village on an island off South Carolina called Frogmore, which later became St. Helena. "It's a dirt simple recipe of sausage, corn, potatoes, and shrimp boiled in a pot with spices. And it follows the old tradition that if you're sittin' down eatin' with your fingers, you've got to be havin' a good time." If you opt to make it the traditional way, be sure to add the shrimp last, just a couple of minutes before you plan to serve it.

*Another favored use of cornmeal, hush puppies combine the goodness of doughy batter with the crispy crust of fried bread. Often served alongside seafood dishes—which are also typically fried—it's unclear exactly where the savory cornmeal croquette earned its name. Perhaps they were used to quiet whining dogs during a fish fry? I find it hard to believe this delicious snack would have been tossed to the dogs when it satisfies the growling within our own stomachs so well.*

# HUSH PUPPIES AND TARTAR SAUCE

*Serves 6 to 8     Hands-on 20 minutes     Total 20 minutes*

**TARTAR SAUCE**

½ cup mayonnaise

2 tablespoons sweet pickle relish

2 tablespoons minced celery
  (from 1 stalk)

1 tablespoon chopped fresh flat-leaf
  parsley

2 teaspoons fresh lemon juice
  (from 1 lemon)

1 teaspoon Dijon mustard

½ teaspoon celery salt

**HUSH PUPPIES**

Vegetable oil

¾ cup plain yellow cornmeal

½ cup (about 2 ⅛ ounces) all-purpose
  flour

1 tablespoon baking powder

1 teaspoon baking soda

1 teaspoon table salt

½ teaspoon garlic powder

¾ cup whole buttermilk

¾ cup grated white onion (from
  1 medium onion)

¾ cup fresh corn kernels (from 1 ear)

¼ cup chopped scallions (from
  2 scallions)

1 large egg, lightly beaten

**1.** Prepare the Tartar Sauce: Stir together all Tartar Sauce ingredients in a small bowl until combined; chill until ready to serve.

**2.** Prepare the Hush Puppies: Pour the oil to a depth of 6 inches into a large saucepan over medium; heat to 350°F.

**3.** Combine the cornmeal, flour, baking powder, baking soda, salt, and garlic powder in a large bowl. Stir in the buttermilk, onion, corn, scallions, and egg until moistened and combined. Let stand 10 minutes.

**4.** Drop the batter by 2-ounce spoonfuls into hot oil, and fry, in batches, until golden brown, 2 to 3 minutes per side. Transfer to a wire rack set over paper towels to drain. Serve warm with the Tartar Sauce.

# THE GRITS THAT BIND

There are many metrics by which different cultures measure the merit of a person. In the South, more important than graduating college, having a successful first hunt, or even learning how to walk, making a good bowl of grits is a true rite of passage. To some, the tiny little ground corn by-product may seem insignificant, but when cooked and served with a pat of butter and sprinkling of salt, it's more than a meal, it's a little taste of Southern soul. That's because whether baked in a cheesy casserole, fried up into tender cakes, served as dinner with tender morsels of shrimp, or simply savored for morning breakfast, grits have seen the South through wars, the Depression, political strife, and cultural division. Regardless of the past, it's the grits that bind us.

FRIED GRITS CAKES,
PG 133

BAKED EASY-CHEESY
GRITS, PG 133

BASIC GRITS,
PG 132

SWEET BREAKFAST
GRITS, PG 132

# BASIC GRITS

Serves 8    Hands-on 35 minutes
Total 8 hours, 35 minutes, including 8 hours soaking

*For the purists, there's only one way to make grits: You've got to boil them with a little salt and butter, and you can't use overprocessed quick or instant grits. For the best batch, find a local mill that sells stone-ground coarse grits, which offers a more toothsome texture.*

1 cup stone-ground grits
4 ½ cups water
2 teaspoons kosher salt

2 tablespoons unsalted butter
½ teaspoon black pepper

**1.** Place the grits in a medium bowl, and cover with 2 ½ cups of the water. Stir and let the grits settle for a few minutes before skimming off and discarding any chaff. Cover bowl, and let the grits soak at room temperature at least 8 hours or overnight. Drain and discard 1 ½ cups soaking water.

**2.** Bring remaining 2 cups water to a boil in a large heavy saucepan over high. Add 1 teaspoon of the salt, and slowly pour in the grits and remaining soaking water. Stir and return to a boil. Reduce heat to medium-low, and simmer, whisking often to prevent a film from forming on the bottom of the pan, until the grits are thick and creamy and the water has been absorbed, about 30 minutes. Stir in the butter, and season with the pepper and remaining 1 teaspoon salt. Serve immediately.

---

# SWEET BREAKFAST GRITS

Serves 6    Hands-on 10 minutes    Total 10 minutes

*I was a warm-grain breakfast kid growing up. I loved oatmeal, cream of wheat, cream of rice, basically anything you could stir butter and brown sugar into. It wasn't until later in life that I found grits was also a great candidate for a warm and creamy breakfast. Make them even dreamier with Praline Bacon (page 167).*

2 cups whole milk
2 cups water
4 tablespoons unsalted butter
2 tablespoons granulated sugar

1 teaspoon kosher salt
1 cup uncooked quick-cooking grits
 (not instant)

Bring the milk, water, butter, sugar, and salt to a boil in a heavy saucepan over medium-high, stirring constantly to keep the milk from scalding. Slowly stir in the grits, and continue to stir until smooth. Reduce heat to medium-low; cover and cook, uncovering to stir halfway through cooking time, until the grits are smooth, about 6 to 8 minutes.

# BAKED EASY-CHEESY GRITS

*Serves 8 to 10     Hands-on 15 minutes     Total 1 hour, 15 minutes*

3 cups whole milk

2 ¼ cups water

1 cup uncooked quick-cooking grits
 (not instant)

4 tablespoons unsalted butter

8 ounces processed cheese, cubed
 (such as Velveeta)

8 ounces colby-Jack cheese, cubed

1 teaspoon kosher salt

1 teaspoon garlic salt

½ teaspoon cayenne pepper

2 large eggs, lightly beaten

*For the home cook in a hurry, there's no shame in substituting the quick-grit for the real thing, especially when the finished product includes a hefty combination of cheese and butter. This is a family recipe from my brother-in-law that has become a fixture at our holiday table.*

**1.** Preheat the oven to 350°F. Bring the milk and the water to a boil in a large saucepan over medium-high, stirring occasionally. Whisk in the grits; reduce heat to medium-low, and cook, whisking constantly, until thickened, about 5 to 7 minutes. Remove from heat, and whisk in the butter, cheeses, kosher salt, garlic salt, and cayenne until the cheeses melt and mixture is smooth. Cool 10 minutes; whisk in the eggs. Pour the mixture into a greased 13- x 9-inch (3-quart) baking dish.

**2.** Bake in preheated oven until the top is lightly browned and mixture is slightly set, about 40 to 45 minutes. Let stand 10 minutes before serving.

---

# FRIED GRITS CAKES

*Serves 6     Hands-on 30 minutes     Total 1 hour, 30 minutes*

3 tablespoons (1 ½ ounces) unsalted
 butter, plus more for greasing pan

Basic Grits (page 132)

1 large egg, beaten

*A crisp-yet-spongy alternative to cornbread with braised meat dishes. Try these with Kentucky Burgoo (page 53) or Brunswick Stew (page 119).*

Grease a 13- x 9-inch pan with butter. Prepare the Basic Grits. Whisk 1 tablespoon of the butter into the hot cooked Basic Grits. Place the beaten egg in a small bowl, and add ¼ cup grits, 1 spoonful at a time, whisking until blended. Add the egg mixture to the warm grits, whisking until blended. Pour the grits mixture into prepared pan, and cool to room temperature, 45 minutes to 1 hour. (If you will not cook the grits cakes within 1 hour, cover and chill.) When ready to cook, turn the grits out of pan, and cut into 12 (3-inch) squares. Heat remaining 2 tablespoons butter in a medium skillet over medium-high until melted. Cook the grits cakes in melted butter, in batches, until crisp and lightly browned, about 5 to 6 minutes per side.

# Vivian Howard

## CONNECTED TO THE COASTAL PLAINS

Vivian Howard sees her little neck of the woods in Deep Run, North Carolina, as resolutely "micro-regional." That's because Deep Run is too far east to be considered Appalachian and too far inland to be coastal. Howard describes her hometown as part of the Coastal Plains. "It's very flat, and though its foodways are affected by the sea, it's not based on the sea," says Howard.

Howard's parents were hog and row crop farmers, which afforded her a perspective on life that championed hard work and relished simplicity and tranquility. Though she would move on to spend a few years in New York as a young adult, earning her culinary degree and working in restaurants such as the critically acclaimed wd-50 and Jean-Georges Vongerichten's Spice Market, Howard's ties to North Carolina's Coastal Plains incessantly tugged at her heart.

It was a call that she answered in 2005 when she returned with her husband, Ben Knight, to open Chef & the Farmer in Kinston, just a few miles away from her hometown. Housed in a former mule stable, the homespun restaurant serves as a tribute to the traditional regional dishes of Howard's home. With more than sixty percent of the ingredients sourced from within a ninety-mile radius, it also acts as a call for local farmers to remain steadfast in their agricultural way of life.

Following a devastating fire to the restaurant in 2012, Howard opened a casual oyster bar, the Boiler Room, to keep her busy while Chef & the Farmer rebuilt. During that time, she was tapped to star in a PBS series, *A Chef's Life*, which documents the joys and hardships of farming and cooking in Howard's neck of the woods.

For Howard, the Coastal Plains best represent the foods of the rural, frugal farmer. To Howard, they take on a specific flavor based on the preparation and the seasonal ingredients unique to her region, including simple root vegetables such as sweet potatoes where more than sixty percent of the country's supply is grown.

"People are often surprised that the foods I grew up on aren't the typical foods you associate with the South. You won't find Apple Stack Cake or fried chicken," says Howard. "We usually steam our collard greens with air-dried sausage rather than stewing them with a ham hock, we make pinch biscuits instead of rolled biscuits, and our ied sausage and biscuits are really unlike any other dish you might find anywhere else in the broader region of the South."

One of her favorite memories from her mother's kitchen is the rich, layered flavor of chicken and rice. "It's a dish that really developed out of the need to use spent laying hens," says Howard. "You would boil them for hours and get this delicious broth. Then we'd pick the meat and put it back in the pot and add rice. It was very simple and so comforting."

Although rice plays a small role in the cuisine, Howard points to corn as the more dominant ingredient with hoecakes and cornbread factoring heavily into day-to-day cooking.

"We very much have a vegetables- and grain-focused diet with meat being more of a condiment."

The one exception would be when the family puts on a fish stew. While the basic ingredients are the same, a fish stew from the Coastal Plains of North Carolina differs from a traditional Carolina Fish Muddle.

"Fish stew is a celebration food for us," says Howard. "And it may most perfectly represent where we are. A farmer might go to the coast for a weekend in the fall and come back with a red drum or sheepshead. To stretch that catch out, you make a fish stew."

Aside from her family, Howard's passion for the Coastal Plains of North Carolina has become her life's pride and joy, a sentiment thoroughly documented in her 2016 book, *Deep Run Roots*. In it, she shares in story and in recipes a snapshot of a region of the South that may be micro in size but stands out as a special place with massive soul.

*A classic dish along the Atlantic Coast, Fish Stew is not to be confused with a Fish Muddle. Though the ingredients are the same, the defining difference is that the stew is more of a layered dish. On the other hand, a muddle allows all the ingredients to be stirred together during the cooking process—hence, the term muddle. The eggs are often used to stretch the soup when serving a lot of people. They're something a farmer always has on hand. The key is to crack the eggs on top to create a blanket. Serve with a bit of all the layers in a bowl, and use white bread to sop it up.*

# VIVIAN HOWARD'S FISH STEW

*Serves 12    Hands-on 25 minutes    Total 45 minutes*

1 pound smoked bacon slices (about 16 slices)

1 (6-ounce) can tomato paste

3 pounds russet or red potatoes, peeled and cut into ½-inch rounds (about 3 cups rounds)

2 pounds yellow onions, peeled, halved, and cut into ¼-inch slices (about 3 cups sliced)

6 garlic cloves, sliced (about 3 tablespoons)

2½ tablespoons kosher salt

1½ teaspoons crushed red pepper

8 cups water

3 pounds halibut, red drum, rockfish, or sheepshead steaks with bones intact (about 3 ounces each)

1 fish head, rinsed well (optional)

1 dozen large eggs

1 (8-ounce) white bread loaf, sliced

**1.** Cut the bacon slices into 1-inch pieces. Cook the bacon in an 8- to 10-quart Dutch oven or cast-iron stockpot over medium-high until crisp, 8 to 10 minutes. Transfer the bacon to a plate lined with paper towels to drain, reserving 2 tablespoons drippings in Dutch oven and discarding remaining drippings. Whisk the tomato paste into reserved drippings, stirring and scraping to loosen browned bits from bottom of Dutch oven.

**2.** Remove from heat. Layer one-third of the potatoes in the Dutch oven over the tomato sauce mixture. Top with one-third of the sliced onion and one-third of the sliced garlic; sprinkle with one-third of the salt and red pepper. Repeat layers twice, ending with the salt and the red pepper. Add 8 cups water or more, if needed, so the water just barely reaches the top of the layers. Cover the Dutch oven with a tight-fitting lid, and bring to a boil over medium. Once the stew starts to boil, reduce the heat to low, and simmer, covered, until the potatoes are just tender, about 15 minutes.

**3.** Uncover and add the fish to the top of the stew, pushing aside the potatoes as necessary to nestle the fish steaks under cooking liquid. Add the fish head, if desired, on top of the stew. Simmer, covered, until the fish and potatoes are tender, about 5 minutes. If using a fish head, remove the head when the fish steaks are tender.

**4.** While the stew simmers, crack the eggs, 1 at a time, in a single layer over the top of the stew. Simmer until the eggs are cooked through, 2 to 3 minutes.

**5.** Ladle the stew into bowls, including at least 1 fish steak, 2 potato rounds, some onions, and 1 egg with broth. Sprinkle with the chopped bacon, and serve with the white bread.

*When it comes to crab cakes, Maryland is the standard-bearer for the humble fried cake. The problem most people run into is including too much breading in the mixture. A good crab cake lets the fresh crab be the star of this dish. You can serve them with rémoulade or lemon aioli, but I prefer a simple squeeze of lemon. Be sure to splurge for the jumbo lump crabmeat. Its plump, tender texture is what makes the ultimate crab cake.*

# MARYLAND-WORTHY CRAB CAKES

*Serves 6    Hands-on 25 minutes    Total 55 minutes*

¾ cup mayonnaise

2 large eggs, beaten

2 tablespoons Dijon mustard

1 teaspoon hot pepper sauce
  (*such as Tabasco*)

2 pounds fresh jumbo lump crabmeat,
  drained and picked over

½ cup sliced scallions (from 4 scallions)

1 teaspoon kosher salt

2 cups panko (Japanese-style
  breadcrumbs)

6 tablespoons canola oil

Lemon wedges

**1.** Whisk together the mayonnaise, eggs, mustard, and hot pepper sauce in a small bowl. Toss together the crabmeat, scallions, salt, and 1 cup of the panko in a medium bowl. Carefully fold in the mayonnaise mixture. (Be careful not to overmix to avoid breaking down the crabmeat.)

**2.** Shape about ½ cup crabmeat mixture into a 3-inch patty, and repeat with the remaining crabmeat mixture to equal 12 patties. Place the patties on a baking sheet; cover and chill at least 30 minutes or up to 8 hours.

**3.** Remove the crab cakes from refrigerator. Place remaining 1 cup panko on a large plate. Dip each crab cake in the panko, pressing the crumbs into the patties to adhere. Heat 3 tablespoons of the oil in a large skillet over medium-high. Cook half of the crab cakes in the hot oil until golden brown, 3 to 4 minutes per side. Transfer the crab cakes to a plate lined with paper towels to drain. Cover with aluminum foil to keep warm. Repeat procedure with the remaining oil and the crab cakes. Serve with the lemon wedges.

*You're not likely to find any wild salmon in the Gulf of Mexico, but you'll find that Salmon Croquettes have long been a popular dish, primarily for their simplicity and affordability. In the 1920s, canned foods began to fill the shelves of regional grocers such as Piggly Wiggly. While the French "croquette," a breaded mixture of meat or potato filling, had long been an accepted style of preparation, the South adopted seasonal crab for crab cakes as its regional variation. But when crab was neither in season nor affordable, canned salmon quickly took its place. You can still make salmon croquettes from a can, but in this case, fresh is most certainly best.*

# SALMON CROQUETTES

*Serves 6     Hands-on 30 minutes     Total 30 minutes*

1 pound skinless salmon fillet

1 ½ teaspoons kosher salt

½ teaspoon black pepper

1 small yellow onion, grated
  (about ⅓ cup)

2 large eggs, beaten

2 tablespoons finely chopped fresh
  flat-leaf parsley

⅓ cup plain yellow cornmeal

⅓ cup dry breadcrumbs

1 teaspoon lemon zest (from 1 lemon)

½ teaspoon cayenne pepper

3 tablespoons unsalted butter

Creole Rémoulade (page 189)

**1.** Preheat the oven to 400°F. Sprinkle the salmon with 1 teaspoon of the salt and the black pepper, and place on a lightly greased baking sheet. Bake in preheated oven until the fish flakes with a fork, 10 to 12 minutes. (Thinner fillets may take less time.) Cool completely, about 20 minutes.

**2.** Flake the cooled salmon into a medium bowl. Add the onion, eggs, parsley, cornmeal, breadcrumbs, lemon zest, cayenne, and remaining ½ teaspoon salt. Gently combine the mixture with hands or a spoon until well blended. Shape the mixture into 6 (3 ¼-inch) patties (about ½ inch thick).

**3.** Melt the butter in a large skillet over medium. Add the patties, and cook until well browned on both sides, 3 to 5 minutes per side. Serve hot with the Creole Rémoulade.

# Ford Fry

## NEVER STUFFY, ALWAYS AUTHENTIC

The journey from chef to restaurateur is more complicated than you might think. It certainly isn't what Atlanta-based chef Ford Fry imagined for himself as a teenager growing up in Houston, Texas. But a lot can happen when you manage to find your passion at a young age—whether you intended to or not.

So how did the child of an accountant and a church administrator growing up in a white-collar part of Houston, making below-average grades become a chef and restaurateur in Atlanta? The answer isn't unlike the way many people come to find their own career path—especially chefs. He became a chef because his dad, who was grasping at straws to give direction to his young-adult son, suggested it might be something he'd be good at doing.

"[My Dad] had read an article about the job of a chef as a fast-track career in the *Wall Street Journal* and shared it with me," says Fry. "It's unclear to me exactly how he came to that conclusion about me in particular. Sure, I liked to eat, but who doesn't? I did enjoy tinkering around the kitchen—and especially with our patio grill—as a teenager, but it didn't seem that unusual to me."

When he suggested culinary school, Fry had his doubts. This was long before the day of cable food channels and celebrity chefs. To him, the prospect of slaving away in a kitchen for the rest of his life didn't seem too appealing.

"But something inside made me take the leap," says Fry. "I think maybe it's because the most impactful memories I had at that time in my life were all strung together by a common thread: food. It was a central part of some of my best life experiences. Whether at holiday occasions of gathering together with my family, roadside stops on road trips, or planning entire vacations where tourist attractions were superseded by the restaurants we would visit along the way, food and family were always the two commonalities."

Fry attended the New England Culinary Institute in Vermont and quickly realized he'd made the right choice. He then worked his way through some inspiring kitchens on the West Coast and in Colorado before moving to Atlanta where he would make his home. In 2007, he opened JCT. Kitchen & Bar in Atlanta's Westside. According to Fry, the neighborhood needed a local joint that was sophisticated but also comfortable for weekly regulars.

When settling on the idea, Fry knew he wanted the food to be thoughtful and responsible with, what he calls, a farmstead approach, and it needed to have a sense of familiarity. To him, there was only one style of cooking that made sense: Southern. And considering its location right on the junction of the railroad tracks, the name JCT. seemed only fitting.

"Growing up in Texas, my experience with true Southern cooking was my grandmother's housekeeper, Lottie Mae. She cooked simple Southern food, but it was always soulful and flavorful," says Fry. "Atlanta had plenty of traditional Southern-style restaurants. I wanted to offer something fresh and seasonal without stepping on the toes of others. There was something kindred to me about the home-style feel of Southern cuisine along with the everyday familiarity of French brasserie fare. JCT. is the culmination of those two ideas."

JCT. Kitchen & Bar quickly became a cornerstone in the revival of Atlanta's Westside, and it solidified for Fry that what people wanted more than just fancy food was a familiar dining experience that could remind them of home. The restaurant has borrowed from Southern tradition with weekly Sunday Suppers that harken back to a time when family would gather to break bread together.

"I think there's a lot of importance to the perfect execution, but really what ends up on the plate is just food. Cooking is more than just about the food, it's about the experience," says Fry. "I've found that the things I love making the most are those things that have a memory associated with them. Like my grandmother's rémoulade sauce that always showed up with warm, fresh boiled shrimp before a holiday meal. Or wood-roasted lamb after church back in Houston; or that perfect cheese enchilada I just have to have when I get back to Texas. To me, cooking has the power to bring you something delicious, but also transport you to a place in life where you've been satisfied, happy, and complete."

Fry has gone on to fill empty gaps for Atlanta neighborhoods with seafood, Italian, Tex-Mex, and steak restaurants and has also spread his wings into Nashville, Charlotte, and back in his home state of Texas. He's received numerous accolades and multiple nominations for a James Beard Award. But in his regular rotations of visiting his restaurant kitchens, it's JCT. Kitchen that reminds him of the importance of staying true to his purpose: cooking delicious food that is never stuffy and always authentic.

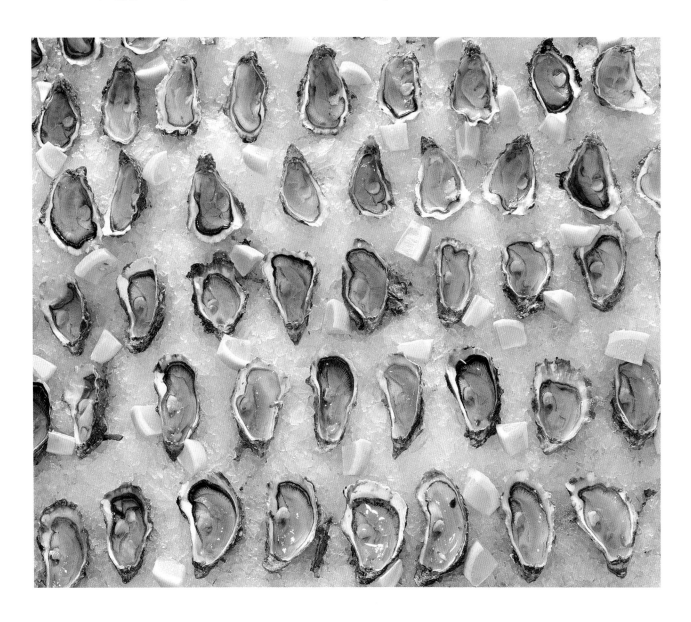

*Traditional oyster stew is thick, but this version from Atlanta's Ford Fry of Southern-inspired JCT. Kitchen & Bar and coastal seafood hot spot, The Optimist, is more like a light cream soup or a thin bisque. It's extremely rich, luscious, and silky, with a faint scent of the ocean. Purchase the freshest, largest oysters you can buy for this recipe. Note: Merkén is a traditional Chilean seasoning with a smoky chipotle-type taste, but not as hot. The "potluck" garlic bread is the best to have on hand for dipping.*

# OYSTER PAN STEW WITH "POTLUCK" GARLIC BREAD

*Serves 6     Hands-on 30 minutes     Total 30 minutes*

**OYSTER PAN STEW**

3 cups fresh shucked large oysters
    (about 30 oysters), plus ½ cup
    reserved oyster liquor
¼ cup unsalted butter
⅓ cup finely chopped shallot
1 garlic clove, sliced
1 cup fish stock or clam juice
1 cup heavy cream
1 tablespoon lemon zest (from 1 lemon)
½ cup plus 2 tablespoons dry vermouth
    (5 ounces)
¼ cup finely chopped fresh chives
2 tablespoons chopped fresh flat-leaf
    parsley

1 teaspoon kosher salt
1 teaspoon black pepper

**"POTLUCK" GARLIC BREAD**

4 ounces (½ cup) unsalted butter,
    softened
1 tablespoon minced garlic (from
    3 garlic cloves)
2 tablespoons finely chopped fresh
    flat-leaf parsley
1 teaspoon kosher salt
½ (6-ounce) baguette, ends trimmed
    and loaf cut into 6 pieces
Merkén or smoked paprika
Olive oil

**1.** Prepare the Oyster Pan Stew: Process ½ cup oyster liquor and ½ cup of the shucked oysters in a blender until smooth, 1 minute; set aside.

**2.** Melt 2 tablespoons of the butter in a large Dutch oven over medium. Add the shallot and garlic; cook, stirring, until fragrant, 1 to 2 minutes. Stir in the stock, heavy cream, lemon zest, oyster mixture, and ½ cup of the vermouth; simmer, stirring occasionally, until liquid is reduced by half, 10 to 12 minutes. Reduce heat to low, stir in remaining 2 tablespoons vermouth and 2 tablespoons butter, and cook, stirring constantly, until the butter is halfway melted, about 30 seconds. Stir in the chives, parsley, salt, pepper, and

remaining 2 ½ cups oysters. When the butter melts completely, remove from heat, cover Dutch oven, and let stand until the oysters are slightly poached, 3 to 4 minutes.

**3.** Prepare the "Potluck" Garlic Bread: Preheat the oven to 400°F. Stir together the butter, garlic, parsley, and salt in a bowl until well blended. Cut 3 slits in the top of each bread piece. Spread the butter mixture evenly among bread pieces, pushing into slits. Wrap each bread piece in parchment paper, leaving ends open, and secure with kitchen twine. Bake in the preheated oven until hot, about 8 to 10 minutes.

**4.** Spoon the stew into bowls, and garnish each serving with a pinch of the Merkén and a drizzle of olive oil. Serve with the hot bread.

*This golden multilayer cake is framed by delicate layers of burnt sugar, or caramel icing. The icing—not to be confused with a thick frosting—is perhaps the rite of passage required by any Southern cook to master. When it has come together in the saucepan, it should coat a wooden spoon and slowly drizzle off. Too thin, and the cake barely looks dressed; too thick, and you've overdone it. This is where the adage is true: Practice makes perfect.*

# CARAMEL CAKE

*Serves 10 to 12     Hands-on 30 minutes     Total 3 hours, 30 minutes*

**CAKE**

1 cup (8 ounces) unsalted butter, softened, plus more for greasing pans

3 cups (about 12 ¾ ounces) all-purpose flour, plus more for dusting pans

1 teaspoon baking powder

1 teaspoon table salt

2 ½ cups granulated sugar

5 large eggs

2 large egg yolks

2 teaspoons vanilla extract

¾ cup whole milk

**ICING**

4 cups granulated sugar

1 tablespoon all-purpose flour

1 ½ cups whole milk

4 ounces (½ cup) unsalted butter

½ teaspoon kosher salt, plus more to taste

1 tablespoon vanilla extract

**1.** Prepare the Cake: Preheat the oven to 350°F. Grease bottom and sides of 2 (9-inch) round cake pans with butter; dust with flour, and tap out excess.

**2.** Whisk together the baking powder, salt, and 3 cups flour in a large bowl.

**3.** Place 1 cup softened butter in the bowl of a heavy-duty electric stand mixer; beat on medium speed until creamy, about 1 minute. Gradually add the sugar, beating on medium speed until well blended after each addition and scraping down the sides of the bowl as needed, 10 to 15 seconds after each addition (about 2 minutes total). Add the eggs and the egg yolks, 1 at a time, beating on low speed just until blended after each addition. Beat in the vanilla. Add the flour mixture alternately with the milk, beginning and ending with the flour mixture. Beat on low speed just until blended after each addition. Divide the batter between prepared pans.

**4.** Bake in the preheated oven until a wooden pick inserted in center comes out clean, about 30 minutes. Cool in the pans on a wire rack 10 minutes; run an offset spatula or knife around edge of the pans to loosen sides; transfer the cakes to a wire rack (rounded side up) to cool completely, about 1 hour.

**5.** Prepare the Icing: Sprinkle ½ cup of the sugar in a large heavy saucepan; cook over medium, shaking the pan occasionally but not stirring, until the sugar is melted and the syrup is amber, about 5 to 7 minutes. Remove from heat.

*continued on next page*

**6.** While sugar caramelizes, whisk together the flour and remaining 3 ½ cups sugar in a separate medium saucepan. Whisk in the milk, and bring to a boil over medium-high, stirring constantly. Gradually pour one-third of the hot milk mixture into the caramelized sugar, whisking constantly to blend. Slowly add remaining hot milk mixture, whisking until the mixture is smooth. Cover and cook on low 2 minutes.

**7.** Uncover and increase heat to medium. Cook, without stirring, until the mixture reaches soft ball stage and a candy thermometer registers 238°F, about 12 to 14 minutes. Remove from the heat, and stir in the butter until melted and well blended. Let stand, without stirring, 30 minutes.

**8.** Pour the mixture into the bowl of a heavy-duty stand mixer. Add the salt and the vanilla, and beat on medium speed until the mixture reaches spreading consistency, 10 to 15 minutes. (Icing should still fall off the spatula but have good structure.)

**9.** Assemble the Caramel Cake: Place 1 cake layer on a cake plate. Working quickly, spread just enough Icing over the cake on plate to cover the top in a thin layer. Top with second cake layer, and spread about one-third of the remaining Icing over top of cake. Spread remaining Icing on sides of cake. Let stand until set, about 20 minutes.

*Black walnuts have a special home in Maryland, and there are numerous cake recipes that showcase black walnuts as the star. This one has been handed down through my family and includes the sweet tastes of apples and warm holiday spices. Served with a scoop of vanilla ice cream, it's a consistent crowd-pleaser.*

# MARYLAND APPLE-WALNUT BUNDT CAKE

*Serves 12      Hands-on 25 minutes      Total 2 hours, 25 minutes*

2 cups granulated sugar

1 cup vegetable oil

2 teaspoons vanilla extract

3 large eggs

3 cups (about 12 ¾ ounces) all-purpose flour, plus more for pan

¾ teaspoon table salt

1 teaspoon baking soda

1 ½ cups black walnuts, toasted and chopped

3 cups finely chopped Golden Delicious or Gala apples (from 2 large apples)

4 ounces (½ cup) unsalted butter, plus more for pan

1 cup packed light brown sugar

2 tablespoons whole milk

2 tablespoons (1 ounce) brandy

**1.** Preheat the oven to 350°F. Whisk together the granulated sugar, oil, vanilla, and eggs in a large bowl. Whisk together the flour, salt, and baking soda in a medium bowl; add the flour mixture to the sugar mixture, stirring until blended. (Batter will be thick; use your hands to combine, if needed.) Fold in the walnuts and the chopped apples. Spoon the batter into a greased and floured 12-cup Bundt pan. Bake in the preheated oven until a wooden pick inserted in center comes out clean, about 1 hour. Remove from the oven, and place the pan on a wire rack.

**2.** While the cake bakes, stir together the butter, brown sugar, milk, and brandy in a saucepan. Bring to a boil over medium, stirring constantly. Pour the brown sugar mixture over the warm cake in pan, gently pulling the cake toward center away from the pan with a knife to allow the brown sugar mixture to flow down side of cake. Let stand in the pan on wire rack 1 hour. Turn the cake out onto a serving plate, and serve warm, or cool completely.

*While New Orleans is known for its settlements of French Catholics, Charleston is known for its settlement of French Protestants, or Huguenots, who were sent by England's King Charles II to establish the community of "Charles Town." There's nothing really related to the Huguenots or to a traditional torte about this cake. It's likely adapted from the classic Ozark Pudding from northwest Arkansas and southwest Missouri. A favorite dessert of the Huguenot community of Charleston, it gained national fame when President Harry S. Truman declared it his favorite dessert. His wife, Bess, made it her contribution to the* Congressional Club Cookbook.

# HUGUENOT TORTE WITH BOURBON WHIPPED CREAM

*Serves 8    Hands-on 15 minutes    Total 1 hour, 25 minutes*

Vegetable shortening, for greasing pan

¼ cup (about 1 ounce) all-purpose flour, plus more for dusting

2 large eggs

1½ cups granulated sugar

1 teaspoon vanilla extract

1½ teaspoons baking powder

¼ teaspoon table salt

1 cup chopped toasted pecans

1 cup peeled, chopped Granny Smith apple (from 1 medium)

1 cup heavy cream

1 tablespoon bourbon

**1.** Preheat the oven to 325°F. Grease and flour a 10-inch pie pan. Whisk together the eggs, sugar, and vanilla in a bowl until well blended and fluffy, about 1 minute. Place ¼ cup flour in a separate bowl, and whisk in the baking powder and the salt. Stir the pecans and apple into the flour mixture. Whisk the flour mixture into the egg mixture until well blended. Pour the mixture into the prepared pie pan, and bake in the preheated oven until the top is browned and crusty, about 45 minutes. Cool in the pan on a wire rack 30 minutes.

**2.** Meanwhile, beat the cream and bourbon with an electric mixer on medium speed until soft peaks form, about 3 to 4 minutes. Serve the warm cake topped with the whipped cream.

*When it comes to dishes that have a sense of place, Key lime pie is synonymous with the Florida Coast. I'll never forget the first time I tasted the tart and creamy indulgence when visiting family friends in Sarasota as a kid. The pie was so tart, I could feel the insides of my cheeks pucker—which is the telltale sign that you're dealing with the real McCoy. For those that like a little less tartness and something a little more tropical, this is my mother's recipe using fresh mango.*

# MANGO-KEY LIME PIE

*Serves 8 to 10      Hands-on 20 minutes      Total 4 hours, 45 minutes*

2 cups graham cracker crumbs
  (from 16 rectangles)
⅓ cup packed light brown sugar
½ teaspoon ground cinnamon
4 ounces (½ cup) salted butter, melted
6 large egg yolks
½ cup bottled Key lime juice
1 (14-ounce) can sweetened condensed
  milk

½ cup pureed fresh mango, plus ½ cup
  diced fresh mango (from 1 mango)
2 cups heavy cream
1 teaspoon vanilla extract
6 tablespoons powdered sugar
Lime zest (optional)

**1.** Preheat the oven to 350°F. Combine the graham cracker crumbs, brown sugar, cinnamon, and butter in a large bowl. Press the mixture into the bottom and up the sides of a lightly greased 10-inch pie pan.

**2.** Combine the egg yolks, lime juice, sweetened condensed milk, and ½ cup pureed mango in a food processor, and process until well incorporated, about 1 minute. Fold in ½ cup diced mango using a rubber spatula. Pour the mixture into the prepared crust, and bake in the preheated oven until set, 20 to 25 minutes. Transfer to a wire rack to cool completely, about 1 hour. Refrigerate at least 3 hours before serving.

**3.** Place the cream and vanilla in bowl of a heavy-duty stand mixer fitted with whisk attachment, and beat on medium-high speed until foamy. Gradually add the powdered sugar, and beat until medium peaks form. Dollop the whipped cream on top of the pie, and garnish with the lime zest, if desired; serve immediately, or chill until ready to serve.

*Too many times I've avoided a bowl of creamy, pink, marshmallow-festooned creation at holiday parties or church gatherings. Mainly because I'm never quite sure what exactly has been stirred in, nor am I confident in its shelf stability to sit out on an outdoor folding table in the summertime. (You never know when that mayonnaise is going to take a turn.) But when you put all the best parts about ambrosia salad in a homemade coconut ice cream, you eschew all concerns from inquiring parties and guarantee a room full of smiling faces.*

# AMBROSIA ICE CREAM

*Serves 8 to 10     Hands-on 10 minutes     Total 5 hours, 10 minutes*

2 cups refrigerated coconut milk beverage

1½ cups granulated sugar

2 cups whole milk

2 cups heavy cream

3 tablespoons orange zest (from 2 medium oranges)

1 teaspoon vanilla extract

1 cup unsweetened flaked coconut, toasted

½ cup canned crushed pineapple in juice, drained (from 1 [8-ounce] can)

½ cup chopped maraschino cherries

1 cup miniature marshmallows

**1.** Heat the coconut milk beverage and the sugar in a small saucepan over medium, stirring occasionally, just until the sugar dissolves, about 5 minutes. Remove from heat, and stir in the whole milk, heavy cream, orange zest, and vanilla. Cover and chill until cold, about 1 hour.

**2.** Remove the milk mixture from refrigerator; slowly pour the mixture into the frozen freezer bowl of a 2-quart electric ice-cream maker, and proceed according to manufacturer's instructions, adding the coconut, pineapple, cherries, and marshmallows during the last 5 minutes of churning. (Instructions and times may vary.) Transfer to an airtight freezer-safe container; freeze until firm, about 4 hours.

**NOTE:** Be sure to use coconut milk from the refrigerated dairy section of the store, not the canned coconut cream.

*No Southern home is without their own family-cherished version of sweet tea. But when you consider that the average amount of sugar served in this revered traditional drink is the equivalent of a 12-ounce can of soda, I like to lean on the virtues of natural sugars—like the kind you find in ripe summer berries—to help balance things out. Throw it in an ice-cream machine for a refreshing sorbet and call this what it really is: dessert!*

# SUMMER BERRY-SWEET TEA SORBET

*Serves 8 to 10     Hands-on 30 minutes     Total 5 hours*

1 ½ pounds fresh berries (such as blackberries, blueberries, or dewberries)

3 cups water

1 cup granulated sugar

4 regular-size tea bags (such as black or iced-tea blend)

**1.** Process the berries, ½ cup of the water, and ¼ cup of the sugar in a blender or food processor until smooth, about 30 seconds.

**2.** Combine remaining 2 ½ cups water and ¾ cup sugar in a medium saucepan, and bring to a boil over medium-high. Remove from heat. Add the tea bags to water mixture, and steep 7 minutes. Discard the tea bags. Pour the pureed berry mixture into the tea, and chill 30 minutes.

**3.** Slowly pour the sweet tea mixture into the frozen freezer bowl of a 2-quart electric ice-cream maker, and proceed according to manufacturer's instructions. (Instructions and times may vary.) Transfer to an airtight freezer-safe container; freeze until firm, about 4 hours.

GULF COAST & THE DELTA

# Gulf Coast & The Delta

**OFTEN REFERRED TO AS THE "DEEP SOUTH,"** this region is bordered by the Gulf of Mexico and heavily influenced by the cultural and economic history of the mighty Mississippi River and the river delta that fans out to its south. The foods of the Gulf Coast reflect the cooking traditions of French and Spanish colonists as well as a deeper dimension of flavor from the resourcefulness of its early Native American and African slave populations. Here, foods reveal a stronger dependence on spice and heat from Creole and Cajun cooking traditions and a dependence on the bounty of the Gulf of Mexico.

## DINING DETOURS

Highlands Bar & Grill, Birmingham, AL

Niki's West, Birmingham, AL

Johnny's Restaurant, Homewood, AL

Lasyone's Meat Pie Restaurant, Natchitoches, LA

Domilise's, New Orleans, LA

Galatoire's, New Orleans, LA

Herbsaint, New Orleans, LA

Rosedale Restaurant, New Orleans, LA

Doe's Eat Place, Greenville, MS

Lusco's, Greenwood, MS

Payne's Bar-B-Que, Memphis, TN

Restaurant Iris, Memphis, TN

The Second Line, Memphis, TN

# John Currence

## GREEK, LEBANESE, AND ASIAN MIGRATION

While many immigrant cultures are often linked to Southern cooking—African, English, German, Irish, Czech, Caribbean—it's important to note that other cultures also made their home in the South, often as pioneers of their own or in small groups to reestablish their own community. In the early twentieth century, Greek, Italian, and Lebanese immigrants made their way to places in Louisiana, Alabama, Mississippi, as well as throughout the South.

Having spent three decades of his restaurant career in New Orleans, Chapel Hill, North Carolina, and Oxford, Mississippi, Chef John Currence brings a deep respect for this diverse heritage to his cooking. His admiration for these immigrant populations in the Delta have helped him better understand the canon of food that represents the flavors of the whole Gulf Coast region.

"When you talk about foods that define Mississippi, I see it as looking back three to four decades at the Lebanese, Italian, German, and even the Chinese populations that thrived in the Delta as merchants or craftsmen. From these cultures sprang small mom-and-pop restaurants that served foods of their heritage. They were Americanized versions of it but still familiar and comfortable for the people of their community."

One of Currence's favorite stops is Wong's Foodland, a Chinese-owned grocery in Clarksdale, Mississippi.

"It's one of the first places in Mississippi that I visited that still has a nose-to-tail butcher shop area where you could buy pig ears, heads, feet, fresh chitlins, and every little piece," recounts Currence. "They had a window and small kitchen in there where they made delicious fried rice and Americanized versions of Chinese food. It's always my stop on the way to duck camp to pick up peanuts to boil and pigs ears to cook."

Not far from Foodland, Chamoun's Rest Haven is an authentic Lebanese diner serving up classic kibbe, stuffed cabbage rolls, and the foods owner Chafik Chamoun, a Lebanese immigrant who came to the Delta in 1954, was raised on. "You see less of the original Lebanese fare on their menu these days and more Americanized meat-and-potatoes dishes, but this is a man that followed his grandfather to the Delta to make a better life."

Greek foodways have also taken a stronghold in certain parts of the region. Currence references one of his former sous chefs, Timothy Hontzas, who opened a place called Johnny's in Birmingham as a tribute to his Greek heritage. His grandfather, Johnny Hontzopolous, migrated to New Orleans in 1921 and opened three restaurants in Mississippi, and inspired his son Gus to open Niki's West in Birmingham, which has become a pillar of the restaurant community. In 2012, Tim opened Johnny's Restaurant in Homewood, Alabama, as a tribute to his grandfather. This new generation of what many have deemed a "Greek and Three" is one of many examples of how Currence has encouraged his stable of chefs to let their heritage shine through as a way to further advance where Southern cuisine is going.

"I love that he's taken the idea of the Southern meat-and-three that his family has long owned and introduced dishes to the menu that his mother and grandmother used to cook for him," says Currence. "That's where Southern foodways are going."

*This tasty breakfast dish reminds us that stale bread doesn't have to be forgotten, or "perdu." John Currence, chef/owner of Big Bad Breakfast, City Grocery, SnackBar, and Nacho Mama's, kicks up the indulgence of this New Orleans-style treat by deep-frying it for a few minutes.*

# PAIN PERDU

*Serves 4     Hands-on 45 minutes     Total 1 hour, 15 minutes*

2 ½ tablespoons powdered sugar, plus more for dusting

¾ cup heavy cream

2 ½ teaspoons vanilla extract

¼ cup packed dark brown sugar

2 tablespoons cold unsalted butter, cubed

2 tablespoons (1 ounce) dark rum

Vegetable oil

5 large eggs

½ cup whole milk

3 tablespoons (1 ½ ounces) brandy

1 tablespoon granulated sugar

¼ teaspoon ground nutmeg

¼ teaspoon ground cinnamon

Pinch of table salt

12 (¾-inch-thick) baguette slices

Sliced bananas

**1.** Preheat the oven to 200°F. Beat the powdered sugar, ½ cup of the heavy cream, and 1 teaspoon of the vanilla with an electric mixer on high speed until stiff peaks form, 1 to 2 minutes. Cover the whipped cream, and chill until ready to serve.

**2.** Bring the brown sugar and butter to a simmer in a saucepan over medium, stirring often. Reduce heat to medium-low, and cook, stirring often, until the sugar melts and mixture is smooth, 3 to 4 minutes. Carefully add the rum and 2 tablespoons of the cream; simmer, stirring occasionally, 1 minute. Remove from heat. (If you want a thicker sauce, let the mixture simmer over low, stirring occasionally, until desired thickness.) Store the rum sauce in an airtight container in refrigerator up to 10 days.

**3.** Pour the oil to a depth of 4 inches into a large deep skillet; heat over medium to 375°F.

**4.** Whisk together the eggs, milk, brandy, granulated sugar, nutmeg, cinnamon, salt, and remaining 2 tablespoons cream and 1 ½ teaspoons vanilla. Dip the bread, 1 slice at a time, into the egg mixture, allowing each slice to soak in the mixture about 30 seconds. Remove the bread from the egg mixture, allowing excess egg mixture to drip off into bowl. Gently place 4 pieces of soaked bread into hot oil, and fry until golden brown, 2 to 2 ½ minutes per side. Remove to a baking sheet lined with paper towels. Keep warm in preheated oven until ready to serve.

**5.** Arrange 3 bread slices on each of 4 serving plates; dust with the powdered sugar, and top with the sliced bananas and the whipped cream; drizzle with the rum sauce.

*These days it's pretty standard to find a shrimp and grits offering on the menu of any restaurant that claims partiality to Southern cooking. It's a particularly popular trend of upscale Southern restaurants to dress up the dish beyond its humble beginnings as a Lowcountry staple served upon the family table after a day of shrimping. This soulful version is a favorite at Oxford's City Grocery where Chef John Currence has long paid tribute to classics such as this.*

# SHRIMP AND GRITS

*Serves 4     Hands-on 20 minutes     Total 20 minutes*

4 cups water

1 cup uncooked quick-cooking grits

2 ounces (¼ cup) unsalted butter

3 ounces extra-sharp Cheddar cheese, shredded (about ¾ cup)

2 ounces Parmesan cheese, grated (about ½ cup)

1½ teaspoons paprika

2 teaspoons hot sauce

1 teaspoon kosher salt

8 ounces thick-cut bacon slices, chopped (about 2 cups chopped)

2 tablespoons olive oil

2 cups sliced white mushrooms (about 6 ounces)

1½ pounds large raw shrimp, peeled and deveined (tails on, if desired)

1 tablespoon minced garlic (from 3 cloves)

3 tablespoons dry white wine

2 tablespoons fresh lemon juice

1 cup sliced scallions (from 8 scallions)

**1.** Bring 4 cups water to a boil in a medium saucepan over high. Gradually whisk in the grits; reduce heat to medium, and simmer, stirring occasionally, until thickened, 5 to 6 minutes. Whisk in the butter, Cheddar, Parmesan, paprika, hot sauce, and ¾ teaspoon of the salt until blended and smooth. Keep warm over low until ready to serve.

**2.** Heat a large skillet over medium-high, and cook the bacon, stirring occasionally, until crisp, 8 to 10 minutes; transfer the bacon to a paper towel-lined plate to drain, reserving 2 tablespoons drippings in skillet and discarding remaining drippings.

**3.** Heat the reserved drippings in the skillet over medium-high until very hot; add the olive oil. Add the mushrooms; cook, stirring occasionally, until lightly browned, about 6 minutes. Add the shrimp; cook, stirring occasionally, until almost cooked through, about 4 minutes. Add the garlic, wine, lemon juice, and remaining ¼ teaspoon salt; cook until liquid has almost evaporated, 30 to 60 seconds. Stir in the scallions, and sprinkle with the bacon. Serve immediately over the warm grits.

*The average Saturday morning pancakes and bacon just got a lot more interesting. Drawing from a Southern classic candy dessert, this sweet and savory treat not only makes a great breakfast side but does wonders for an ordinary scoop of ice cream. The key is to make sure the brown sugar is spread evenly enough on the bacon to caramelize completely.*

# PRALINE BACON

*Serves 6     Hands-on 15 minutes     Total 1 hour, 5 minutes*

¾ cup packed light brown sugar
1 cup finely chopped pecans

1 pound thick-cut bacon slices (12 slices)

**1.** Preheat the oven to 350°F, and line a rimmed baking sheet with aluminum foil. Stir together the brown sugar and finely chopped pecans in a small bowl.

**2.** Place an ovenproof rack on prepared baking sheet, and lightly coat rack with cooking spray. Dredge the bacon slices in pecan mixture, pressing to adhere, and arrange the slices on rack. Bake in preheated oven until crisp, 30 to 40 minutes. Cool in pan on rack 20 minutes before serving.

---

## SOUTHERN STAPLE

## Beignets & Chicory

No visit to New Orleans is complete without breakfast, or at least an afternoon snack, at the Café du Monde in the French Quarter. It's possible there are other things to order on the menu, but really the only thing you need to request are beignets and a cafe au lait. There's a reason it's one of the most romanticized spots in the city. Every culture has their own version of sugar-coated fried dough—American donuts, Italian zeppole, Mexican churros—but in New Orleans, the only fried pillow of pastry dough you need comes in the shape of a square and heavily dusted with powdered sugar. And its only appropriate pairing is the nutty, dried-fruit character of dark-roasted coffee laced with chicory root. Chicory was once considered a simple "filler" to help extend coffee during times of scarcity. Native to France, chicory was used as a culinary ingredient but served as a stand-in for coffee during the early 1800s under Napoleon's rule. Naturally, it made its way to the French colonies of America soon after.

# THE BETTER BISCUIT

When it comes to breakfast breads, the biscuit is all I need. Fresh from the oven, I like to pull one apart, slowly watching the steam escape, and then smear a pat of butter on one side and watch it fade into the white, fluffy goodness.

When it comes to biscuits there are a few points to consider:

**Use good flour**, one that is light and low in gluten, but not gluten-free. White Lily is the best.

**Choose your fat wisely.** Lard is harder to come by, but makes great layers. Butter offers the best flavor, but poor structure, and shortening is short on flavor, but adds fluffiness.

**Always keep ingredients cold.** Refrigerate everything as much as possible right up until the moment you pop the biscuits in the oven.

**Pat and cut, never knead.** The idea is to protect the gluten from activating until just the right moment. If you knead the dough, the fat begins to melt; instead cut with a dough cutter and work quickly and efficiently. Once the liquid has been added, pat the dough gently rather than kneading it.

**Use something sharp**—a metal biscuit cutter or cookie cutter—to cut the biscuits. Coat the cutter in flour to avoid pinching the dough as it cuts, and never twist the cutter while cutting.

BEATEN BISCUITS,
PG 171

BUTTERMILK BISCUITS,
PG 170

SWEET POTATO
BISCUITS, PG 173

# BUTTERMILK BISCUITS

*Makes 20 biscuits    Hands-on 20 minutes    Total 30 minutes*

*Before refrigeration, sweet whole milk was hard to keep on hand. Once it began to sour, it was often used to make butter. With the rise of baking soda in the mid-1800s, the need for something acidic practically bound buttermilk to Southern baking for eternity. The slight sour flavor it brings to biscuits, cornbread, and bread has become part of the distinctive flavor profile.*

2 cups (about 8 ½ ounces) all-purpose flour, plus more for work surface
¼ cup granulated sugar
¼ teaspoon baking soda
1 tablespoon baking powder
1 teaspoon table salt
6 tablespoons cold unsalted butter, cubed
1 cup whole buttermilk, plus more if needed

**1.** Preheat the oven to 450°F. Sift together the flour, sugar, baking soda, baking powder, and salt in a large bowl. Cut the butter into the flour mixture until the mixture resembles coarse meal. Gradually add the buttermilk, stirring just until combined. (If dough appears dry, add a bit more buttermilk. Dough should be wet.)

**2.** Turn the dough out onto a floured work surface. Dust hands with flour, and gently press the dough out to ½-inch thickness. Fold the dough in half, and gently press to 1-inch thickness. Repeat folding and pressing 4 more times. Cut the biscuits, using a 2-inch round cutter. Transfer the biscuits to an ungreased baking sheet. (If you like biscuits with soft sides, place them touching each other. If you like crisp sides, place the biscuits about 1 inch apart.) Gently knead remaining dough scraps together, and press out the dough to make a few more biscuits; transfer to baking sheet. Bake in preheated oven until light golden brown on top and bottom, 10 to 12 minutes.

---

# ANGEL BISCUITS

*Serves 6 to 8    Hands-on 20 minutes    Total 4 hours, 45 minutes*

*What makes these biscuits so angelic isn't just their light and fluffy texture but the double-leavening agents of baking soda and yeast, which ensure your biscuits couldn't possibly fall flat.*

1 cup whole buttermilk
1 (¼-ounce) envelope active dry yeast
2 ½ cups (about 10 ⅝ ounces) all-purpose flour, plus more for work surface and kneading
1 teaspoon baking soda
1 teaspoon table salt
2 teaspoons granulated sugar
4 tablespoons cold vegetable shortening
4 tablespoons cold unsalted butter, cubed
2 tablespoons melted unsalted butter

**1.** Heat the buttermilk in a saucepan over low until lukewarm (between 100° to 110°F). Remove from heat, and add the yeast, stirring until dissolved. Let cool to room temperature, about 20 minutes.

**2.** Sift together the flour, baking soda, salt, and sugar. Cut the shortening and butter into the flour mixture until dough comes together in pea-size crumbles. Cover and chill 10 minutes.

**3.** Stir the buttermilk mixture into the flour mixture just until dough comes together. Cover and chill at least 4 hours or up to 24 hours.

**4.** Preheat the oven to 400°F. Turn the dough out onto a floured surface, and knead gently, about 10 to 15 times, adding more flour, if necessary, to keep the dough from sticking. Pat the dough to an even ½-inch thickness. Cut the biscuits, using a 2-inch round cutter, and place 1 inch apart on an ungreased baking sheet. Let rise at room temperature until doubled in size, 15 to 20 minutes.

**5.** Bake in preheated oven until the tops are lightly browned, 10 to 15 minutes. Brush tops with the melted butter.

# BEATEN BISCUITS

*Makes about 30 biscuits    Hands-on 20 minutes    Total 40 minutes*

2 cups (about 8 ½ ounces) all-purpose
  flour, plus more for work surface
½ teaspoon table salt
½ teaspoon granulated sugar
2 ounces (¼ cup) cold unsalted
  butter, cubed
1 cup whole milk

*Don't be bashful with the dough—these biscuits get their name from the beating during the "kneading" process. This is a fun and easy biscuit for kids to make.*

**1.** Preheat the oven to 400°F. Sift together the flour, salt, and sugar into a bowl. Gently work in the butter with fingertips until the mixture resembles small peas.

**2.** Gradually add the milk, stirring until the dough comes together. Pound the dough with the bottom sides of your fists on a floured work surface, folding the dough back onto itself as it is pounded flat, 10 to 15 minutes.

**3.** Pinch off a 1 ½-inch piece of the dough, and roll into a ball between your palms. Place on an ungreased baking sheet, and press the biscuit to flatten slightly; press tines of a fork into top of the biscuit making an X pattern. Repeat with remaining dough.

**4.** Bake in the preheated oven until the biscuits are golden and dry in the middle, 20 to 25 minutes.

*Influenced by Caribbean and African heritage where most breads were made from the starchy root vegetables rather than grain flours, these biscuits are a little moister than other biscuits.*

# SWEET POTATO BISCUITS

*Makes a baker's dozen    Hands-on 15 minutes    Total 35 minutes*

1 cup cooked, cooled, mashed sweet potato (from 1 [12-ounce] sweet potato)

¼ cup whole milk

2 cups (about 8 ½ ounces) all-purpose flour, plus more for work surface

2 tablespoons granulated sugar

1 tablespoon baking powder

1 teaspoon kosher salt

4 ounces (½ cup) cold unsalted butter, cut into ¼-inch pieces

**1.** Preheat the oven to 400°F. Whisk together the sweet potato and the milk in a medium bowl until thoroughly combined.

**2.** Whisk together the flour, sugar, baking powder, and salt in a large bowl. Add the cold butter, and toss to coat. Cut the butter into the flour mixture using a pastry blender until mixture resembles coarse meal.

**3.** Add the sweet potato mixture to the flour mixture, and gently stir using a spatula until the mixture is just incorporated.

**4.** Line a baking sheet with parchment paper. Turn the dough out onto a floured surface, and pat to ½-inch thickness. Cut the dough with a 2-inch round cutter, rerolling scraps once. Place the biscuits on prepared baking sheet.

**5.** Bake in preheated oven until the bottoms are browned and the tops are golden, 15 to 18 minutes. Serve warm, or cool completely on a wire rack.

*Anyone can slap together some shredded Cheddar, mayonnaise, and jarred pimientos for a quick cheese spread. But it's hardly anything in which a whole region such as the South should stake such pride. If you ask me, what makes a good pimiento cheese spread is very sharp Cheddar, in this case Irish, and home-roasted peppers and garlic. Truth be told, it's not my Nana who is credited for this dip but the mother-in-law of my chef friend Joshua Thomas, who would only part with the recipe if she received the credit. Whip up a quart of this time-honored spread, which is altogether sharp, perky, and not too mayonnaise-y, and you'll see why the credit is more than deserved.*

# NANA'S PIMIENTO CHEESE

*Makes 1 quart     Hands-on 15 minutes*
*Total 4 hours, 25 minutes, including 4 hours chilling*

3 unpeeled garlic cloves
1 red bell pepper
1 pound Irish Cheddar cheese, shredded
  (about 4 cups)

1 cup mayonnaise
2 teaspoons chopped fresh thyme
1 teaspoon black pepper
¼ teaspoon freshly grated nutmeg

**1.** Preheat the oven to 350°F. Place the garlic on a rimmed baking sheet, and roast in preheated oven until soft, 15 to 20 minutes. Peel the garlic, and mash with side of a knife blade until creamy.

**2.** Using tongs, hold the bell pepper over the open flame of a burner on a gas cooktop, and heat each side of the pepper until charred, 5 to 6 minutes total. (If you do not have a gas cooktop, place the pepper in a small skillet over high, and cook, turning often, until slightly charred on each side, 10 to 12 minutes total.) Place the charred bell pepper in a bowl. Cover with plastic wrap, and let stand 15 minutes. Peel, seed, and cut the bell pepper into small pieces. Let cool 5 minutes.

**3.** Combine the cheese, mayonnaise, thyme, black pepper, nutmeg, mashed garlic, and chopped bell pepper in a medium bowl; cover and refrigerate at least 4 hours before serving. Store in an airtight container in refrigerator up to 5 days.

CITRUS CHICKEN
SALAD, PG 176

SPICY PICKLED
SHRIMP, PG 177

NANA'S PIMIENTO
CHEESE

*What Southern family doesn't have a good chicken salad recipe? It's the sort of thing grandmothers have handed down scrawled onto a 3 x 5 index card for generations. Ever since my mom began serving it with fruit and a bit of poppy seed dressing stirred in, I haven't been able to enjoy it any other way. This recipe uses canned mandarin oranges, but fresh oranges when in season are a must. And if you want to change it up, use sliced red grapes.*

# CITRUS CHICKEN SALAD

*Serves 4    Hands-on 15 minutes    Total 1 hour, 15 minutes*

1 (3- to 4-pound) whole rotisserie chicken, shredded (about 3 ½ cups shredded)

⅓ cup mayonnaise

¼ cup Poppy Seed Dressing (recipe follows)

1 celery stalk, chopped (about ⅓ cup)

3 scallions (green parts only), chopped (about ⅓ cup)

¾ teaspoon kosher salt

½ teaspoon black pepper

¾ cup walnuts, chopped

1 cup drained mandarin oranges (from 1 [11-ounce] can)

Crackers or sandwich bread

Stir together the chicken, mayonnaise, Poppy Seed Dressing, celery, scallions, salt, pepper, and ½ cup of the walnuts in a medium bowl; gently fold in the oranges so they stay intact. Chill at least 1 hour before serving. Garnish with remaining ¼ cup walnuts, and serve with the crackers or on sandwich bread.

# POPPY SEED DRESSING

⅓ cup granulated sugar

½ cup white wine vinegar

1 teaspoon kosher salt

1 teaspoon dry mustard

1 teaspoon grated yellow onion

1 cup vegetable oil

1 tablespoon poppy seeds

Combine the sugar, vinegar, salt, mustard, and onion in a blender or food processor, and process until incorporated, about 20 seconds. With blender or food processor on high, gradually add the oil in a slow, steady stream. Stir in the poppy seeds. Store in an airtight container in refrigerator up to 3 days. Makes 1 ¾ cups

*Pickled shrimp symbolize the footloose summer days of walking the sandy shoreline and enjoying the plump, sweet goodness of Gulf Coast bounty. There's really nothing to them, just make sure you don't overcook them during the poaching process. For a less spicy version, omit the jalapeño.*

# SPICY PICKLED SHRIMP

*Serves 8      Hands-on 25 minutes*
*Total  7 hours, 25 minutes, including 7 hours chilling*

2 pounds medium-size raw shrimp,
    peeled and deveined (tails on)
8 cups water
½ cup diced yellow onion (from 1
    onion)
1 teaspoon chopped fresh thyme
½ teaspoon dried oregano
½ tablespoon black pepper
1 cup rice vinegar
4 tablespoons fresh lime juice
    (from 2 limes)

4 teaspoons kosher salt
¼ cup olive oil
¾ cup chopped scallions (from
    6 scallions)
1 fresh jalapeño chile, sliced
    (about 2 tablespoons)
2 tablespoons chopped fresh cilantro
1 teaspoon granulated sugar
Thin lime slices

**1.** Rinse the shrimp under cold water, and drain in a colander.

**2.** Heat 8 cups water, diced onion, thyme, oregano, black pepper, ¾ cup of the rice vinegar, 2 tablespoons of the lime juice, and 1 tablespoon of the salt in a medium saucepan over medium-high until flavors come together, about 5 minutes. Increase heat to high, and bring to a boil. Add the shrimp; reduce heat to medium, and simmer until the shrimp turn bright pink, 3 to 5 minutes. Reserve 1 cup cooking liquid, and place in a large glass bowl with a lid. Drain the shrimp in a colander, and place in ice water to cover 2 minutes. Drain the shrimp, and place the shrimp in an airtight container in the refrigerator until ready to use.

**3.** Stir the olive oil, scallions, jalapeño slices, cilantro, sugar, remaining ¼ cup rice vinegar, remaining 2 tablespoons lime juice, and remaining 1 teaspoon salt into reserved cooking liquid. Add the shrimp, and toss to coat. Cover with lid, and chill at least 7 hours before serving. (Store in refrigerator up to 1 week.) Garnish the shrimp with lime slices.

---

SOUTHERN STAPLE

## Gulf Shrimp Taste a Rainbow of Colors

Unlike Gulf crab and oysters, which are harvested as only one species, the shrimp that flourish from Florida to the southwestern tip of the Texas coast are a different story. Instead of being labeled by species, they're labeled by color. Each have their own distinctive flavor.

**Brown Shrimp:** Due to their iodine-rich diet, brown shrimp have a meaty flavor; ideal for gumbo and jambalaya.

**Pink Shrimp:** Delicate and sweet, these shrimp have a mild flavor and are best served with light sauces.

**White Shrimp:** Also mild, these shrimp are sweet and a little briny; excellent for shrimp cocktail.

**Royal Red Shrimp:** They're called "royal" for a reason. Rich and buttery, these shrimp are the cream of the crop but are harder to find and are at a premium when in season.

*Chowchow takes many forms depending on where you are in the country. Some people believe pickled vegetable relish found its way to the South during the expulsion of Acadian people from Nova Scotia during the settlement of Louisiana. Whatever the history, it's found a particular home in different parts of the region as a way to preserve summer ingredients to be enjoyed long into the winter. Served as a condiment with fish cakes, mashed potatoes, soup beans, hot dogs, and hamburgers, it's a Southern staple. Green tomatoes are delicious as the base ingredient, but cabbage also works well as a substitute.*

# GREEN TOMATO CHOWCHOW

*Serves 16    Hands-on 30 minutes*
*Total 6 hours, 45 minutes, including chilling and stand times*

8 cups chopped green tomatoes
   (about 3 pounds)
1 cup chopped yellow onion
   (from 1 onion)
1 cup chopped green bell pepper
   (from 1 bell pepper)
1 cup chopped red bell pepper
   (from 1 bell pepper)
1 jalapeño chile, seeded and chopped
   (about 2 tablespoons)

2 tablespoons pickling salt or fine
   sea salt
3 cups white vinegar
2 cups granulated sugar
2 teaspoons mustard seeds
1 teaspoon celery seeds
¼ teaspoon ground turmeric

**1.** Place the tomatoes, onion, green and red bell peppers, jalapeño, and salt in a large glass or stainless-steel bowl, and toss well to combine. Cover and let stand at room temperature 4 hours, tossing every hour, or refrigerate 8 hours or overnight.

**2.** Drain the tomato mixture in a colander, discarding the liquid. Bring the vinegar, sugar, mustard seeds, celery seeds, and turmeric to a boil in a large stockpot over high. Stir in the tomato mixture, and return to a boil. Reduce heat to medium-low, and simmer gently, stirring occasionally, until the tomato mixture becomes very yellow and tender, about 30 minutes.

**3.** Cool completely; cover and chill 2 hours. Store in an airtight container in the refrigerator up to 5 days.

*Cucumbers and corn can be magical summer ingredients, but when a bumper crop comes in, it can be hard to find creative new ways to use them. This refreshing chilled soup is a great way to spotlight them and makes a beautiful starter course for entertaining friends.*

# CHILLED CUCUMBER-CILANTRO SOUP WITH SPICY CORN RELISH

*Serves 6     Hands-on 25 minutes     Total 3 hours, including 2 hours chilling*

## CORN RELISH

1 cup fresh corn kernels, blanched (from 2 ears)

¼ cup chopped fresh cilantro

1 jalapeño chile, seeded (if you prefer less heat) and diced (about 2 tablespoons)

1 tablespoon fresh lime juice (from 1 lime)

¼ teaspoon kosher salt

## SOUP

2 English cucumbers, peeled and coarsely chopped (about 3 cups)

1 tablespoon red wine vinegar

1 teaspoon kosher salt

½ cup chopped fresh cilantro

¼ cup fresh dill leaves

2 tablespoons fresh lemon juice (from 1 lemon)

16 ounces plain whole-milk Greek yogurt (about 2 cups)

¼ cup chicken broth

**1.** Prepare the Corn Relish: Stir together all the Corn Relish ingredients; cover and chill until ready to serve.

**2.** Prepare the Soup: Toss together the cucumbers, vinegar, salt, cilantro, dill, and lemon juice in a medium bowl, and let stand at room temperature 30 minutes to let the cucumber lightly pickle.

**3.** Process the cucumber mixture, Greek yogurt, and chicken broth in a blender until smooth and herbs are well incorporated, about 2 minutes. Cover and chill the soup at least 2 hours or up to 24 hours. Serve the soup topped with the Corn Relish.

*There's something inextricably linked between okra and tomatoes in the South. Perhaps it's simply because they're so abundant in the summer garden. While a simple panfry of the two sautéed with some onions and garlic makes a fine dish, this savory soup makes the two a main course.*

# GARDEN OKRA AND TOMATO SOUP

*Serves 8     Hands-on 40 minutes     Total 1 hour, 20 minutes*

4 bacon slices, cut crosswise into thin strips

1 large yellow onion, chopped (about 2 cups)

1 cup chopped celery (from 3 stalks with leaves)

1 green bell pepper, chopped (about 1 cup)

2 garlic cloves, minced (about 2 teaspoons)

2 pounds fresh okra, sliced (about 6 cups)

2 pounds tomatoes, chopped (about 4 ¾ cups)

1 ½ cups fresh corn kernels (from 3 ears)

1 teaspoon kosher salt

1 teaspoon black pepper

1 (32-ounce) container chicken broth

1 (15.5-ounce) can cannellini beans, drained and rinsed

1 teaspoon Worcestershire sauce

1 Parmesan cheese rind

Hot sauce (*such as Tabasco*)

Country Cornbread (page 86)

Freshly grated Parmesan cheese (optional)

**1.** Cook the bacon in a large heavy Dutch oven over medium until crisp, about 6 minutes. Transfer the bacon to a plate lined with paper towels, reserving 2 tablespoons drippings in Dutch oven. Discard the remaining drippings.

**2.** Heat the reserved drippings in Dutch oven over medium; add the onion, celery, and bell pepper, and cook, stirring often, until almost tender, about 8 minutes. Add the garlic, okra, tomatoes, and corn, and cook, stirring occasionally, until the tomatoes have released their juices, 3 to 4 minutes. Stir in the salt and the pepper. Add the bacon, broth, beans, Worcestershire sauce, and cheese rind, and bring to a boil. Reduce heat to low, and simmer, stirring occasionally, until thickened and the vegetables are very tender, 45 minutes to 1 hour; remove the cheese rind.

**3.** Serve in bowls with the hot sauce and the Country Cornbread, and garnish with the grated Parmesan, if desired.

# Frank Stitt

## GODFATHER OF SOUTHERN CUISINE

There's a reason Frank Stitt is often referred to as the Godfather of Southern cuisine. He's a man who single-handedly turned Birmingham fine dining into a reality in the 1980s, and he's managed to inspire and mentor young chefs throughout the South along the way.

Born in the 1950s in the northern Alabama town of Cullman, Stitt's first real understanding of cuisine growing up was through the lens of his grandparents' farm. Here, he got his hands dirty with chickens, Jersey cows, and digging around in his grandmother's vegetable garden for potatoes, sweet potatoes, asparagus, and more. Their land had apple orchards and Concord grape vines, their own smokehouse, and on Sundays after church, they'd churn butter for the week. It was at their dinner table where he got his first exposure to how true farm-raised food should taste.

Another culinary epiphany arrived while studying philosophy at the University of California at Berkeley, where he discovered Alice Waters and her groundbreaking restaurant, Chez Panisse, which celebrated the glory of European-inspired cuisine using seasonal, locally farmed ingredients. Stitt worked with the Chez Panisse team, honing his kitchen skills before launching a culinary sabbatical to Europe, where he became an assistant to food writer Richard Olney, traveling through kitchens and farms in Southern France, Bordeaux, Paris, and a brief foray into Italian cooking in Florence. He quickly developed an abiding appreciation for the philosophy and technique of "Old World" food.

While his experiences could easily have afforded him opportunities in New York, San Francisco, or other big city kitchens across the country, Stitt brought his passion for food back home to Alabama. Here, he revitalized the restaurant scene in Birmingham with Highlands Bar & Grill in 1982, which married the soul of Southern hospitality with good farm-raised food and the traditions and techniques of French cuisine. Since then, he has opened the Italian-inspired Bottega and Bottega Café, the French bistro Chez Fonfon, and has gone on to do tireless work in developing an area farmers' market, The Market at Pepper Place.

Inspired by his travels, Stitt could have started with French or Italian cuisine, but the foods of his native South first captured his heart.

"As Southerners we have a romantic and sentimental attachment to the land, and we feel connected to our past through the tradition of being at the table together," says Stitt.

Among the ingredients he most loves to work with, he has a fondness for the blueberries, honey, and sorghum of Appalachia, the flavorful rice-driven food culture of the Lowcountry, and the simplicity of greens, squash, green beans, and field peas of the Mississippi Delta. "These are the food traditions that shaped who we are," says Stitt. "We're all separated into a regionality within the South, but we're all bound by an agricultural commonality. When people say, 'Let's go get a bowl of beans,' we all know it means, 'Let's go eat!'"

Frank Stitt has garnered numerous accolades including a James Beard Award for Best Chef Southeast and his Highlands Bar & Grill was named Most Outstanding Restaurant in America. More impressive are the number of chefs from around the South, including Hugh Acheson, Sean Brock, Mike Lata, Travis Milton, and more, who point to him as the inspiration for their own careers.

"That summertime lunch at the farm where you would have all of these vegetables from corn and potatoes to fresh dill, onions, and tomatoes, those are my fondest food memories," says Stitt. "I know I'm on the right track when someone says, 'That's so much like what my aunt or grandmother used to make.' When there's a light in their eyes when they eat something as simple as a pea cake that takes them to a familiar place, that's why I do what I do."

*When you're looking for something to do with a bounty of summer shell peas, pea cakes make a great appetizer or side dish. This easy panfried recipe from* Frank Stitt's Southern Table *cookbook celebrates the bright flavors to be found in your own backyard garden. Serve with a drizzle of* Mississippi Comeback Sauce *(page 226).*

# PEA CAKES

*Serves 5     Hands-on 40 minutes*
*Total 1 hour, 20 minutes, including cooking peas*

2 cups Cooked Butter Peas (page 186), such as pink-eyes, butter peas, or crowders, cooking broth reserved

1 cup crumbled Country Cornbread, plus more if needed (page 86)

2 tablespoons chopped chives

1 tablespoon minced hot red chile pepper, such as a ripe jalapeño

1 tablespoon extra-virgin olive oil

1 tablespoon all-purpose flour, plus extra for dredging

Kosher salt and freshly ground black pepper to taste

1 large egg, beaten

2 tablespoons vegetable oil

**1.** Puree ¾ cup of the peas with ¼ cup of the reserved broth in a blender until smooth. Pour into a medium bowl, add the remaining whole peas, 1 tablespoon of the reserved broth, the cornbread, chives, hot pepper, olive oil, flour, and salt and pepper, and mix well. Add the egg, and mix again. You may need to adjust the "wetness" by adding a little more cornbread or broth to the mixture; it should be just moist enough to hold together.

**2.** Form 8 to 10 small cakes by shaping about 3-tablespoon portions of the mixture into 2-inch-wide disks, compressing the mixture with your fingers and patting it together.

**3.** Heat the vegetable oil in a heavy skillet over medium-high heat. Dust the cakes with a little flour and gently place them, in batches if necessary, in the hot oil. Lower the heat to medium and cook, turning once, until golden brown, about 4 minutes on each side. Serve hot.

*continued on next page*

# COOKED BUTTER PEAS

6 cups water, preferably spring water

1 onion, quartered

1 bay leaf

4 thyme sprigs, plus a scattering of leaves for garnish

4 savory sprigs, plus a scattering of leaves for garnish

Kosher salt

1 pound peas, such as pink-eyes, butter peas, or crowders, picked over and rinsed

2 tablespoons fruity extra-virgin olive oil, bacon fat, or unsalted butter, melted

Freshly cracked black pepper

Combine the water, onion, herbs, and salt in a medium saucepan, and bring to a boil. Reduce the heat to a simmer, and cook gently for 15 minutes. Add the peas, adjust the heat to maintain a simmer, and cook until the peas are just tender, 15 to 20 minutes. Taste for seasoning, and add salt if necessary. Remove the pan from the heat, and let the peas rest in their liquid for 10 minutes. Serve sprinkled with the herbs and drizzled with olive oil. Sprinkle with cracked black pepper. Makes 6 cups

PEA CAKES,
PG 185

*Boudin sausage is a Cajun specialty made from a mixture of pork and rice with spices and packed into a sausage casing. While you can certainly make your own boudin, many great selections are readily available at the average supermarket. Like the tasty Italian risotto-filled arancini balls, I love using boudin in the same way, fried as an appetizer. Serve with spicy Creole Rémoulade and you'll have a room full of happy guests.*

# BOUDIN BALLS

*Serves 4    Hands-on 20 minutes    Total 30 minutes*

## CREOLE RÉMOULADE

⅔ cup mayonnaise

1 tablespoon Dijon mustard

2 to 3 dashes of hot sauce (*such as Tabasco*)

½ teaspoon Worcestershire sauce

1 tablespoon ketchup

1 tablespoon fresh lemon juice (from 1 lemon)

1 tablespoon finely chopped fresh flat-leaf parsley

Dash of cayenne pepper

Dash of black pepper

Dash of kosher salt

## BOUDIN BALLS

Vegetable oil

2 links Cajun-style boudin sausage (about 12 ounces)

¼ cup finely chopped scallions (from 2 scallions)

½ cup (about 2 ⅛ ounces) all-purpose flour

1 large egg, lightly beaten

¼ cup fine dry breadcrumbs

¼ cup panko (Japanese-style breadcrumbs)

½ teaspoon kosher salt

½ teaspoon black pepper

½ teaspoon cayenne pepper

**1.** Prepare the Creole Rémoulade: Combine all the rémoulade ingredients in a medium bowl. Cover and chill until ready to serve.

**2.** Prepare the Boudin Balls: Pour the oil to a depth of 2 inches in a deep 9-inch cast-iron skillet; heat the oil in skillet over medium-high to 365°F.

**3.** Meanwhile, remove the sausage from the casings, and crumble into a bowl. Add the scallions, mixing well with hands. Shape the boudin mixture into 12 (1-inch) balls.

**4.** Place the flour in a small bowl; place the egg in a separate small bowl. Combine the breadcrumbs, panko, salt, black pepper, and cayenne in a third small bowl. Gently roll the boudin balls in the flour to coat, and dip in the egg; gently roll in the breadcrumb mixture, coating thoroughly.

**5.** Fry the coated balls in the hot oil, 2 or 3 at a time, turning as needed, until golden brown on all sides and cooked through, 2 to 3 minutes. Transfer to a plate lined with paper towels to drain. Serve warm with the Creole Rémoulade.

*Though commonly associated with Latin and South American cooking, hot tamales have long been a staple of Delta communities. Generally made using similar methods, the distinguishing characteristics of Delta tamales are that they are typically simmered in a meat sauce, rather than steamed. The texture tends to be grittier due to the use of cornmeal rather than masa. The addition of cayenne makes them considerably spicier than their Latin counterparts. This version comes from South-meets-Texas restaurant State of Grace in Houston.*

# MISSISSIPPI DELTA TAMALES

*Serves 5     Hands-on 1 hour, 20 minutes     Total 2 hours, 30 minutes*

**TAMALE SAUCE**

1 (10-ounce) yellow onion, coarsely chopped (about 2 ½ cups)

10 garlic cloves

4 cups water

1 pound ground chuck

1 beef bouillon cube

¼ cup chili powder

1 tablespoon kosher salt

1 tablespoon ground cumin

1 tablespoon black pepper

2 teaspoons dried oregano

½ tablespoon ancho chile powder

¼ teaspoon ground cloves

½ cup lard (about 3 ½ ounces)

½ cup (about 2 ⅛ ounces) all-purpose flour

**MEAT FILLING**

2 pounds ground chuck

½ cup tomato sauce

2 tablespoons kosher salt

2 tablespoons chili powder

2 teaspoons harissa

½ teaspoon garlic powder

½ teaspoon cayenne pepper

½ teaspoon ground cumin

¼ teaspoon black pepper

**TAMALES**

25 to 30 dried corn husks

4 cups (about 23 ounces) fine plain yellow cornmeal

2 cups chicken stock

**1.** Prepare the Tamale Sauce: Combine the onion, garlic, and 4 cups water in a blender, and process until pureed, about 30 seconds. Combine the onion mixture, ground chuck, bouillon cube, chili powder, salt, cumin, black pepper, oregano, ancho chile powder, and cloves in a large stockpot. Bring to a boil over high, and boil 3 to 4 minutes. Reduce heat to medium-low, and simmer meat mixture while preparing roux in Step 2.

**2.** Melt the lard in a small saucepan over medium-high. Slowly add the flour, stirring to combine; cook, stirring often, until lightly browned, about 5 minutes. Slowly add about 2 cups of simmering meat mixture to roux, stirring to blend well. Transfer the roux mixture to the meat mixture in stockpot, and simmer 15 to 20 minutes.

*continued on next page*

**3.** Prepare the Meat Filling: Stir together all the Meat Filling ingredients in a medium bowl until well blended.

**4.** Prepare the Tamales: Bring a large stockpot of water to a boil. Place the husks in boiling water, and boil until they become pliable and free of dust, 3 to 4 minutes. Gently separate the husks into single sheets, being careful not to tear them.

**5.** Stir together the cornmeal and 5 cups of the Tamale Sauce in a medium bowl until well combined and the mixture forms a tight paste.

**6.** Pat 1 corn husk dry, and place on a flat surface; spread about 5 tablespoons of the cornmeal-sauce mixture in an even 2 ½-inch square in center of husk, leaving at least 1 inch of clean husk around all edges. Spread about 3 tablespoons of the Meat Filling in a line down the center of the cornmeal mixture. Roll the husk so that the cornmeal mixture surrounds the Meat Filling and forms a cylinder. Fold the narrow bottom end of the husk up, and then continue rolling to seal. Place the tamale, seam side down, on a baking sheet to prevent it from unrolling. (The top of the tamale should remain open.) Repeat with the remaining corn husks, cornmeal mixture, and Meat Filling.

**7.** Stir together the remaining Tamale Sauce and the chicken stock in a large, tall stockpot. Arrange the tamales standing up side by side, open end up, in the sauce mixture in pot. Cover and bring to a boil over medium-high; reduce heat to medium-low, and cook until the cornmeal mixture easily separates from husk when unwrapped, 45 minutes. Serve the tamales with the cooking liquid.

---

SOUTHERN STAPLE

## The Delta Defined

Is it the Mississippi Delta or the Mississippi River Delta? Technically, they're actually two different things. The Mississippi River Delta is the three million acres of wetland that fans out from the Mississippi River and stretches from Louisiana's Vermilion Bay to the west to the Chandeleur Islands to the east in the Gulf of Mexico near Mississippi. But the Mississippi Delta is the smaller alluvial plain between the Mississippi and Yazoo rivers that begins just south of Memphis, Tennessee, and extends 200 miles south to Vicksburg, Mississippi. Its flat, fertile soil was once covered with hardwood forest but was developed into one of the richest areas for cotton-growing in the country before the Civil War. It's a region unique in its racial, cultural, and economic history. The Delta essayist David Cohn, author of *God Shakes Creation,* and a Greenville native, once wrote, "The Delta begins in the lobby of the Peabody Hotel in Memphis and ends on Catfish Row in Vicksburg."

*The first thing to know about Natchitoches Meat Pies is they're not pronounced the way they're spelled. Instead of Natch-ih-toe-ches, it's Nack-a-tish. It's important to know that because whether you walk into a place world-renowned for these savory fried pies such as Lasyone's, or a local hole-in-the wall, which could be the gas station down the street, you better know how to order one. This version includes a beef filling, but they're just as delicious with the commonly found crawfish filling as well.*

# NATCHITOCHES MEAT PIES

*Serves 10    Hands-on 30 minutes    Total 40 minutes*

2 cups plus 1 tablespoon all-purpose
  flour (about 8 ½ ounces), plus more
  for work surface
1 teaspoon baking powder
½ teaspoon table salt
3 tablespoons cold shortening
½ cup whole milk
1 large egg, lightly beaten

½ tablespoon vegetable oil, plus
  more for frying
½ pound ground chuck
¼ cup chopped scallions (from
  2 scallions)
½ teaspoon kosher salt
½ teaspoon black pepper
⅛ teaspoon cayenne pepper

**1.** Place 2 cups of the flour in a medium bowl; whisk in the baking powder and the table salt. Cut in the shortening with a pastry blender until mixture resembles coarse meal. Add the milk and the egg; stir to form a soft dough. Cover and chill until ready to use.

**2.** Heat ½ tablespoon vegetable oil in a medium skillet over medium-high. Add the ground chuck, scallions, salt, black pepper, and cayenne; cook, stirring occasionally to crumble beef, until beef is browned, about 6 to 8 minutes. Gently sift remaining 1 tablespoon flour over meat mixture, and stir to combine well. Remove from heat, and drain in colander to remove excess drippings. Let cool 30 minutes.

**3.** Remove the dough from refrigerator. Knead the dough 3 or 4 times on a heavily floured surface, and roll to about ⅛-inch thickness. Cut into 8 (5-inch) circles, using a small plate as a guide; reroll scraps once, and cut 2 more 5-inch circles. Place a rounded tablespoon of meat mixture on 1 side of each circle. Using fingertips or a pastry brush dipped in water, moisten edges of circles, fold the dough over the meat mixture, and crimp to seal with tines of a fork. Prick upper surface of the pies twice with fork tines.

**4.** Pour the vegetable oil to a depth of 2 inches in a deep skillet, and heat over medium-high to 350°F. Gently place 2 to 3 pies in the hot oil, and fry until golden brown, about 2 to 3 minutes per side. Repeat with the remaining pies. Serve immediately.

# RED BEANS AND RICE

*Serves 8 to 10     Hands-on 25 minutes*
*Total 10 hours, 45 minutes, including 8 hours soaking*

*Hearty and rich, red beans and rice are as much a part of the Louisiana cuisine as gumbo, jambalaya, and étouffée. The longer the beans cook with the andouille sausage, the more soul is revealed on the spoon. The beans will get soft and creamy on their own with enough cook time, but I like to add some of the bean mixture to push that texture along by blending about a third of them in a food processor before stirring back into the pot to serve.*

1 pound dried red kidney beans, rinsed
1 tablespoon vegetable oil
1 pound andouille sausage, halved lengthwise and cut into ½-inch-thick slices
1 cup chopped yellow onion (from 1 onion)
1 cup chopped green bell pepper (from 1 medium bell pepper)
4 celery stalks, chopped (about 1 ½ cups)
3 garlic cloves, minced (about 1 tablespoon)

1 teaspoon kosher salt, plus more to taste
1 teaspoon black pepper, plus more to taste
1 teaspoon cayenne pepper, plus more to taste
½ teaspoon ground sage
½ teaspoon dried thyme
1 (13-ounce) smoked ham hock
2 bay leaves
8 cups hot cooked white rice
½ cup thinly sliced scallions
Hot sauce (*such as Tabasco*)

**1.** Place the beans in a large bowl, and cover completely with water. Let stand at room temperature 8 hours or up to overnight. Drain and rinse.

**2.** Heat the vegetable oil in a large Dutch oven over medium-high. Add the sausage, and cook, stirring occasionally, until edges are nicely browned, about 5 to 7 minutes. Add the onion, bell pepper, and celery, and cook, stirring often, until the vegetables are softened and beginning to brown, about 8 to 10 minutes. Add the garlic, and cook 2 minutes. Stir in the salt, black pepper, cayenne, sage, and thyme.

**3.** Add the soaked beans and enough water to cover beans by 1 inch. Place the ham hock deep into the center of the beans, and add the bay leaves. Bring to a boil over high; reduce heat to low, cover, and simmer until the beans are completely tender, about 2 hours.

**4.** Uncover and cook until liquid has thickened and become creamy, about 6 minutes. Discard the bay leaves. Remove the ham hock. Transfer about 3 cups bean mixture from Dutch oven to a food processor, and pulse until creamy, about 6 times. Return the processed bean mixture to Dutch oven, and stir to combine. Stir in additional salt, black pepper, and cayenne to taste. Spoon the bean mixture over the rice, and sprinkle with the scallions; serve with the hot sauce.

# MAQUE CHOUX

*Serves 4    Hands-on 15 minutes    Total 15 minutes*

3 bacon slices
1 cup finely chopped yellow onion (from 1 small onion)
¾ cup finely chopped red bell pepper
1½ cups fresh corn kernels (from 3 ears)
¼ cup whipping cream
1 teaspoon chopped fresh thyme

½ teaspoon cayenne pepper
1 scallion, finely chopped (about 3 tablespoons)
½ teaspoon kosher salt
¼ teaspoon black pepper
3 dashes of hot sauce (*such as Tabasco*) (optional)

Cook the bacon in a large skillet over medium until crisp, about 7 minutes, turning once. Transfer the bacon to a plate lined with paper towels to drain, reserving drippings in the skillet. Crumble the bacon. Heat the reserved drippings in the skillet over medium-high, and add the onion; cook, stirring often, until tender, about 3 to 4 minutes. Add the bell pepper and corn, and cook, stirring often, 2 minutes. Stir in the cream, thyme, and cayenne. Simmer, stirring occasionally, 3 to 5 minutes. Remove from the heat, and stir in the scallion, crumbled bacon, salt, pepper, and, if desired, hot sauce.

*Though French in pronunciation, the name for this mixed vegetable sauté likely derives from the Native Americans who first created it. A humble side dish of corn, bell peppers, onion, and often a few Creole spices, this dish inherits a little more richness with the addition of butter or cream. Toss in shrimp or crawfish to sauté and you've got a meal!*

---

## SOUTHERN STAPLE

## The Tabasco Pepper

People along the Gulf Coast have always liked their spice. It's rare to find diners or restaurants without salt, pepper, hot sauce, and pepper vinegar on the tables. Though the Southwest has its style of hot sauces, derived primarily from jalapeño and serrano chiles, the hot peppers of the Gulf Coast are made almost exclusively with Tabasco peppers fermented with vinegar and salt and transformed into a concentrated hot sauce. Named for the Mexican state of Tabasco, these small peppers are commonly used in all brands of hot pepper sauce, though the term Tabasco is often confused for a brand name. In fact, when most people reach for a bottle with the word boldly emblazoned across the label, they're grabbing a McIlhenny Company Tabasco Pepper Sauce, which is responsible for the pepper's rise to fame. In 1868, Edmund McIlhenny first made the sauce by grinding the peppers into a mash and combining them with salt in a barrel to age for three years before combining with vinegar and bottling. While there are many other Tabasco pepper sauce producers, it's McIlhenny's that has given it an international reputation.

*Nothing says "taste of summer" like succotash. Add to it the sweet, delicate taste and texture of Royal Red shrimp, the rarest of the Gulf shrimp breeds, as they are pulled from the deepest waters during their limited season. To keep them fresh, they are often flash-frozen—sometimes right on the boat. Their flavor is best served with the bounty of summer produce, such as succotash.*

# BLISTERED SUMMER SUCCOTASH AND ROYAL RED SHRIMP

*Serves 4     Hands-on 20 minutes     Total 25 minutes*

2 ounces (¼ cup) unsalted butter

1 cup 1-inch fresh green bean pieces (about 3 ounces)

1 cup fresh corn kernels (from 2 ears)

2 scallions, chopped (about ¼ cup)

½ cup chopped red bell pepper (from 1 bell pepper)

1 cup half-moon zucchini slices (from 1 zucchini)

1 cup cherry tomatoes, halved (about 4 ounces)

2 tablespoons (1 ounce) dry white wine

1 pound raw Royal Red shrimp, peeled and deveined (tails on, if desired)

½ teaspoon kosher salt

¼ teaspoon black pepper

4 cups hot cooked long-grain white rice

**1.** Heat 2 tablespoons of the butter in a large skillet over medium-high until melted. Add the green beans and corn, and cook, stirring constantly, until tender and slightly charred, 4 to 5 minutes. Add the scallions and the bell pepper, and cook, stirring occasionally, until slightly softened, 3 to 4 minutes. Add the zucchini, and cook, stirring occasionally, until charred and crisp on the edges, about 4 minutes. Add the tomatoes, and cook, stirring occasionally, until warm, 1 to 2 minutes. Transfer the vegetables to a medium bowl, and cover with aluminum foil to keep warm. Do not clean skillet.

**2.** Return skillet to medium-high. Add the wine and remaining 2 tablespoons butter to skillet. Sprinkle the shrimp with the salt and the pepper, and add the shrimp to skillet; cook until the shrimp turn pink and opaque, 1 to 2 minutes on each side. Serve the vegetables and the shrimp over the hot cooked rice.

*Étouffée is the French word for "smothered," an apt description for the way this classic Louisiana dish envelops plump morsels of shrimp. Crawfish is also commonly used and is easily substituted when in season.*

# SHRIMP ÉTOUFFÉE

*Serves 6 to 8    Hands-on 50 minutes    Total 1 hour*

## Rice Reliant

Rice has been grown commercially in the South for more than three centuries. In fact, it produces about ninety percent of the rice eaten in the United States and exports about half of its annual crop to other countries. Though it first had a stronghold in South Carolina after the Civil War, rice farming moved farther west around the coast to Louisiana and Texas. Today Arkansas is the largest rice-producing state (about thirty percent of the nation's total). But it's Louisiana where the humble cereal grain is a staple in its culinary heritage. Sure, the Atlantic Coast will always have its purloos, but can you imagine red beans, gumbo, étouffée, or jambalaya without rice? Banish the thought!

6 ounces (¾ cup) unsalted butter
¾ cup (about 3¼ ounces) all-purpose flour
1½ cups diced yellow onion (from 2 onions)
1 cup diced green bell pepper (from 1 bell pepper)
1 cup diced celery (from 3 celery stalks)
1 (6-ounce) can tomato paste
2 garlic cloves, minced (about 2 teaspoons)
2 teaspoons dried oregano
4 teaspoons kosher salt

2 teaspoons black pepper
1 teaspoon cayenne pepper
6 cups water
¼ cup heavy cream
2 pounds large raw shrimp, peeled and deveined
2 tablespoons fresh lemon juice (from 1 lemon)
4 cups hot cooked long-grain white rice
½ cup chopped scallions (from 3 scallions)
½ cup chopped tomato (from 1 tomato)

**1.** Melt the butter in a heavy saucepan over medium. Add the flour; cook, whisking often, until caramel in color. Add the onion, bell pepper, and celery, and cook, stirring often, until the vegetables are softened, 6 to 8 minutes.

**2.** Stir in the tomato paste, garlic, oregano, salt, black pepper, and cayenne. Gradually add 6 cups water, 1 cup at a time, stirring until incorporated after each addition. Increase heat to high, and bring to a boil, stirring occasionally. Reduce heat to medium, and simmer, stirring occasionally, until slightly thickened, about 10 minutes.

**3.** Stir in the cream, and simmer, stirring often, until slightly thickened, about 30 minutes. Add the shrimp, and simmer, until the sauce thickens and the shrimp turn pink and opaque, about 6 to 10 minutes. Stir in the lemon juice.

**4.** Serve over the hot cooked rice, and sprinkle with the chopped scallions and the tomato.

*Crayfish. Crawdads. Mudbugs. Yabbies. There are a number of endearing terms given to this flaming red freshwater crustacean. While few of the nicknames sound very appealing, there's no denying the simply addictive quality of the buttery meat found within their thick shell. There's no official season for fresh crawfish, but you can typically find them from March through June, before it gets too hot. And when the crawfish are ready to boil, so are Louisianans.*

# CAJUN CRAWFISH BOIL

*Serves 15     Hands-on 35 minutes     Total 45 minutes*

### CAJUN BUTTER

1 pound (2 cups) unsalted butter,
  softened
6 garlic cloves, minced (about
  2 tablespoons)
½ cup Old Bay seasoning

### CRAWFISH BOIL

12 lemons, halved
5 heads garlic, halved horizontally
5 cups Old Bay seasoning
6 pounds medium-size red potatoes,
  scrubbed
8 ears fresh corn, husked and halved
30 pounds live crawfish

**1.** Prepare the Cajun Butter: Place the butter, minced garlic, and ½ cup Old Bay seasoning in a food processor; process until well blended and smooth. Set aside.

**2.** Prepare the Crawfish Boil: Rinse the crawfish with fresh water in a large cooler or stockpot until water runs clear, 2 or 3 times.

**3.** Fill a 30-quart stockpot halfway with water; bring to a boil over high. Add the lemons, garlic, and 3 cups of the Old Bay seasoning, and stir until dissolved. Add the potatoes; cook 15 minutes. Add the corn; cover and cook until potatoes and corn are tender, about 15 minutes. Transfer the potatoes and the corn to a large baking sheet, and cover with aluminum foil; keep warm in a warming drawer or in a 250°F oven.

**4.** Stir remaining 2 cups Old Bay seasoning into pot; return to a boil over high. Place one-third of the crawfish in the pot, and stir until they are submerged. Cover; cook until bright red and cooked through, about 5 minutes. Using a mesh strainer, remove the crawfish, and place them in a large, clean cooler to keep warm. Repeat with remaining crawfish in 2 batches.

**5.** Toss the warm crawfish, in batches, with some of the Cajun Butter (about 2 tablespoons per batch) in 2-gallon ziplock plastic bags. Serve immediately with the corn and the potatoes, and plenty of paper napkins and cold beer.

Court bouillon, *pronounced "coo-bee-on," is conventionally a French light poaching broth commonly used for fish. The French "court" or "short" and "bouillon" or "broth" was fused into Louisiana cuisine with the Creole addition of roux and tomato. This recipe comes from a childhood neighbor who used to make it often and scribbled it down for my mother before moving back home to Jennings, Louisiana. Any mild white fish such as catfish or cod will suffice.*

## Iced Tea: Sweet or Unsweet

Confirmed origins of that cold class of iced tea that has long quenched the thirst of Southerners are unknown, but it's believed to have its birthplace in the late 1860s in New Orleans. It later found a concession spot at the 1904 World's Fair in St. Louis, which significantly elevated its popularity throughout the country. The question is: How do you take it, sweet or unsweet? Newcomers to the South for the first time are often surprised to find their order of iced tea arrives already sweetened when ordered at a restaurant. (Word to the wise, you usually have to specify if you want it unsweet.) The farther west you move in the region, the more common it is to see both options, if not completely unsweet altogether.

# LOUISIANA COURT BOUILLON

*Serves 4 to 6     Hands-on 20 minutes     Total 1 hour, 25 minutes*

½ cup (about 2 ⅛ ounces) all-purpose flour

½ cup vegetable oil

1 cup chopped yellow onion (from ½ medium onion)

1 cup chopped celery (from 3 celery stalks)

½ cup chopped green bell pepper (from 1 bell pepper)

2 garlic cloves, minced (about 2 teaspoons)

1 (6-ounce) can tomato paste

1 (14.5-ounce) can diced tomatoes with green chiles

2 quarts water

2 pounds skinless white fish fillets (such as bass or cod), cut into 1- to 2-inch pieces

5 teaspoons kosher salt

1 teaspoon black pepper

¼ cup chopped fresh flat-leaf parsley

1 tablespoon hot sauce (*such as Louisiana Original Hot Sauce*)

4 cups hot cooked white rice

**1.** Cook the flour and the oil in a large deep skillet over medium, whisking constantly, until the mixture is a deep tan color, 5 to 6 minutes.

**2.** Add the onion, celery, bell pepper, and garlic, and cook, stirring often, until vegetables are soft, 5 to 6 minutes.

**3.** Add the tomato paste and diced tomatoes, and slowly stir in 2 quarts water. Simmer over medium 45 minutes. Sprinkle the fish pieces with salt and pepper. Gently add the fish pieces to simmering tomato mixture, and cook until the fish is just flaky and opaque, 20 to 25 minutes.

**4.** Stir in the parsley and hot sauce. Serve immediately over the hot cooked rice.

# Vishwesh Bhatt

## BRIDGING THE AMERICAN SOUTH WITH THE GLOBAL SOUTH

Chef Vishwesh Bhatt is not from the South, though he's lived in quite a few Southern locales throughout the course of his adult life—from Austin and Lexington to Miami and his current home of Oxford, Mississippi. But from the beginning of his time in the South, his food experiences, particularly strolling through the produce and spice aisles of supermarkets, made him feel right at home. Bhatt's native home is Gujarat, India. When his family moved to the United States during his teenage years, one of the first things that struck him was the irrefutable similarities of commonly used ingredients, such as beans, tortillas, chiles, cumin, and cilantro in the South, that his mother and grandmothers had long used in India.

"Looking at things like okra, chiles, eggplant, cilantro, and summer melons, these were all things that I recognized," says Bhatt. "Though people cooked things differently in the South than how my family did, I, at least, had an idea of what they should taste like in my head. It was my first connection between how similar things were between the U.S. and India."

As a child in India, he spent many hours helping his mother prepare large family feasts. What may have seemed like menial work was invigorating for Bhatt, not necessarily for the culinary skills he was beginning to learn but for the familial environment it provided. Despite his young age, he was part of family conversations and interactions. Even when he didn't always understand what was going on, the simple task of shelling peas allowed him to be a part of the family.

Today, as the executive chef at Oxford's Snackbar, a Southern-meets-French restaurant owned by longtime friend and mentor John Currence, Bhatt has mastered the art of weaving flavors of his native India with traditional Southern ingredients such as field peas, grits, catfish, mac 'n' cheese, and pot roast. Okra chaat, his most-requested dish, sits humbly on the list of sides.

But it wasn't always so. It wasn't until he was pursuing graduate studies at Ole Miss that the culinary bug bit him, something Bhatt attributes to the influence of Currence. He decided to start with culinary school in Miami, and then worked in restaurants with several different food categories, including French, Caribbean, English, and Southern. It wasn't until Currence offered him the reins at Snackbar that the influences of his culinary heritage began to show in his cooking.

"It became clear to me that it's part of who I am and even though I've spent the majority of my life in America, it was still an important part of my identity," says Bhatt. "As I've gotten older, members of my family have passed away and what's left for me are just memories of celebrations and gatherings where food played an important role. Food is what keeps me connected to those parts of my life."

When asked if he feels like his style of cooking has introduced something new to Oxford, Bhatt thoughtfully considers his answer, "You know, Oxford is a different place. I think because of the university it brings a more diverse population to this small town. People who come here have traveled all over the world. At the same time it's intrinsically Southern in its culture. I think it's influenced me more than my cooking has influenced it," says Bhatt.

Among his favorite Southern things to cook are cornbread, squash, fried chicken, and especially okra. Add to that, field peas and the many varieties and flavors they represent. Though he's been known to sop up a bowl of pea potlikker with a slice of cornbread, he also finds ways to marry them with different seasonal ingredients, such as tomatoes sautéed with chiles, cilantro, cumin, and chaat masala.

Now, at age fifty-three, Bhatt is a five-time James Beard Award finalist for Best Chef of the South—a sign that he must be doing something right. But for him, it's more about the Snackbar regulars and the visitors who stroll through the doors to discover something new. In many ways, Bhatt is telling the story of where Southern food comes from, but also where it's going.

*Chef Bhatt's delightful summer salad showcases a few ingredients from his Indian heritage. Not surprisingly, these flavors meld beautifully, offering a different approach to traditional Southern fare.*

# LADY PEA-AND-TOMATO SALAD

*Serves 10      Hands-on 25 minutes      Total 1 hour, 15 minutes*

4 cups vegetable or chicken stock

4 cups fresh or frozen lady peas or white acre peas

2 medium (6-ounce) heirloom tomatoes

1 small red onion, finely chopped (½ cup)

2 serrano chiles, cut into thin rings

¼ cup chopped fresh mint

¼ cup chopped fresh cilantro

¼ cup chopped fresh chives

2 tablespoons lemon zest, plus 5 tablespoons fresh lemon juice (from 2 lemons)

1 ½ tablespoons sorghum syrup

3 tablespoons olive oil or pecan oil

2 teaspoons cumin seeds, toasted and crushed

2 teaspoons brown mustard seeds, toasted

1 ½ teaspoons chaat masala

½ teaspoon kosher salt

**1.** Bring the stock to a boil in a saucepan over medium-high; add the peas, and return to a boil. Reduce heat to medium, and cook until the peas are tender but not mushy, 25 to 30 minutes. (Check peas after 15 minutes so they do not overcook.) Drain and transfer to a rimmed baking sheet; cool completely, about 30 minutes.

**2.** Dice 1 tomato to equal 1 cup. Slice remaining tomato. Gently toss the cooled peas with diced and sliced tomatoes, onion, chiles, mint, cilantro, chives, lemon zest and juice, sorghum syrup, oil, cumin and mustard seeds, chaat masala, and salt in a bowl to serve.

*An authentically New Orleans dish, jambalaya is essentially a descendent of paella brought over by Spanish immigrants that was then fused with the blend of cultural influences in the region including African, Caribbean, and French. Like paella, the common ingredient in jambalaya is rice, followed by any number of meats and seafood including pork, chicken, and shrimp. The more Creole style, which is also called "red jambalaya," includes tomato, while Cajun "brown jambalaya" goes without.*

# CREOLE JAMBALAYA

*Serves 8     Hands-on 20 minutes     Total 1 hour, 5 minutes*

2 tablespoons unsalted butter

1 pound andouille sausage, cut into ½-inch-thick slices

3 celery stalks, chopped (about 1 cup)

1 medium-size green bell pepper, chopped (about 1 cup)

1 medium-size yellow onion, chopped (about 2 cups)

2 garlic cloves, minced (about 2 teaspoons)

1 teaspoon kosher salt

1 teaspoon black pepper

1 teaspoon dried thyme

½ teaspoon dried oregano

½ teaspoon paprika

½ teaspoon cayenne pepper

2 cups uncooked long-grain white rice

2 tablespoons tomato paste

5 cups chicken broth

1 (28-ounce) can whole tomatoes, drained and crushed

1 pound medium-size raw shrimp, peeled and deveined

1 cup sliced scallions (from 4 scallions)

**1.** Preheat the oven to 350°F. Melt 1 tablespoon of the butter in a Dutch oven over medium-high. Add the sausage, and cook, stirring constantly, until browned, 7 to 9 minutes. Reserve drippings in Dutch oven.

**2.** Add the remaining 1 tablespoon butter to the sausage and the drippings in Dutch oven, and cook until melted. Add the celery, bell pepper, and onion; cook, stirring often, until tender, about 10 minutes. Add the garlic, and cook, stirring often, 2 more minutes. Reduce heat to medium, and add the salt, pepper, thyme, oregano, paprika, and cayenne; cook, stirring constantly, 1 minute. Add the rice and tomato paste, and cook, stirring constantly, until toasted, about 3 minutes. Add the broth and the tomatoes, stirring to loosen browned bits from bottom of Dutch oven. Increase heat to high, and bring to a boil. Stir in the shrimp and half of the scallions. Cover and bake in the preheated oven until the rice is tender, about 30 minutes. Let stand 5 minutes. Sprinkle with the remaining scallions just before serving.

# DUCK AND ANDOUILLE GUMBO

*Serves 8    Hands-on 45 minutes*
*Total 10 hours, 55 minutes, including 8 hours chilling*

*Gumbo is the culinary illustration of Louisiana's cultural melting pot borrowing from the Creole, African, and Native American cultures of the region. A hearty stew, it spotlights the fruits of the sea when closer to the coast and the bounty of the land when farther inland. There's something indulgent about duck gumbo. Combined with spicy andouille sausage and a nutty, dark roux, it's a robust dish that duck just makes richer. If you're using wild duck during hunting season, you may need three instead of two depending on their size.*

3 large yellow onions (about 1 ½ pounds)
8 celery stalks (about 1 pound)
2 (6-pound) whole ducks, dressed
6 quarts water
5 fresh bay leaves
2 tablespoons minced garlic (from 6 garlic cloves)
3 teaspoons kosher salt
3 teaspoons black pepper
6 ounces (¾ cup) unsalted butter
1 pound andouille sausage, halved lengthwise and cut into ⅓-inch-thick slices

1 cup (about 4 ¼ ounces) all-purpose flour
1 cup diced green bell pepper (from 1 large bell pepper)
1 tablespoon Worcestershire sauce
1 (14.5-ounce) can diced tomatoes, undrained
2 teaspoons dried oregano
2 teaspoons dried thyme
Hot cooked white rice (optional)
½ cup chopped scallions (from 2 scallions)

**1.** Dice 1 onion; set aside. Cut each of the 2 remaining onions into quarters. Dice 4 celery stalks to equal 1 ½ cups; set aside. Quarter each of the 4 remaining celery stalks. Place the ducks, 6 quarts water, quartered onions, quartered celery, 3 bay leaves, 1 tablespoon garlic, and 1 teaspoon each salt and pepper in a large stockpot. Bring to a boil over high. Reduce heat to medium-low; simmer until ducks are cooked through and tender, about 1 ½ hours. Remove ducks, and cool slightly, about 15 minutes. Shred the meat into large pieces, discarding skin and bones. Chill in an airtight container. Pour the stock through a mesh strainer into a large bowl, discarding solids. Cover and chill stock 8 hours or overnight, and discard solidified fat from top of stock. Reserve 5 cups of the stock for gumbo; reserve remaining stock for another use.

**2.** Melt 1 tablespoon of the butter in a Dutch oven over medium. Add the sausage, and cook, stirring occasionally, until browned, about 6 minutes. Transfer the sausage to a plate lined with paper towels to drain, reserving drippings in Dutch oven. Add the remaining butter to reserved drippings in Dutch oven. Gradually whisk in the flour; cook, whisking constantly, until the flour is a rich milk chocolate color, 8 to 10 minutes.

**3.** Add the bell pepper, diced onion, diced celery, Worcestershire sauce, and remaining 1 tablespoon garlic and 2 teaspoons each salt and pepper; cook, stirring often, until the vegetables are tender, about 8 minutes. Gradually add 5 cups stock, stirring until combined. Add the tomatoes, oregano, thyme, and remaining 2 bay leaves. Bring to a boil over medium-high; reduce heat to medium-low, and simmer, stirring until slightly thickened, about 30 minutes.

**4.** Return the sausage to Dutch oven; cover and simmer, stirring occasionally, until flavors meld, about 15 minutes. Stir in the shredded duck meat; cover and cook until heated through, about 10 minutes. Remove and discard bay leaves. Serve the gumbo over the hot cooked rice, if desired, and top with the scallions.

---

# SEAFOOD GUMBO

*Serves 10      Hands-on 45 minutes      Total 1 hour*

¾ cup vegetable oil

1 cup (about 4 ¼ ounces) all-purpose flour

2 cups diced yellow onion (from 2 onions)

1 ½ cups diced green bell pepper (from 2 bell peppers)

1 ½ cups diced celery (from 5 stalks)

1 cup sliced scallions (from 8 scallions)

2 garlic cloves, minced (about 2 teaspoons)

2 bay leaves

1 tablespoon kosher salt

1 tablespoon black pepper

½ tablespoon filé powder

½ teaspoon dried thyme

½ teaspoon dried oregano

¼ teaspoon cayenne pepper, plus more if preferred

6 cups seafood or chicken stock, warmed

½ cup chopped fresh flat-leaf parsley

1 ½ pounds medium-size raw shrimp, peeled and deveined

1 pint medium-size fresh shucked oysters with oyster liquid

1 pound fresh crabmeat, picked over

5 cups hot cooked long-grain white rice

*The secret to good gumbo is the roux, a dark nutty-flavored base. Slowly cooking fat and flour until it achieves a deep golden-brown color is where the soul comes in. This recipe is strictly Cajun, using oil rather than butter for the roux and eschewing any sign of tomatoes, which would put it more in the Creole category. Okra features well in this stew, but the seafood is the star.*

**1.** Heat a small saucepan over medium-high, and add the vegetable oil. Slowly whisk in the flour to make a smooth roux. Reduce heat to medium, and cook, stirring often, until the roux becomes nutty brown in color, 10 to 15 minutes.

**2.** Stir in the onion, bell pepper, celery, and ½ cup of the scallions, and cook, stirring occasionally, until the vegetables start to soften, about 5 minutes. Stir in the garlic, bay leaves, salt, black pepper, filé powder, thyme, oregano, and cayenne, and cook, stirring occasionally, until toasted and fragrant, 3 to 4 minutes. (Mixture will be gummy and sticky.) Slowly stir in the warmed stock.

**3.** Bring to a boil over high; reduce the heat to medium-low, and simmer, stirring occasionally, 15 minutes. Add the parsley, shrimp, and remaining ½ cup scallions, and cook, stirring, 3 minutes. Add the oysters and crabmeat, and cook until the shrimp is cooked through, 2 to 3 minutes. Serve in bowls over the hot cooked rice.

*A New Orleans original, this tasty sandwich got its name from the round, white sesame-coated Sicilian style of bread on which it's made. It first appeared at the French Quarter's Central Grocery when Sicilian shop owner Salvatore Lupo layered Italian cold cuts and cheese on a bread smeared with a savory olive mix. Of course, when muffuletta bread isn't available, you can always substitute with focaccia or French bread. I personally like a little more crunch with the sandwich and opt for a quick toast in the oven. The key is to let the olive mix sit for a minute or two on the bread to give it a chance to soak in.*

# TOASTED MUFFULETTA

*Serves 4 to 8     Hands-on 25 minutes     Total 25 minutes*

1 cup pitted black olives

1 cup large pimiento-stuffed green olives

¼ cup coarsely chopped celery

¼ cup olive oil

2 tablespoons coarsely chopped shallot

2 tablespoons fresh flat-leaf parsley leaves

2 garlic cloves, coarsely chopped (2 teaspoons)

1 jalapeño chile (seeded, if desired), coarsely chopped

1 teaspoon black pepper

2 tablespoons unsalted butter, softened

1 (1-pound) fresh French bread loaf, halved lengthwise

4 ounces provolone cheese slices

4 ounces mozzarella cheese slices

¼ pound thin deli ham slices

¼ pound thin mortadella slices

¼ pound thin Genoa salami slices

**1.** Preheat the oven to 450°F. Pulse the black olives, green olives, celery, olive oil, shallot, parsley, garlic, jalapeño, and black pepper in a food processor just until combined, but still chunky, 3 to 5 times.

**2.** Spread the butter on cut side of bottom half of bread loaf. Spread 1 cup olive mixture on cut side of top half of the bread, and layer the provolone and mozzarella cheese slices over the olive mixture. Place both halves on a baking sheet, and bake in preheated oven until the bread is toasted on edges and the cheese is bubbly, 7 to 10 minutes. Remove from oven, and let cool 3 to 4 minutes.

**3.** Spread remaining olive mixture (about 1 cup) over the buttered side of bottom half of bread. Layer the meat slices over the olive mixture on bottom half. Place the top half of the bread, cheese side down, on bottom half of the loaf. Carefully slice into desired number of wedges, and serve immediately.

*As great as a pork shoulder can be when smoked and served up as barbecue, there's something special about the spicy flavors that fill your home when roasting a Cuban-style pork shoulder. These flavors made their way to the South by way of the Cuban immigrants who settled along the Florida coastline in the early 1960s. This roast makes a delicious Sunday supper, but be sure to save some for toasty Cuban sandwiches, another savory delight.*

# CUBANO PORK ROAST

*Serves 20    Hands-on 30 minutes*
*Total 8 hours, 30 minutes, including 3 hours chilling*

1 yellow onion, diced

1 cup fresh orange juice (from 2 oranges)

1 cup light beer (*such as Miller Lite*)

⅓ cup extra-virgin olive oil

⅓ cup fresh oregano leaves, coarsely chopped

8 garlic cloves, minced (about 8 teaspoons)

2 teaspoons ground cumin

2 teaspoons chili powder

2 teaspoons kosher salt

2 teaspoons black pepper

1 (9-pound) boneless pork shoulder

**1.** Whisk together the onion, orange juice, beer, oil, oregano, garlic, cumin, chili powder, salt, and pepper in a small bowl. Reserve half of the marinade mixture in an airtight container, and chill. Transfer remaining marinade mixture to a large ziplock freezer bag. Tie the pork with kitchen twine, securing at 1-inch intervals. Add the pork to the marinade mixture in bag, remove as much air from bag as possible, and seal; massage the mixture into the pork. Place in a shallow baking dish, and chill at least 3 hours or up to overnight.

**2.** Preheat the oven to 275°F with oven rack in center of oven. Line a rimmed baking sheet with a double layer of heavy-duty aluminum foil. Place another double layer of foil on top, and place the pork in center. Fold up foil to create a shell around pork, and pour the marinade mixture over pork. Crimp foil to seal loosely while allowing air to circulate inside. Roast in preheated oven 3 hours. Remove from oven, and fold back foil to expose pork; pour the reserved chilled marinade mixture over pork. Increase oven temperature to 325°F, and roast the pork, basting with pan juices occasionally, until a meat thermometer inserted into thickest portion registers 180°F, 2 to 3 more hours. Remove the pork from oven, and let rest 10 to 15 minutes before serving. If not serving the same day, reserve the cooking liquid, and after thinly slicing pork, reheat the slices in the reserved cooking liquid.

*Of course, it's the Cuban bread that makes this sandwich extra special, but if you don't have that, you can use a fresh, wide French loaf. For the pickles, while it's possible to buy them presliced, it's best to slice them thinly yourself.*

# CUBAN SANDWICHES

*Serves 4    Hands-on 30 minutes    Total 6 hours, 30 minutes*

1 French bread loaf, cut into
  4 quarters and split
4 tablespoons yellow mustard
8 Swiss cheese slices
4 medium-size whole dill pickles,
  very thinly sliced

8 thin smoked ham slices
3 cups thinly sliced Cubano Pork Roast
  (page 212)
1½ ounces (3 tablespoons) unsalted
  butter

**1.** Heat a griddle over medium on a cooktop, or preheat a panini press. Place the bread pieces, cut side up, on a work surface, and spread cut sides of both halves with the mustard; top both halves with the cheese. Layer the pickles, ham, and pork on bottom half. Close the sandwiches, gently pressing together.

**2.** Melt half of the butter on griddle, and place the sandwiches on griddle close together. (You may have to cook sandwiches in batches.) Place a large heavy skillet on sandwiches to weight them, and cook 3 to 4 minutes. Remove the sandwiches, and melt remaining butter on griddle. Turn the sandwiches over, place on griddle; top with skillet. Cook until the bread is toasty and crisp. Halve the sandwiches diagonally. Serve immediately.

## Nashville Hot Chicken

Fried chicken needs no add-ons to disrupt its indisputable goodness. But in Nashville—and more recently at any newer restaurant throughout the South—the good old finger lickin' classic has been reborn with a fiery power you could say comes straight outta the pits of Hell. The local legend is that in the 1930s the spirited chicken emerged out of a lover's jealousy when a girlfriend of Thornton Prince waited for him to arrive home after an evening of tomcatting with a breakfast of fried chicken laced with a lip-flaming chili sauce. To her chagrin, Prince fell in love with the revenge recipe and began selling it in batches. Today, Prince's is still a family-run operation with two locations in Nashville. You can find Hot Chicken just about anywhere these days, but in Nashville, you can't beat the original at Prince's Hot Chicken Shack on Ewing Drive. Be sure to go when you have time to wait; at Prince's they make their chicken to-order in cast-iron skillets. "Medium" is about the upper limit of heat tolerance for most people, but plenty take the challenge of "hot" or "extra hot." To raise the heat on your own batch of Hot Chicken, just add another tablespoon of cayenne at a time to the basting sauce.

*There's a reason this style of chicken is a classic: It starts with a long soak in buttermilk, incorporates the simplicity of five ingredients, and gets cooked to perfection in a cast-iron skillet. A little Chinese five-spice powder gives this a dose of warm spice. The chicken will release from the pan when ready to turn. If it resists, wait a minute or two or the crust will come off. To up the heat quotient, go for Nashville Hot Baste (at right).*

# CLASSIC FRIED CHICKEN + NASHVILLE HOT BASTE

### Serves 4    Hands-on 30 minutes
### Total 7 hours, 50 minutes, including 6 hours chilling

1 (3- to 4-pound) whole chicken, cut into 8 pieces
2 cups whole buttermilk
1 ½ tablespoons plus 1 teaspoon kosher salt
2 cups (about 8 ½ ounces) all-purpose flour
½ teaspoon cayenne pepper
½ teaspoon Chinese five-spice powder
1 teaspoon black pepper
Vegetable oil

**1.** Place the chicken in a baking dish. Combine the buttermilk and 1 ½ tablespoons of the salt; pour over chicken. Cover and chill 6 hours or overnight.

**2.** Preheat the oven to 250°F. Stir together the flour, cayenne pepper, five-spice, black pepper, and remaining 1 teaspoon salt in a shallow dish. Remove the chicken from the buttermilk mixture, discarding the mixture. Dredge each piece in the flour mixture until well coated. Place the pieces on a baking sheet, and let stand at room temperature 30 minutes.

**3.** Pour oil to a depth of ½ inch in a large cast-iron skillet, and heat the oil to 350°F over medium-high. Working in batches, carefully add the chicken pieces to the skillet. (The temperature of the oil will drop to 320° to 325°F when you add the chicken.) Fry the chicken until the crust is golden brown and the breading releases easily (about 4 minutes per side for wings and drumsticks, 4 to 5 minutes per side for thighs, 5 to 6 minutes per side for breasts).

**4.** Transfer the fried chicken to an ovenproof dish lined with paper towels; keep warm in the oven. Let stand 10 to 15 minutes before serving.

# NASHVILLE HOT BASTE

3 tablespoons cayenne pepper
2 tablespoons light brown sugar
1 teaspoon garlic powder
1 teaspoon paprika

1 tablespoon onion powder
1 cup hot frying oil from batch of
 fried chicken

Whisk together all the ingredients, and brush evenly over the hot fried chicken, and
serve. Makes about 1 cup

# Kelly English

## A BAYOU HEART BEATS FOR THE HEARTLAND OF THE SOUTH

Memphis, founded in the early nineteenth century as a hub for trade and transportation along the banks of the Mississippi River, has a long and storied past steeped in social, religious, and racial activism. Its stronghold as the northern tip of the Mississippi Delta, which fans out for 200 miles directly south and was considered one of the richest cotton-growing areas in the country before the Civil War, has given Memphis a particularly unique perspective over the story of the South. It's as rich in a culture of true Southern food as it is in the home of soul, blues, and gospel. It's the raw character and heritage of this city that drew Louisiana-born chef Kelly English to make it his home.

In the near decade in which English has lived in Memphis, his inspiration has derived from scouring every corner of his adopted home to discover its beauty; whether it's watching the sun set over the mythical Mississippi River, strolling through the gilded lobby of the historic Peabody Hotel, taking in the myriad scales of blues music emanating from bars along Beale Street, or sinking his teeth into the best barbecue bologna sandwich in town. (You'll find it at the no-frills counter-service Payne's Bar-B-Que, where the ribs are tender and doused with sauce, the coleslaw is made with mustard, Cokes come in a can, and English is a regular.)

"As a guy from New Orleans, I was immediately struck by the contrast in the food culture of Memphis," says English. "It's rich and layered, but I feel like it was my first introduction to true Southern cooking, even though I'd technically been living in the South my whole life. I guess growing up in southern Louisiana will do that to you."

English is referring to the dominance of New Orleans and by extension, most all of Louisiana's culinary strongholds, which are rooted in both Cajun and Creole cooking.

He remembers the first real serving of collard greens he had when studying prelaw at the University of Mississippi in Oxford. "It was like that scene in that Disney movie, *Ratatouille*, where the mouse closes his eyes when he takes a bite of cheese and all of these images of different foods pop into his mind followed by what seems like fireworks. That's how my first bite of greens was. I'll never forget it."

It's a romantic memory without question, but English also refers to the deeper meaning of how greens really garnered such a stronghold in Southern cooking. "Greens and ham hocks, these were essentially the cheapest, easiest form of food to get for the African slaves working the cotton fields. It sustained them, and they sustained this part of the country. Greens say as much to me about our history as they do our foodways."

English helped pay his way through college while working in restaurants in Oxford where he was inspired by the work of John Currence, whose approach to Southern cuisine was both deliberate and delicious. It prompted English to switch tracks and get his culinary degree from the Culinary Institute of America, an experience that would later land him an opportunity to cook in some of New Orleans's most prestigious restaurants. But in his years of cooking both in Louisiana and in Mississippi, a handful of visits to Memphis began to foster a love for the city. In 2008, he set down roots in the Blues City with the opening of Iris, a French-Creole fine dining homage to his Louisiana heritage.

"I wanted to bring the taste of New Orleans to Memphis using ingredients that are more commonly found here. I basically look at it as what settlers in Louisiana would have cooked if they settled in Memphis instead. I try not to reinvent a cuisine that's already really pure; I'd rather just use what local purveyors can provide, cook it the best way I can, and give that to people."

English points to chefs like Currence, who, having no native ties to Mississippi, revived a celebration of flavors from the

South in Oxford. "Currence was an inspiration before he became a friend," says English. "He stuck his foot out there and showed me that it could be done. He taught me that you don't have to be from somewhere to make a home somewhere. I wanted to do the same thing in Memphis."

In his career, Kelly has garnered an admirable collection of awards and accolades, not the least of which includes multiple James Beard Award finalist nominations. But if you ask him, becoming a chef had nothing to do with gaining a certain level of status.

"Making a career as a chef seemed like a natural thing to me," says English. "Especially because where I'm from, that old adage that cooking is somehow woman's work was not a reality. In our family, part of becoming a man is learning how to cook.

Yes, I learned a lot from watching my grandmothers cook, but I also watched my dad cook. And not just as a stereotypical dad does at a backyard grill but with the oven, on the stove top. My dad is one hell of a cook."

In 2013, English opened The Second Line, a baby sister to Iris that he says "lovingly represents the crappy bars I grew up going to." At the more casual bar and grill, guests find everything from classic po'boys and fried Gulf seafood to skillet cornbread and cheese grits. For him, it was the perfect next step to solidify his commitment to the city.

"I love Memphis, wouldn't want to be anywhere else. It's a hyper-genuine town with good, hardworking people. It has a storied history that has defined its people for the good, and I'm thankful to be a part of that."

*A consummate Gulf Coast loyalist by way of his Louisiana roots, Chef Kelly English always looks for ways to spotlight the beauty of the coastal seafood.*

# AMANDINE OF SPECKLED TROUT, GULF CRAB, AND CAULIFLOWER

*Serves 6     Hands-on 30 minutes     Total 30 minutes*

1 head cauliflower (2 ½ pounds), cut into florets

1 cup heavy cream

4 ounces (½ cup) unsalted butter

2 ¼ teaspoons kosher salt

1 cup whole buttermilk

2 cups (8 ½ ounces) all-purpose flour

1 ½ teaspoons Creole seasoning

6 (4-ounce) speckled trout fillets

Canola oil

½ cup sliced almonds, toasted

¼ cup chopped fresh flat-leaf parsley

1 ½ tablespoons fresh lemon juice

6 ounces fresh jumbo lump crabmeat

**1.** Preheat the oven to 300°F. Bring a large saucepan of water to a rolling boil; add the florets, and cook until tender, about 8 minutes. Drain and place on a baking sheet. Bake until dry, about 5 minutes. Remove from oven, and transfer the florets to a blender.

**2.** Bring the cream and 2 tablespoons of the butter to a simmer in a small saucepan over medium-high, stirring occasionally. Remove from heat, and pour over the cauliflower in blender; process until smooth, about 1 minute. Season with ½ teaspoon of the salt, and return the mixture to small saucepan. Cover and keep warm over low.

**3.** Pour the buttermilk into a shallow dish. Combine the flour, 1 teaspoon of the Creole seasoning, and 1 teaspoon of the salt in a separate shallow dish. Season the fish with ½ teaspoon of the salt and remaining ½ teaspoon Creole seasoning. Dip the fish in the buttermilk and dredge in the seasoned flour; place on a clean plate.

**4.** Pour oil to a depth of 1 inch in a large cast-iron skillet, and heat over medium-high until shimmering. Cook the fillets, in 2 batches, until golden brown and the fish flakes with a fork, 2 to 3 minutes per side. Drain on a baking sheet lined with paper towels.

**5.** Discard any remaining oil from skillet, and wipe skillet clean. Cook the remaining 6 tablespoons butter in skillet over medium, stirring often, until butter begins to brown, about 2 minutes. Add the almonds, and cook, stirring constantly, until butter and almonds are deeply browned, about 2 minutes. Remove the sauce from heat, and stir in the parsley, lemon juice, and remaining ¼ teaspoon salt.

**6.** Place a large spoonful of the cauliflower puree on each of 6 serving plates; top with the fish fillets, crab, and sauce. Serve immediately.

*This bright and flavorful dish owes its origins to the wave of Greek immigrants who settled in the South in the early 1900s—particularly in the Birmingham, Alabama, area. This dish blends fragrant herbs, sweet tomato, and briny olives with the beauty of Gulf Coast snapper in a one-pot dish that is both easy and never fails to impress.*

# GREEK SNAPPER

*Serves 4     Hands-on 15 minutes     Total 30 minutes*

1 tablespoon olive oil

1 small yellow onion, diced (about 1 cup)

1 garlic clove, minced (about 1 teaspoon)

1 (14.5-ounce) can diced tomatoes, drained

½ cup chicken broth

½ cup pitted kalamata olives, sliced

1 teaspoon dried oregano

1 teaspoon kosher salt

½ teaspoon black pepper

1½ pounds skinless red snapper fillet, cut into 4 pieces

Hot cooked long-grain white rice

3 ounces feta cheese, crumbled (about ¾ cup)

2 tablespoons chopped fresh flat-leaf parsley

1 teaspoon lemon zest (from 1 lemon)

**1.** Preheat the oven to 425°F. Grease a 13- x 9-inch baking dish. Heat the olive oil in a medium skillet over medium-high until shimmering; add the onion, and cook, stirring often, until tender, 3 to 4 minutes. Add the garlic, and cook, stirring often, until fragrant, about 1 minute. Stir in the tomatoes, broth, olives, oregano, salt, and pepper, and cook until hot and bubbly, 5 to 6 minutes.

**2.** Place the snapper in prepared baking dish. Spoon the tomato mixture over the fish. Bake in preheated oven until fish flakes with a fork, 15 to 17 minutes. Place the snapper over hot cooked rice on individual plates, and spoon the tomato mixture over the fish. Sprinkle each serving evenly with the feta, parsley, and lemon zest, and serve immediately.

MISSISSIPPI COMEBACK
SAUCE, PG 226

FRIED CATFISH,
PG 227

GREEK SNAPPER

*It's no secret that warm hospitality is a definitive trait throughout the South. Often times a simple "goodbye," is offered in the form of an invitation, "Y'all come back!" It's doubtful that this sauce got its name from the friendly gesture when it was whipped up for the first time at the Rotisserie, a Greek restaurant in Jackson, Mississippi, but it's certainly good enough to prompt another taste, or two. Serve the sauce with shrimp cocktail, fried seafood, as a spread on sandwiches, or as a salad dressing or dip. This recipe suggests prepared horseradish, which strengthens in the sauce when served on the second day.*

# MISSISSIPPI COMEBACK SAUCE

*Serves 6 to 8     Hands-on 5 minutes     Total 1 hour, 5 minutes*

1 cup mayonnaise

3 celery stalks, chopped (about 1 cup)

½ cup prepared horseradish

4 scallions, chopped (about ½ cup)

2 teaspoons lemon zest, plus
  3 tablespoons fresh lemon juice
  (from 1 lemon)

1 tablespoon Dijon mustard

1 tablespoon kosher salt

1 tablespoon black pepper

½ teaspoon cayenne pepper

Process all the ingredients in a food processor until well blended, stopping to scrape down sides as needed. Transfer to an airtight container, and chill at least 1 hour before serving. Serve with boiled shrimp, crudités, or smeared on a hamburger bun. Store in refrigerator up to 1 week.

*In his memoir,* Life on the Mississippi, *Mark Twain said, "The catfish is a plenty good enough fish for anybody." When it's deep-fried in cornmeal and served with hush puppies and tartar sauce, I couldn't agree more. The farm-raised catfish, which is what you'll likely find unless you catch it yourself, is said to have a flakier consistency than the muddier wild-caught fish.*

# FRIED CATFISH

*Serves 6     Hands-on 20 minutes     Total 20 minutes*

2 cups whole milk

2 large eggs, beaten

2 cups (about 11 ½ ounces) fine plain
   yellow cornmeal

4 teaspoons kosher salt

2 teaspoons black pepper

1 teaspoon cayenne pepper

6 (6-ounce) skinless catfish fillets,
   each cut into 3- to 4-inch strips

4 cups peanut oil

Lemon wedges

Mississippi Comeback Sauce (page
   226) or Tartar Sauce (page 128)

**1.** Whisk together the milk and the eggs in a shallow bowl. Stir together the cornmeal, salt, pepper, and cayenne in a separate shallow bowl. Dip the fish in the milk mixture, then dredge in the cornmeal mixture, coating thoroughly. Let stand 5 to 10 minutes.

**2.** Meanwhile, heat the oil in a large, deep cast-iron skillet over medium-high to 350°F. Gently add half of the fish strips, a few at a time (do not crowd skillet), and fry until golden brown on each side, 3 to 4 minutes total. Transfer to a plate lined with paper towels to drain. Cover with aluminum foil to keep warm. Repeat with remaining fish strips. Serve with the lemon wedges and the desired sauce.

*An homage to the original baked appetizer at Antoine's in New Orleans, this makes oysters a main event, with the added flavor of smoke from the grill. The trick to this is to try to find fairly large oysters such as the ones you'll find in the Gulf.*

# GRILLED OYSTERS WITH ROCKEFELLER BUTTER

*Serves 6    Hands-on 20 minutes    Total 4 hours, 20 minutes*

2 bacon slices

1 shallot, coarsely chopped

2 garlic cloves, coarsely chopped

4 ounces fresh baby spinach, stems removed

2 tablespoons dry white wine

1 tablespoon fresh lemon juice (from 1 lemon)

1 tablespoon coarsely chopped fresh flat-leaf parsley

½ teaspoon kosher salt

½ teaspoon black pepper

1 ¾ ounces Parmesan cheese, grated (about ½ cup)

4 ounces (½ cup) unsalted butter, at room temperature

2 dozen oysters, on the half shell

Lemon wedges

**1.** Cook the bacon in a medium skillet over medium-high, turning occasionally, until browned, 8 to 10 minutes. Drain the bacon on a plate lined with paper towels, reserving 1 tablespoon drippings in skillet. Discard the remaining bacon drippings. Return the skillet with the reserved drippings to medium-high. Add the shallot, and cook, stirring occasionally, until translucent, 2 to 3 minutes. Add the garlic, and cook, stirring occasionally, until fragrant, about 2 minutes. Add the spinach, wine, and lemon juice, and cook, stirring occasionally, until the spinach is wilted. Add the parsley, salt, pepper, and cheese. Remove from heat.

**2.** Combine the butter, spinach mixture, and bacon in a food processor, and pulse until smooth, stopping to scrape down the sides as needed, 12 to 14 times. Transfer to an airtight container, and chill 4 to 6 hours.

**3.** Preheat the grill to medium-high (400° to 450°F). Arrange the oysters in a single layer on the grill grates. Carefully spoon about 2 teaspoons of the butter mixture onto each oyster. Grill, uncovered, until the edges of the oysters curl, 6 to 7 minutes. Serve immediately with lemon wedges.

*Nothing celebrates the bounty of the Gulf Coast more than grilled redfish on the half shell, especially if it's fresh-caught from a day on the water. The skin on the fish hardens as it cooks, creating a cup or "shell" that holds the delicious sauce on the fish and allows the flesh to easily come away from the skin as you eat. Add to it the brightness of seasonal citrus fruit and an ice-cold beer, and you have the perfect ending to a day.*

# REDFISH ON THE HALF SHELL WITH FLORIDA CITRUS-SHALLOT VINAIGRETTE

*Serves 4 to 6    Hands-on 30 minutes    Total 40 minutes*

→→ ·—· ←←
## SOUTHERN STAPLE
→→ ·—· ←←

### Florida Citrus

For as long as I can remember, any and all orange juice that ever hit our breakfast table was from Florida oranges—the result, no doubt, of a great marketing campaign. The truth is, much of it also came from California and Texas as well. But the image of Florida as the seat of American citrus farming isn't simply the result of a marketing gimmick. Citrus seeds are thought to have been planted in Florida as early as the mid-sixteenth century. The tropical climate of the Sunshine State made for a perfectly hospitable environment. Since then, Florida has become the primary citrus producer for the U.S., accounting for more than 70 percent of overall production.

**VINAIGRETTE**

½ cup diced shallot (from 2 shallots)

¼ cup sherry vinegar

2 tablespoons Dijon mustard

2 tablespoons chopped fresh basil

½ teaspoon kosher salt

½ teaspoon black pepper

1 cup olive oil

2 oranges, peeled and sectioned

1 grapefruit, peeled and sectioned

**FISH**

2 (5-pound) whole redfish, halved lengthwise with skin and scales on

2 ½ ounces (5 tablespoons) unsalted butter, softened

2 ½ teaspoons kosher salt

2 teaspoons black pepper

2 tablespoons chopped fresh basil

**1.** Prepare the Vinaigrette: Whisk together the shallot, vinegar, Dijon, basil, salt, and pepper in a medium bowl until well combined. Gradually whisk in the olive oil. Stir in the orange and the grapefruit sections until well coated.

**2.** Prepare the Fish: Preheat the grill to medium-high (400° to 450°F). Rub the flesh side of the fish with the butter, and sprinkle with the salt and pepper. Place the fish on lightly greased grill grate, skin side down, and grill, covered, until the fish flakes with a fork, 12 to 15 minutes. Do not turn the fish over. Transfer the fish to a serving platter. Drizzle half of the Vinaigrette over the fish; sprinkle with the chopped basil. Serve with remaining Vinaigrette.

*During the early 1900s, a large sum of satsuma trees were imported from Japan and planted throughout the lower Gulf Coast states from Florida to Texas. The fruit is similar to a tangerine but has far fewer seeds, and its thinner rind is easier to peel. Satsumas were pricier than oranges but had the benefit of being ripe well in advance of other popular citrus. When in season, they're perfect to peel and eat on their own, but, for an indulgent dessert, the aromatics they lend to the everyday pound cake are too good to pass up.*

# SATSUMA POUND CAKE

*Serves 12    Hands-on 20 minutes    Total 3 hours, 15 minutes*

8 ounces (1 cup) unsalted butter, softened, plus more for greasing pan

3 cups (about 12 ¾ ounces) all-purpose flour, plus more for dusting pan

3 cups granulated sugar

6 large eggs

2 tablespoons satsuma zest (from 4 satsumas or 6 tangerines)

1 teaspoon vanilla extract

½ teaspoon table salt

¼ teaspoon baking soda

1 cup sour cream

**1.** Preheat the oven to 325°F. Grease a 10-inch Bundt pan with butter, and dust with flour. Place 1 cup butter in the bowl of a heavy-duty stand mixer, and beat on medium speed until creamy, about 2 minutes. Gradually add the sugar, beating on medium speed until light and fluffy, about 3 minutes. Add the eggs, 1 at a time, beating just until blended after each addition. Stir in the zest and vanilla.

**2.** Place 3 cups flour in a bowl. Whisk in the salt and baking soda. Add the flour mixture to the butter mixture alternately with the sour cream, beginning and ending with the flour mixture. Beat at low speed just until blended after each addition.

**3.** Pour the batter into prepared pan. Bake in the preheated oven until a long wooden pick inserted in the center of the cake comes out clean, 1 hour and 15 minutes to 1 hour and 20 minutes, shielding with aluminum foil after 1 hour to prevent excessive browning, if necessary. Cool in the pan on a wire rack 10 minutes; remove the cake from the pan to wire rack, and cool completely, about 1 ½ hours.

*When you look into the history behind red velvet cake, the truth is it likely did not originate from anywhere south of the Mason-Dixon Line. (Early references show that it may have originated at New York's Waldorf Astoria Hotel.) But when the Louisiana-based film* Steel Magnolias *illustrated it as the consummate groom's cake—shaped as a grey-frosted armadillo—the South heartily claimed this cake as one of its own. This version adds the richness of cheesecake in a layer cake form.*

# RED VELVET CHEESECAKE

*Serves 10 to 12      Hands-on 20 minutes      Total 7 hours*

**CHEESECAKE LAYER**

2 quarts water

Vegetable shortening for greasing pan

2 (8-ounce) packages cream cheese, softened

⅔ cup granulated sugar

½ teaspoon table salt

2 large eggs

⅓ cup sour cream

⅓ cup whole milk

1 teaspoon vanilla extract

**RED VELVET CAKE LAYERS**

Salted butter for greasing pans

2 ½ cups (about 10 ⅝ ounces) all-purpose flour, plus more for dusting

1 ½ cups granulated sugar

3 tablespoons unsweetened cocoa

1 ½ teaspoons baking soda

1 teaspoon table salt

2 large eggs

1 ½ cups vegetable oil

1 cup whole buttermilk

2 tablespoons red liquid food coloring (about 1 [1-ounce] bottle)

2 teaspoons vanilla extract

2 teaspoons white vinegar

**CREAM CHEESE FROSTING**

2 ½ cups (about 10 ounces) powdered sugar, sifted

2 (8-ounce) packages cream cheese, softened

4 ounces (½ cup) salted butter, softened

1 tablespoon vanilla extract

**1.** Prepare the Cheesecake Layer: Preheat the oven to 325°F. Place a large roasting pan on the lower rack of the oven. Boil 2 quarts water in a saucepan over high; reduce the heat to low; keep warm. Grease a 9-inch springform pan; line the bottom of the pan with a round of parchment paper. Double-wrap the exterior bottom and up the outer sides of the pan with aluminum foil to protect the cheesecake while baking in the water bath.

**2.** Place the cream cheese in the bowl of a heavy-duty stand mixer fitted with paddle attachment, and beat on medium speed until creamy. Add the sugar and the salt, and beat until well blended. Scrape down the sides of the bowl; add the eggs, 1 at a time, beating well after each addition. Add the sour cream, milk, and vanilla, and beat until smooth. Pour the cream cheese mixture into the prepared pan. Place in the roasting pan in the preheated oven. Carefully pour 2 quarts hot water into the roasting pan, allowing it to surround cheesecake in the springform pan. Bake until cheesecake is set to the touch, 40 to 45 minutes.

**3.** Carefully remove the cake from the roasting pan; let cake cool on a wire rack 1 hour. Remove foil from the outside of the pan. Cover the cheesecake in the pan. Place in the freezer until completely frozen, at least 3 hours or overnight.

**4.** Prepare the Red Velvet Cake Layers: Preheat the oven to 350°F. Butter and flour 2 (9-inch) round cake pans. Whisk together the flour, sugar, cocoa, baking soda, and salt in a bowl. Combine the eggs, oil, buttermilk, food coloring, vanilla, and vinegar in bowl of a heavy-duty stand mixer fitted with paddle attachment; beat on medium speed until well blended, stopping to scrape down sides as needed. Gradually add the flour mixture, beating on low speed just until blended after each addition. Beat on high speed until well blended, 1 to 2 minutes.

**5.** Pour the batter evenly into the prepared pans. Bake in the preheated oven until a wooden pick inserted in center comes out clean, 25 to 30 minutes. Cool in the pans on wire racks 10 minutes. Carefully remove from the pans to wire racks; cool completely, about 1 hour.

**6.** Prepare the Cream Cheese Frosting: Combine all the frosting ingredients in the bowl of a heavy-duty stand mixer fitted with the paddle attachment, and beat on medium-high speed until smooth and creamy.

**7.** Assemble the Cake: Place 1 Red Velvet Cake Layer in the center of a cake platter. Remove the Cheesecake Layer from the freezer. Carefully remove it from the springform pan. Remove the parchment paper, and place the Cheesecake Layer on top of the Red Velvet Cake Layer on platter. (You may want to measure the 2 cake layers to ensure the Cheesecake Layer is not too large for the Red Velvet Cake Layer. Shave off the sides of the Cheesecake Layer on a cutting board before placing it on the Red Velvet Cake Layer, if needed.) Place the remaining Red Velvet Cake Layer on top of the Cheesecake Layer.

**8.** Gently apply a thin layer of Cream Cheese Frosting around the assembled cake. (It's okay if there are crumbs on this first layer. Clean the spatula each time you dip into frosting bowl, to keep from transferring crumbs to the frosting.) Chill the cake until the frosting is set, about 30 minutes. Remove from the refrigerator, and apply a second layer of frosting, using a large scoop on the top of the cake and spreading it evenly across the top with a large spatula before spreading frosting down the sides of the cake. Serve immediately, or refrigerate the cake, covered, until ready to serve (up to 24 hours).

**9.** Remove the cake from the refrigerator; let stand at room temperature 15 to 20 minutes before serving. Cake may stand at room temperature up to 1 hour; store in the refrigerator up to 5 days.

*If there's anything I love more than bourbon whipped into sweet potatoes, it's pecan streusel on top. So why not put them all together and call it Thanksgiving? This pie is as rich as it sounds, but the streusel helps give it a little texture. Serve with a scoop of ice cream to create perfection.*

# BOURBON-SWEET POTATO PIE WITH PECAN STREUSEL

*Serves 8    Hands-on 30 minutes*
*Total 4 hours, 40 minutes, including 3 hours cooling*

1 pound unpeeled sweet potatoes
½ cup (about 2 ⅛ ounces) all-purpose flour
⅓ cup packed light brown sugar
1 ⅓ cups granulated sugar
2 ½ ounces (5 tablespoons) cold salted butter, plus 4 ounces (½ cup) salted butter, softened

¼ cup chopped pecans
¼ cup whipping cream
¼ cup (2 ounces) bourbon
¼ teaspoon ground nutmeg
½ teaspoon ground cinnamon
1 teaspoon vanilla extract
2 large eggs
1 (9-inch) frozen deep-dish piecrust shell

**1.** Place the sweet potatoes in a large Dutch oven, and add water to cover by 2 to 3 inches. Bring to a boil over medium-high; reduce heat to medium, and cook until tender, about 40 minutes.

**2.** Meanwhile, combine the flour, brown sugar, and ⅓ cup of the granulated sugar in a medium bowl. Cut in 5 tablespoons cold butter with a pastry blender or your fingertips until well blended and crumbly; stir in the pecans.

**3.** Preheat the oven to 350°F. Drain the sweet potatoes, and run under cold water, about 2 minutes. Peel and break apart the sweet potatoes into bowl of a heavy-duty stand mixer or large bowl. Add ½ cup softened butter, and beat on medium speed until well blended, about 30 seconds. Add the cream, bourbon, nutmeg, cinnamon, vanilla, eggs, and remaining 1 cup granulated sugar, beating on medium speed until smooth, about 1 minute. Pour the filling into the piecrust, and sprinkle with the pecan mixture.

**4.** Bake in the preheated oven until a knife inserted in center comes out clean, 55 to 60 minutes. (Pie will puff up like a soufflé and then will sink down as it cools.) Cool completely on a wire rack, about 3 hours.

# GINGER PEACH FRIED PIES

*Makes 10 pies    Hands-on 30 minutes    Total 1 hour, 40 minutes*

*A common kitchen philosophy throughout much of the South is that anything that's good is better fried. And if you think pie is something that simply cannot be improved upon, you've obviously never held in your hand a warm half-moon of flaky pastry filled with a core of molten sweet fruit. You can use any seasonal fruit to make these delicious hand pies, but if you ask me, nothing beats the marriage of ginger and fresh peaches. In a pinch, you can use store-bought pie dough, but this homemade pastry from my friend and bakery owner, Sibby Barrett, is decidedly better.*

**PEACH FILLING**

2 cups fresh or frozen peach slices (about 1 pound fresh)
½ cup granulated sugar
½ tablespoon grated fresh ginger
1 teaspoon ground cinnamon

**PASTRY DOUGH**

3 cups (about 12 ¾ ounces) all-purpose flour, plus more for dusting
3 tablespoons granulated sugar
¼ teaspoon table salt
½ cup vegetable shortening, chilled
1 large egg, beaten
1 cup whole buttermilk

**ADDITIONAL INGREDIENTS**

Canola oil
Vanilla ice cream

**1.** Prepare the Peach Filling: Bring the peaches and sugar to a boil over medium, stirring often; reduce the heat to low, and simmer, stirring often, until very soft, about 20 minutes. Add the ginger and cinnamon, and use a potato masher to blend well. Let cool completely, about 1 hour.

**2.** Prepare the Pastry Dough: Sift together the flour, sugar, and salt. Using a pastry blender, cut in the shortening until the mixture looks crumbly. Add the egg, and stir with a fork until blended. Add the buttermilk, and stir until the dough just comes together. Press the dough together into a disk, and wrap in plastic wrap. Chill the dough 1 hour.

**3.** Assemble the Pies: Roll the dough to ⅛-inch thickness on a lightly floured surface. Cut out 10 (5-inch) circles, rerolling the scraps once, and place the circles on a baking sheet lined with wax paper. Scoop a rounded tablespoon of the Peach Filling into the center of each circle. Moisten the edge of half of each circle with cold water; fold the circles in half, and crimp the edges to seal. Cover and chill at least 10 minutes or until ready to fry.

**4.** Pour the oil to a depth of 1 inch into a large deep skillet, and heat the oil to 350°F over medium. Fry the pies, 2 or 3 at a time, until golden brown, about 3 minutes on each side. Transfer to a baking sheet lined with paper towels to drain. Serve warm with a scoop of the vanilla ice cream.

# PEANUT BUTTER PIE

*Serves 8 to 10     Hands-on 30 minutes     Total 4 hours, 45 minutes*

½ cup creamy peanut butter

1 cup (about 3 ¼ ounces) sifted
  powdered sugar

Crust (page 114), baked and cooled

⅓ cup (about 1 ½ ounces) all-purpose
  flour

¾ cup granulated sugar

⅛ teaspoon table salt, plus 1 pinch

2 cups whole milk

4 large eggs, separated

1 ½ ounces (3 tablespoons) unsalted
  butter

1 teaspoon vanilla extract

¼ teaspoon cream of tartar

**1.** Preheat the oven to 350°F. Pulse the peanut butter and the powdered sugar in a food processor until mealy, 8 to 10 times. Sprinkle the peanut butter mixture evenly over bottom of the Crust.

**2.** Whisk together the flour, ½ cup of the granulated sugar, and ⅛ teaspoon of the salt in a medium saucepan. Whisk together the milk and the egg yolks in a 4-cup glass measuring cup; gradually whisk the milk mixture into the flour mixture. Cook over medium, whisking constantly, just until the mixture begins to bubble, about 12 minutes. As soon as the mixture begins to bubble, cook, whisking constantly, exactly 1 more minute. Remove the mixture from heat, and whisk in the butter and the vanilla. Pour the hot milk mixture over the peanut butter mixture in the Crust.

**3.** Beat the egg whites and remaining pinch of salt in a stainless-steel bowl with an electric mixer on low speed until frothy, about 1 minute. Add the cream of tartar, and beat on medium speed until fluffy with large bubbles forming around edges, about 30 seconds. With mixer running, add remaining ¼ cup granulated sugar, a few teaspoons at a time, until all the sugar is incorporated. Beat until glossy and stiff peaks form. (Do not overbeat.) Spoon the meringue over the pie, spreading to edges to seal in the filling. Make decorative peaks across top of the pie with back of a spoon.

**4.** Bake in preheated oven until peaks are golden brown, 10 to 15 minutes. Chill the pie at least 4 hours and up to 24 hours before serving.

*It's funny how the memory holds on to certain moments in life; I'll never forget the first time I had peanut butter pie. My great-aunt received the recipe when she was living in Huntsville, Alabama, while my uncle was working for NASA. Years later, when they were living in California, she made it for me while I was visiting on vacation. I was thirteen years old. That pie was so good, I never forgot it. Thankfully, she never parted with the recipe, until now.*

# MOON PIES

*Serves 24    Hands-on 1 hour, 10 minutes    Total 2 hours, 40 minutes*

*A decadent cookie treat made famous by the Chattanooga Bakery in Tennessee in the early 1900s, the moon pie, a dressed up s'more, earned the tradition of being paired with an RC Cola in the 1950s with the Big Bill Lister song, "Gimmee an RC Cola and a Moon Pie." Personally, I think you're better served to enjoy these with a glass of cold milk, but as they say, "to each his own taste." Don't be intimidated, these cookies are a lot easier to make than you think, and there's nothing more fun than making homemade marshmallow!*

## GRAHAM CRACKERS

2 cups (about 8 ½ ounces) all-purpose flour, plus more for work surface
¾ cup (about 4 ounces) whole-wheat flour
1 cup packed light brown sugar
¾ teaspoon baking soda
½ teaspoon table salt
3 ounces (6 tablespoons) cold unsalted butter, cubed
¼ cup honey
¼ cup whole milk
1 tablespoon vanilla extract

## MARSHMALLOW FILLING

1 (¼-ounce) envelope unflavored gelatin (2 ½ teaspoons)
⅓ cup cold water
1 cup granulated sugar
¼ cup water
2 teaspoons vanilla extract

## CHOCOLATE DIP

3 cups semisweet chocolate chips or 2 (12-ounce) packages dark chocolate candy wafers

**1.** Prepare the Graham Crackers: Preheat the oven to 350°F. Pulse the flours, brown sugar, baking soda, and salt in a food processor until combined, about 15 times. Add the butter; pulse, scraping down sides, until the mixture resembles peas, about 13 times.

**2.** Whisk together the honey, milk, and vanilla in a medium bowl until combined. With the processor running, gradually add the honey mixture through the food chute, until the dough forms a ball, about 30 seconds, scraping sides as necessary. Flatten the ball into a 1-inch disk, wrap in plastic wrap; chill 30 minutes.

**3.** Divide the dough in half. Roll out 1 half on a lightly floured surface into a 9 ½- x 11 ½-inch rectangle (about ⅛ inch thick). Using a 2 ¼-inch cookie cutter, cut out 24 rounds. Transfer to parchment paper-lined baking sheets, rerolling scraps once. Prick the crackers with the tines of a fork. Bake in the preheated oven, 10 minutes. Repeat rolling procedure with the remaining dough. Transfer to wire racks to cool, about 10 minutes.

**4.** Prepare the Marshmallow Filling: Sprinkle the gelatin evenly over ⅓ cup cold water in the bowl of a heavy-duty stand mixer fitted with whisk attachment. Gently stir with a spoon. Let gelatin soften, 5 minutes.

**5.** Combine the sugar and ¼ cup water in a saucepan. Bring to a boil over medium-high, stirring until the sugar dissolves. Once dissolved, cook, without stirring, until a candy thermometer registers 238°F (soft ball stage). Remove from the heat, and with the mixer on low speed, gradually pour the syrup into the gelatin. Increase speed to medium-high, and beat until white and fluffy with

stiff peaks, 8 to 10 minutes. Add the vanilla, beating just until incorporated. Quickly spoon 1 to 2 tablespoons Marshmallow Filling on 24 of the cooled Graham Crackers; top with remaining crackers. Place the filled graham cracker sandwiches on wire racks, and chill 20 minutes.

**6.** Prepare the Chocolate Dip: Microwave the chocolate according to package directions, until melted and smooth, stirring at 30-second intervals.

**7.** Using tongs, dip each filled sandwich into the chocolate until covered, letting excess drip off. Place on parchment paper-lined baking sheets. Chill until the chocolate is firm, about 30 minutes. Store in an airtight container.

SOUTHWEST

# The Southwest

**FROM THE OZARKS DOWN THROUGH TEXAS,** this part of the region was considered the wild frontier for much of the history of the Deep South. The western expansion of the railroads brought the South to the edge of American civilization. While the region is influenced by French and Spanish colonists as well as slavery and Native Americans, it also includes German, Czech, Irish, and Mexican influences who migrated from ports in Galveston, Indianola, and the Mexican border. Flavors include influences from chiles, Latin spices, campfire cooking, and a heavier reliance on beef.

## DINING DETOURS

The Hive, Bentonville, AK

Mexico Chiquito, Little Rock, AK

South on Main, Little Rock, AK

Sid's Diner, El Reno, OK

Cattlemen's Steakhouse, Oklahoma City, OK

The Miller Grill, Yukon, OK

Barley Swine, Austin, TX

Franklin Barbecue, Austin, TX

Valentina's Tex-Mex BBQ, Austin, TX

Rapscallion, Dallas, TX

Stampede 66, Dallas, TX

Ninfa's on Navigation, Houston, TX

La Gloria, San Antonio, TX

*The only problem with a breakfast taco is that you can't stop with just one. This clever casserole version makes a happy morning of breakfast tacos for an army of friends or family—and the best part: You make them a day ahead. I like to slice these into two-inch bite-sized pieces, making them a great brunch or tea party option.*

# BREAKFAST TACO ENCHILADAS

*Serves 10 to 12    Hands-on 40 minutes    Total 9 hours, 30 minutes, including 8 hours chilling*

2 ½ cups cooked, crumbled, and
    drained ground pork sausage
    (about 1 pound)
2 cups frozen potato tots, baked
    according to package directions
    until crisp and then diced (from
    1 [32-ounce] package)
½ cup chopped scallions
    (from 4 scallions)
12 ounces pepper Jack cheese,
    grated (about 2 ½ cups)

10 (8-inch) flour tortillas
1 cup whole milk
5 large eggs
½ teaspoon kosher salt
½ teaspoon black pepper
1 tablespoon all-purpose flour
Chopped fresh cilantro (optional)
Salsa
Sour cream

**1.** Grease a 13- x 9-inch baking dish. Combine the sausage, potato tots, scallions, and 1½ cups of the cheese in a medium bowl. Spoon ½ cup sausage mixture down center of each tortilla. Roll up the tortillas, and place, side by side tightly, in prepared baking dish.

**2.** Whisk together the milk, eggs, salt, pepper, and flour in a medium bowl until well blended. Pour the egg mixture over the filled tortillas. Cover with lightly greased aluminum foil, and refrigerate overnight.

**3.** Preheat the oven to 350°F. Remove the enchiladas from the refrigerator, and let stand at room temperature 15 to 20 minutes. Bake in the preheated oven, covered with foil, 25 minutes. Remove and discard the foil; sprinkle the remaining 1 cup cheese over the enchiladas. Return to the oven, and bake, uncovered, until browned and set, about 20 more minutes. Garnish with the cilantro, if desired, and serve warm with the salsa and sour cream.

---

**SOUTHERN STAPLE**

## Sonic Tater Tots

In 1953, the prototype for the first Sonic Drive-In opened in Shawnee, Oklahoma. Originally named "Top Hat," the fast-casual drive-in concept solidified the 1950s carhop as a classic part of American pop culture. The name was changed to Sonic in 1959, with crispy fried Tater Tots™ and cherry limeades topping the list of menu favorites.

## Southwestern Cuisine

Bored with the standard French-inspired continental cuisine of 1980s upscale restaurants, many chefs around the U.S. began looking at the regional flavors and heritage in their own backyards. New Orleans-based Paul Prudhomme championed Cajun cuisine; Alice Waters and Wolfgang Puck reinvented California cooking. At the behest of culinary consultant and cookbook writer Anne Lindsay Greer, who was consulting for Dallas's Anatole Hotel, Dallas chefs Stephan Pyles, Dean Fearing, and Avner Samuel along with Houston chefs Robert Del Grande and Amy Ferguson met to define a new regional cuisine for the Southwest. Thus Southwestern Cuisine was born. Though broad in scope, its foundations drew on Southern, Mexican, German, and Cowboy heritage using wood-fired grills and smokers, and ingredients such as chiles, black beans, cumin, cilantro, limes, squash and their seeds, and rice.

*No Tex-Mex table is complete without a dish of salsa and a basket of tortilla chips for dipping. A basic salsa picante is a combination of tomatoes, onions, a chile pepper such as jalapeño or serrano, and sometimes cilantro, with a squeeze of lime and a dash of salt. There are a million different ways to bring this combination together with an assortment of appropriate additions such as corn, black beans, garlic, vinegar, and even sugar. I personally like the added depth you get from roasting the vegetables before blending them.*

# ROASTED SONORAN SALSA

*Serves 8    Hands-on 15 minutes    Total 30 minutes*

6 plum tomatoes (about 1½ pounds)

4 fresh tomatillos, husks removed, rinsed (about 12 ounces)

2 cups water

1 serrano chile, stemmed and, if desired, seeded

½ cup chopped yellow or white onion (from 1 small onion)

2 tablespoons roughly chopped garlic (from 6 garlic cloves)

1 tablespoon kosher salt

1 tablespoon fresh lime juice (from 1 lime)

**1.** Preheat the broiler with oven rack 6 inches from heat. Place the tomatoes and the tomatillos on a large rimmed baking sheet, and roast in preheated oven until skin blisters, about 8 to 10 minutes, turning at least once during roasting.

**2.** Bring the water, chile, and onion to a boil in a medium saucepan over medium-high, and boil until softened, about 10 minutes. Drain well.

**3.** Place the roasted tomatoes and tomatillos, drained onion mixture, garlic, salt, and lime juice in a food processor; process until mostly smooth, about 30 seconds. Serve immediately, or cover and chill up to 2 weeks.

*Growing up, no Frito corn chip was complete without a scoop of bean dip curled up inside of it. Of course, I grew up on the processed canned concoction, but this homemade recipe will make any game-day spread complete. I used to think you really only needed a big pot of queso to satisfy a Super Bowl party, but now I'm not so sure.*

# DREAMY TEXAS BEAN DIP

*Serves 12     Hands-on 15 minutes     Total 35 minutes*

1 tablespoon vegetable oil

1 small yellow onion, grated (about ½ cup)

1 fresh poblano chile, seeded and diced or 1 (4.5-ounce) can green chiles, undrained

½ teaspoon kosher salt

1 (8-ounce) package cream cheese, softened

2 (16-ounce) cans refried beans

4 ounces preshredded Mexican 4-cheese blend (about 1 cup)

Preheat the oven to 350°F. Grease a 9- x 7-inch baking dish with cooking spray. Heat the oil in a medium saucepan over medium-high until shimmering, about 1 minute. Add the grated onion and the chopped chile, and cook, stirring occasionally, until tender, 3 to 4 minutes. Stir in the salt. Break the cream cheese into 16 pieces, and add to the onion mixture; cook, stirring occasionally, until the cream cheese softens, about 2 minutes. Gradually add the beans, and cook, stirring occasionally, until the mixture begins to become smooth. Pour into prepared baking dish, and sprinkle with the shredded cheese. Bake in preheated oven until the cheese is melted and bubbly, about 20 minutes.

*If you've never had Arkansas Cheese Dip (read The Great Queso Debate, page 254), Mexico Chiquito in Little Rock is really where you should have your first experience. (You'll find many other variations throughout the state.) Though it still relies on your standard easy-to-melt American-style processed cheese, this creamy bowl of goodness relies more on Mexican spices than the chiles and pico de gallo ingredients you tend to find in the Texas version. Serve with tortilla chips, and devour!*

# ARKANSAS CHEESE DIP

*Serves 16     Hands-on 30 minutes     Total 30 minutes*

2 ounces (4 tablespoons) unsalted butter

⅓ cup (about 1 ½ ounces) all-purpose flour

2 cups whole milk

16 ounces processed cheese (*such as Velveeta*), cut into 1-inch cubes

8 ounces Monterey Jack cheese, shredded (about 2 cups)

2 teaspoons ancho chile powder or other dark chile powder

2 teaspoons ground cumin

1 teaspoon cayenne pepper

1 teaspoon garlic powder

1 teaspoon dry mustard

1 teaspoon hot sauce (*such as Tabasco*)

½ teaspoon kosher salt

Tortilla chips

Melt the butter in a medium saucepan over medium. Gradually add the flour, and cook, whisking constantly, until lightly browned, about 1 minute. Gradually whisk in the milk, and cook, whisking often, until thickened, about 5 minutes. Stir in the cheeses, chile powder, cumin, cayenne, garlic powder, mustard, hot sauce, and salt. Cook, stirring often, until the cheese has melted completely and all the ingredients are well incorporated. Serve warm with the tortilla chips.

THE HOMESICK
TEXAN'S
AUSTIN-STYLE
QUESO,
PG 255

ARKANSAS
CHEESE DIP

DREAMY TEXAS
BEAN DIP,
PG 251

ROASTED
SONORAN SALSA,
PG 250

# Lisa Fain

## THE GREAT QUESO DEBATE

Ask any Texan about the foods of the Lone Star State and you'll likely get a list that would include barbecue, burgers, chicken fried steak, fajitas, enchiladas, and tacos. But without question, any such list would be inherently unTexan if it didn't include queso. To Texans, queso is sacred, and it's heartily welcomed at the table at any meal—breakfast, lunch, and dinner. I've even known occasions where an order of it has been savored as a sole dinner item.

Though its more formal name, chile con queso, has its most direct link to Mexico in the late 1800s as chiles poblanos, which showcased poblano chiles as the star relegating the cheese and tomatoes to a supporting role, its origins in Texas and beyond are a little less straightforward. Many may even be surprised to learn that its origins as a Texas invention have been hotly disputed.

The topic arose from a 2016 *Wall Street Journal* article entitled "Don't Tell Texas, But Arkansas Is Laying Claim to Queso." Naturally, such a headline caused quite a few spilled bowls of queso in the Lone Star State, so much so that a few Texas and Arkansas U.S. senators held an official blind taste test—a "queso-off" on the Senate floor—and Arkansas Cheese Dip was the undisputed winner. (Another headline topic that stopped most Texans dead in their tracks.)

It's a bone of contention so troubling that noted Texas-born food writer Lisa Fain, aka the Homesick Texan, dedicated an entire book to the topic simply entitled *Queso!*.

"When I first saw the news reported, I couldn't believe it," says Fain. "There wasn't any real evidence in anything that I read about it. I even called the Arkansas Library to see if they had any, and I never got a response. I became so obsessed, I felt I had to defend Texas's honor."

Fain delved deeper into the matter to find that W. F. "Blackie" and Margaret Donnelly first included a version of queso, or "cheese dip," on the menu of their Little Rock restaurant,

Mexico Chiquito, which opened in 1938. But that didn't settle the matter for Fain, especially when she learned that they had previously owned a restaurant with the same name in Kilgore, Texas, in 1936, thereby establishing the origins of their cheese dip back in Texas.

In truth, according to Fain's research, the revered bowl of melted cheese essentially evolved out of a combination of its aforementioned Mexican predecessor and the popular British cheese-covered toast dish known as Welsh Rarebit. She even found articles from Kentucky and San Francisco that published recipes for "Mexican Rarebit" that predate a 1910 appearance of chile con queso at the Gunter Hotel in San Antonio and a recipe that the *Boston Cooking School Magazine* published in 1914, almost a decade before Texas's first published recipe in 1922. But Texans try not to dwell on such things.

In 1922, O. M. Farnsworth, owner of San Antonio's Original Mexican Restaurant, asserted that he had been serving chile con queso at his restaurant since 1900, but Fain came up empty when trying to track down any proof. Her research led her to the conclusion that, at the very least, chile con queso did beat Arkansas Cheese Dip to the punch in establishing a recipe and a regularity for the beloved side dish with the early 1920s publishing of the *Woman's Club Cook Book of Tested and Tried Recipes* published by the Woman's Club of San Antonio. Following that, the recipe flourished through a wide range of Texas publications and community cookbooks. (For the record, the first appearance of the dip using processed cheese by Velveeta was in 1939 from the First Christian Church of Lubbock, and its favored partner, Ro-Tel tomatoes with green chiles, arrived on the scene in 1949.)

Whether it's queso or cheese dip to you, this basic bowl of thick, molten, chile-laced cheese binds friends—new and old—together, regardless of state boundaries.

*Queso has many variations. In Austin, there was one standard for me growing up. After Friday night football games, my friends and I drove to Kerbey Lane Cafe on South Lamar for a late-night bowl of queso. Not surprisingly, queso expert Lisa Fain, aka the Homesick Texan, whose book* Queso! *explores more than fifty styles of the beloved Texas appetizer, references that same diner with this recipe. Scoop a spoonful of classic guacamole (page 264) in the middle for a "compuesto" version.*

# THE HOMESICK TEXAN'S AUSTIN-STYLE QUESO

*Serves 8     Hands-on 30 minutes     Total 30 minutes*

2 fresh Anaheim chiles (3 ounces)

2 tablespoons unsalted butter

¼ cup diced yellow onion (from 1 onion)

4 jalapeño chiles, seeded and finely diced (about ½ cup)

2 garlic cloves, minced (about 2 teaspoons)

2 tablespoons cornstarch

1 cup whole milk

1 cup water

1 pound yellow American cheese, shredded or sliced

2 tablespoons chopped fresh cilantro

1 teaspoon ground cumin

¼ teaspoon cayenne pepper

½ teaspoon kosher salt

Tortilla chips

**1.** Cook the Anaheim chiles, 1 at a time, over an open flame of a gas burner, turning often, until each side of the chile is charred, about 5 minutes. (If you do not have a gas cooktop, place the chiles in a skillet over high, and cook, turning often, until each side is slightly charred, about 5 to 8 minutes.) Place the charred chiles in a bowl, and cover with plastic wrap; let steam 15 minutes. Peel, seed, and dice the Anaheim chiles into small pieces.

**2.** Melt the butter in a medium saucepan over medium. Add the onion and jalapeño, and cook, stirring occasionally, until the onion and the jalapeños start to soften, about 5 minutes. Add the garlic and the diced Anaheim chiles, and cook, stirring often, 30 seconds.

**3.** Whisk together the cornstarch, milk, and 1 cup water in a small bowl until well blended, and add to saucepan. Bring to a simmer, stirring constantly, and cook, stirring often, until the mixture has thickened. Reduce heat to medium-low. Gradually add the cheese, stirring often and making sure the cheese melts before stirring in more. Stir in the cilantro, cumin, cayenne, and salt.

**4.** Transfer the cheese mixture to a serving bowl, a small slow cooker, or a chafing dish over a flame. Serve with the tortilla chips.

*The average cheese ball gets quite an upgrade from smoky ancho chile and the bitterness of beer. This recipe is a surefire winner from my mother's arsenal. Make a day ahead for the flavors to really set in.*

# ANCHO-DUSTED BEER CHEESE

*Serves 10 to 12    Hands-on 20 minutes    Total 1 hour, 20 minutes*

1 pound sharp Cheddar cheese, shredded (about 4 cups)

1 pound cold cream cheese

1 teaspoon cayenne pepper

1 teaspoon garlic powder

½ teaspoon black pepper

⅓ cup medium-dark beer (*such as Shiner Bock*)

Dash of hot sauce (*such as Tabasco*)

1 teaspoon kosher salt

2 ounces (¼ cup) salted butter

1 tablespoon ancho chile powder

1 tablespoon paprika

2 cups chopped pecans

Assorted crackers

**1.** Pulse the Cheddar, cream cheese, cayenne, garlic powder, black pepper, beer, hot sauce, and ½ teaspoon of the salt in a food processor until combined, 6 or 7 times. Divide the mixture in half, and carefully roll each half into a ball, working quickly to avoid sticking. (Use damp hands for easier handling.)

**2.** Melt the butter in a large nonstick skillet over medium. Add the chile powder and paprika; cook, stirring constantly, until fragrant, about 1 minute. Add the pecans and remaining ½ teaspoon salt; cook, stirring often, until the pecans are lightly toasted, 3 to 4 minutes. Spread the nut mixture in a single layer on a rimmed baking sheet; cool completely, about 10 minutes. Roll the cheese balls in pecan mixture until coated. Wrap each cheese ball in plastic wrap, and chill 1 hour before serving with crackers.

⤜⟶⤛

**SOUTHERN STAPLE**

⤜⟶⤛

## The Origin of Chiles

The wide array of capsicum pods found in Texas today owes its heritage to the tiny chile pequin, the perfect size for migrating birds to pick and eat on their way north through the Central Americas.

Today, there are five domesticated species of chiles noted around the world, including the Caribbean's *Capsicum frutescens* and *Capsicum chinense*; South America's *Capsicum pubescens* and *Capsicum baccatum*; and North America's *Capsicum annuum*, from which bell peppers, jalapeños, serranos, poblanos, and guajillos derive.

*Some say the fried pickle got its start at the Duchess Drive-In in Atkins, Arkansas, while others hold that the Hollywood Cafe in Robinsonville, Mississippi, is where these tasty snacks got their start. Dill pickle chips are the most common type for these, but I also love to use kosher dill spears, which offer a juicy kick to follow the initial crunchy bite.*

# CRISPY FRIED PICKLES

### Serves 6     Hands-on 15 minutes     Total 15 minutes

1 cup (about 4 ¼ ounces) all-purpose
  flour
¾ cup (about 4 ⅛ ounces) fine plain
  yellow cornmeal
2 tablespoons garlic powder
4 teaspoons black pepper

1 tablespoon kosher salt
1 teaspoon cayenne pepper
6 cups peanut oil
1 (16-ounce) jar dill pickle chips
Mississippi Comeback Sauce
  (page 226)

**1.** Combine the flour, cornmeal, garlic powder, black pepper, salt, and cayenne in a medium bowl. Pour the oil into a large cast-iron skillet, and heat over medium-high to 350° to 360°F.

**2.** Meanwhile, remove the pickles from jar; drain well. Place on a plate lined with paper towels, and pat completely dry with a paper towel.

**3.** Drop the pickles into the flour mixture, and coat well using a fork. Carefully add half of the pickles to oil, 1 at a time, and fry, stirring occasionally to prevent the pickles from sticking to each other, until browned, about 3 minutes. Remove the pickles using a metal frying spatula or spider, and drain on a separate plate lined with paper towels. Repeat with the remaining pickles. Serve warm with the Mississippi Comeback Sauce.

→→——←←
**SOUTHERN STAPLE**
→→——←←

## Oklahoma's Fried Onion Burger

The basic hamburger has seen any number of toppings between its two buns since it first grew to popularity in the early twentieth century. The gamut runs from blue cheese, sautéed mushrooms, and chili to bacon, foie gras, and guacamole. But the only place you'll find a stack of sliced onions fried right into the burger patty is in Oklahoma. Born during the Depression in El Reno, Oklahoma, the owners of the Hamburger Inn sought to stretch the size of a meager portion of meat by pressing it into a mound of shredded onions with the back of a heavy-duty spatula. The charred edges of the onions cooked into the flat-top, singed meat turned out to be a winning combination. So much so that it's a treat folks continue to line up for at three local diners in El Reno: Robert's Grill, Sid's Diner, and Johnnie's Grill.

*They say you can't put lipstick on a pig, but when it comes to the black-eyed-pea, famed Texas cook Helen Corbitt did exactly that in the mid-1900s. Though not a native Texan herself—she was from New York, far above the Mason-Dixon Line—she cleverly coined a simple black-eyed pea salad as Texas Caviar, and the rest is history. I like the textures both black-eyed peas and black beans bring to the mix.*

# WEST TEXAS CAVIAR

*Serves 10     Hands-on 20 minutes     Total 50 minutes*

1 (15-ounce) can black-eyed peas, drained and rinsed

1 (15-ounce) can black beans, drained and rinsed

2 cups cherry tomatoes, quartered

3 scallions, chopped (about ½ cup)

1 garlic clove, minced (about 1 teaspoon)

1 cup chopped green bell pepper (from 1 bell pepper)

1 jalapeño chile, seeded and chopped (about 2 tablespoons)

1 cup fresh or frozen corn kernels

3 tablespoons fresh lime juice (from 2 limes)

2 tablespoons extra-virgin olive oil

2 ounces cotija cheese, crumbled (about ½ cup)

1¼ teaspoons kosher salt

Thick tortilla chips

Toss together all the ingredients except the chips in a medium bowl. Cover and chill at least 30 minutes or up to 2 days before serving. Toss again, and serve with the chips.

# GUACAMOLE

Guacamole has been around since the Aztecs dominated what is now Mexico, where avocados were first cultivated. Mashed down into a sauce, it's been a staple part of the Mexican diet not only because it's simply delicious but for its nutrition value as well. Guacamole made its way to North America as Tex-Mex cuisine proliferated in Texas throughout the twentieth century. Often served as "aguacate salad" on early Tex-Mex menus, guacamole began to stake a major claim as an appetizer dish as well as a common condiment on fajita, nacho, and taco plates. Today, you'll find it at just about every social event from holiday gatherings to football tailgating. In its simplest form, guacamole is avocado mashed with pico de gallo, diced tomatoes, onions, jalapeño, and a little garlic and lime juice.

GRAPEFRUIT-AND-COTIJA
GUACAMOLE,
PG 265

PERFECT
GUACAMOLE,
PG 264

TOMATILLO
GUACAMOLE,
PG 265

BLACK BEAN-AND-CORN
GUACAMOLE,
PG 264

# PERFECT GUACAMOLE

*Serves 4 to 6    Hands-on 15 minutes    Total 15 minutes*

*Once you have the first three ingredients—avocado, citrus, and salt—the standard version includes the same ingredients you would find in a pico de gallo: tomato, onion, and jalapeño or serrano chile.*

4 to 5 ripe avocados, peeled, halved, and pitted
¼ cup grated red onion (from 1 onion)
2 ripe plum tomatoes, peeled, seeded, and diced
¼ cup chopped fresh cilantro
2 tablespoons fresh lime juice (from 1 lime)

1 serrano chile, seeded and chopped (about 1 tablespoon)
1 garlic clove, minced (about 1 teaspoon)
1 teaspoon table salt
½ teaspoon ground cumin
Tortilla chips

Place avocados in a medium bowl, and mash, using a fork. Add onion, tomatoes, cilantro, lime juice, serrano, garlic, salt, and cumin; stir vigorously until well combined. Serve with chips or alongside any Tex-Mex dish.

# BLACK BEAN-AND-CORN GUACAMOLE

*Serves 4 to 6    Hands-on 10 minutes    Total 10 minutes*

*Adding the common Tex-Mex ingredients of black beans and corn to this humble side dish almost makes it a meal. Serve it with chips, alongside chicken fajitas, or spooned over a morning breakfast taco.*

4 ripe avocados, peeled, halved, and pitted
1 cup canned seasoned black beans, drained and rinsed
1 cup fresh or frozen corn kernels
¼ cup sour cream

1 jalapeño chile, seeded and chopped (about 2 tablespoons)
2 tablespoons fresh lime juice (from 1 lime)
2 teaspoons kosher salt

Place the avocados in a medium bowl, and mash using a fork. Add the black beans, corn, sour cream, jalapeño, lime juice, and salt, and stir until well blended. Serve immediately.

# GRAPEFRUIT-AND-COTIJA GUACAMOLE

*Serves 4 to 6     Hands-on 15 minutes     Total 15 minutes*

4 ripe avocados, peeled, halved, and pitted
2 tablespoons grated white onion (from 1 onion)
1 small grapefruit, peeled, sectioned, and chopped (about 1 cup)
1 ounce cotija cheese, crumbled (about ¼ cup), plus more for garnish
¼ cup roasted, salted pumpkin seed kernels (pepitas), plus more for garnish
2 tablespoons fresh lime juice (from 1 lime)
1 teaspoon kosher salt
Tortilla chips

Place the avocados into a medium bowl, and mash using a fork. Add the onion, grapefruit, cotija, pumpkin seed kernels, lime juice, and salt; stir vigorously until well blended. Garnish with additional cotija and pumpkin seed kernels, if desired. Serve with the tortilla chips or alongside grilled seafood.

*It's not unusual to see avocado and grapefruit paired up as adornments to salads throughout the Southwest. If you ask me, blending together in a guacamole is a natural combination. Salty cotija cheese and toasted pumpkin seeds round out the mix. Serve this with grilled fish or ceviche.*

# TOMATILLO GUACAMOLE

*Serves 4 to 6     Hands-on 15 minutes     Total 25 minutes*

4 medium tomatillos, husked and quartered (about 12 ounces)
2 tablespoons water
4 ripe avocados, peeled, halved, and pitted
1 jalapeño chile, seeded and chopped (about 2 tablespoons)
2 tablespoons fresh lime juice (from 1 lime)
3 teaspoons kosher salt
Tortilla chips

Combine the tomatillos and 2 tablespoons water in a small saucepan; cook over medium-high, stirring often to prevent sticking, until tomatillos are tender, 10 to 12 minutes. Transfer the tomatillo mixture to a food processor, and let cool with the lid off 15 minutes. Place the avocado in food processor. Add the jalapeño, lime juice, and salt, and pulse until well blended, 8 to 10 times. (The mixture should be creamy.) Serve with the tortilla chips or alongside fajitas.

*I love the creaminess of mashed avocado for guacamole, but there's something about the tart character tomatillos bring that make them a perfect combination, especially for pork carnitas or steak fajitas.*

*Barbecue beans—along with coleslaw, potato salad, and, in some parts of the region, braised collard greens—are necessary sides for a barbecue feast. Some prefer sweeter baked beans, usually made with white navy beans; others prefer savory pintos. This recipe brings them together. And with the addition of bacon and sausage, it's practically a meal. Best to make these a day before you plan to serve them so that the flavors meld.*

# BARBECUE BEANS

*Serves 20     Hands-on 45 minutes     Total 11 hours, 45 minutes*

2 pounds dried pinto beans
½ pound bacon slices, diced
2 cups diced yellow onion (about 2 onions)
1½ cups diced red bell pepper (about 1½ bell peppers)
1½ cups diced celery (about 4 stalks)
2 tablespoons minced garlic (from 6 cloves)
1 pound smoked sausage, diced
8 cups water
1 (14.5-ounce) can diced tomatoes, undrained

1 (12-ounce) dark beer (*such as Negra Modelo*)
¾ cup packed light brown sugar
1 (6-ounce) can tomato paste
1 (4.5-ounce) can diced green chiles, undrained
¼ cup Worcestershire sauce
2 tablespoons yellow mustard
1 tablespoon black pepper
1 tablespoon chili powder
1 teaspoon kosher salt

**1.** Rinse and sort the beans, discarding any stones or shriveled beans. Place in a stockpot; add water to cover by 2 inches. Refrigerate 8 hours or overnight. Drain.
**2.** Preheat the oven to 350°F. Cook the bacon in a Dutch oven over medium-high, stirring often, until crispy, 10 to 15 minutes. Using a slotted spoon, transfer the bacon to a plate lined with paper towels, reserving drippings in the Dutch oven.
**3.** Add the onion, bell pepper, celery, and garlic to the reserved drippings in the Dutch oven, and cook over medium, stirring occasionally, until softened, 6 to 7 minutes. Add the smoked sausage and cooked bacon, and cook, stirring often, until the sausage is lightly browned, about 8 minutes. Add the drained beans and 8 cups water; bring to a boil over high. Cover and transfer to the preheated oven. Bake until the liquid is mostly absorbed, about 1 hour.
**4.** Remove the Dutch oven from the oven, uncover, and stir in the tomatoes, beer, brown sugar, tomato paste, green chiles, Worcestershire sauce, mustard, black pepper, chili powder, and salt. Bring to a boil on stove-top over high. Return the Dutch oven to the oven, and bake until the beans are creamy and tender and the liquid is reduced and thickened, about 2 more hours. Serve hot.

## SOUTHERN STAPLE

## Chuck Wagon Lore

Charles Goodnight is credited with inventing the first chuck wagon. A former Texas Ranger, Goodnight became a cattle rancher in the Palo Duro Canyon of the Texas Panhandle. His JA Ranch worked cattle that were driven up through New Mexico and Colorado on what was called the Goodnight-Loving Trail. Chuck boxes were common Civil War mess tents and proved useful to Goodnight, who placed his on top of a large wagon. Aside from beef and the occasional bison or deer kill from the trail, chuck wagons carried shelf-stable goods like beans, black-eyed peas, corn-meal, flour, and spices. For cowboys out on the trail, it was a familiar home with everything from eating utensils, water barrels, and tools to bedrolls and medical supplies. Chuck wagon cooks not only made meals but mended clothing and boots, gave medical help, and often served as the sole entertainment around the evening campfire.

# BEER CAN SMOKED CHICKEN

*Serves 8     Hands-on 1 hour     Total 24 hours, including 18 hours chilling*

*Of the many factors that are key to smoking meats, managing humidity in balance with heat and oxygen is crucial. While many use a simple water pan in the bottom of the smoker, the old "beer can chicken" method works just as well for keeping the chicken perfectly moist and tender. You can use any beer of choice, but I prefer a good strong IPA, which imparts a nice herbal character to the chicken. I love doing three to four chickens at once, breaking down the meat once it's finished, and freezing in small freezer bags for later use in soups, casseroles, or last-minute nachos.*

**BRINE**

2 cups granulated sugar

2 cups kosher salt

6 cups very hot water

6 cups ice water, plus more as needed

**SMOKED CHICKEN**

2 (5-pound) whole chickens

2 teaspoons black pepper

2 teaspoons kosher salt

2 teaspoons seasoned salt
  (such as Lawry's)

2 teaspoons paprika

2 teaspoons chili powder

2 teaspoons garlic powder

2 teaspoons dried oregano

¼ cup mayonnaise

2 (12-ounce) cans beer

**1.** Prepare the Brine: Stir together the sugar, salt, and hot water in a large food-safe container (big enough to hold the chickens), stirring until the sugar and salt are dissolved. Stir in the ice water.

**2.** Prepare the Smoked Chicken: Add the chickens to the Brine in the container, and add water, if necessary, to cover the chickens. Chill 18 to 24 hours.

**3.** Prepare a charcoal fire in smoker according to the manufacturer's instructions, bringing the internal temperature to 250° to 275°F; maintain temperature for 15 to 20 minutes.

**4.** Meanwhile, stir together the black pepper, kosher salt, seasoned salt, paprika, chili powder, garlic powder, and oregano in a small bowl. Remove the chickens from the Brine; rinse, pat dry with paper towels, and place on a large rimmed baking sheet. Coat the outside of the chickens evenly with the mayonnaise. Sprinkle with the spice mixture.

**5.** Remove half of the beer from each can, and discard. Place half-filled beer cans on the grate of the smoker. Carefully stand 1 chicken over each beer can, sliding can inside cavity of each chicken and standing the chickens using beer cans as the base and the chicken legs for stability. Smoke the chickens on indirect heat until a meat thermometer inserted into the breast of each chicken registers 165°F, about 4 ½ hours. Remove the chickens from the smoker. Discard the beer cans. Let the chickens stand for 20 to 30 minutes before cutting into pieces.

# BIEROCKS

*Serves 16     Hands-on 35 minutes     Total 2 hours, 15 minutes*

**DOUGH**

1 (¼-ounce) envelope active dry yeast

2 cups warm water (110° to 115°F)

½ cup granulated sugar

2 large eggs

2 ⅔ ounces (⅓ cup) unsalted butter, melted, plus more for brushing rolls

1 tablespoon table salt

7 to 8 cups (29 ¾ ounces to 34 ounces) all-purpose flour, plus more for rolling out dough

**FILLING**

1 ½ cups finely chopped onion (from 1 onion)

1 pound ground chuck

4 cups finely shredded cabbage (from 1 head)

1 teaspoon table salt

1 teaspoon black pepper

German mustard or stone-ground mustard

*A carryover from German immigrants to Appalachia who settled in parts of Texas and Oklahoma, these warm little pockets of homemade rolls stuffed with beef and cabbage make for a delicious casual meal. Just be sure not to skimp on the meat filling; the dough will rise, so you want to make sure it's well filled.*

**1.** Prepare the Dough: Combine the yeast, ½ cup warm water, and 1 tablespoon of the sugar in a small bowl; stir to dissolve. Let stand until foamy, about 10 minutes.

**2.** Combine the eggs, butter, salt, remaining 1 ½ cups water, and 7 tablespoons sugar in a heavy-duty stand mixer fitted with a dough hook. Stir in the yeast mixture. Gradually add the flour, 1 cup at a time, beating on medium speed until well blended after each addition. Beat on medium speed until the dough is smooth and elastic, about 8 minutes. Place in a large greased bowl, turning to grease top. Cover the dough loosely with a clean towel or plastic wrap, and let rise in a warm place (80° to 85°F), free from drafts, until doubled in size, about 1 hour.

**3.** Prepare the Filling: Cook the onion and ground chuck in a large skillet over medium-high, stirring to crumble beef, until the onion is tender and beef is browned, 8 to 10 minutes. Stir in the cabbage. Cook, stirring often, until tender, 3 to 4 minutes. Remove from heat; stir in the salt and pepper. Cool 10 minutes.

**4.** Assemble Bierocks: Divide the Dough in half; knead 2 or 3 times on a heavily floured surface. Roll each half into a 16-inch square. Cut each into 16 (4-inch) squares. Place about 3 tablespoons Filling in the center of each square. Bring the corners of each square together over the Filling. Pinch the corners and sides together until the Filling is completely enclosed. Place the rolls, seam-side down, 2 to 3 inches apart on a rimmed baking sheet lined with parchment paper. Cover each baking sheet with plastic wrap. Let the rolls rise in a warm place (80° to 85°F), free from drafts, until lightly risen, about 30 minutes.

**5.** Preheat the oven to 375°F. Discard the plastic wrap. Brush the tops of the rolls with the melted butter. Bake in the preheated oven until golden brown, 22 to 25 minutes. Serve warm with the German or stone-ground mustard.

# Bryce Gilmore

## TEXAS'S ODD DUCK

Unlike many chefs, Bryce Gilmore didn't stumble into a career in restaurants, he was born into it. As a young boy, he was accustomed to the manic hours of restaurant life as the son of Jack Gilmore, an Austin-based restaurateur and chef. He got his first taste of the industry in high school, bussing tables and running food to customers at Austin's Z'Tejas Grill where his dad was the founding chef.

"I basically did whatever they asked me to do. I was only fourteen, and it was a great way to earn some money," says Gilmore. "But I hated it. I wasn't much for dealing with people back then—I much prefer to be behind the scenes."

Eventually, he talked his way into working in the kitchen, a move that led him to take cooking more seriously. After graduating high school, he left for the California Culinary Academy, which afforded him experience at top restaurants in San Francisco, Aspen, and Austin before he honed in on his own restaurant concept.

In 2009, he launched the Odd Duck farm-to-food trailer that gained such a following it drove him to open Barley Swine, a restaurant where he refined his thoughtful approach to Texas cuisine through the lens of strictly focused local, seasonal ingredients. Myriad accolades later, including consecutive James Beard Award nominations, Gilmore has become one of the Lone Star State's top chefs.

At its core, his style of food is as authentically regional to Texas as you can get, but it's more than that, which gives Gilmore's food a distinctive sense of place. "I think most chefs pull inspiration from a variety of things but for the most part I look to what's familiar to me, what I grew up eating, and I build out from there," says Gilmore.

Tex-Mex cuisine and its flavors were an integral part of Gilmore's everyday life growing up. As a result, his home and restaurant pantry abound with seasonal, dried, and powdered chiles; cumin; cilantro; and garlic. He also always has local goat cheese on hand as one of his favorite Central Texas representative ingredients. Barbecue also played a key role, not so much as a specific cuisine—although he certainly had his fair share of brisket and ribs—but as a method of cooking that simply relies on hardwood fire and smoke. "Cooking over an open flame, or using the smoke from that flame to cook, is the way they did things on cattle drives here more than a hundred years ago. That process is woven into our barbecue food culture today. The smoke acts as its own ingredient. It's a layer of flavor that makes our style of cooking particularly recognizable. While there are other parts of the country that use wood for cooking meats, Texas has a way of doing it that makes it a distinctive regional flavor."

In his restaurants, he and his chefs don't stay particularly locked in to one specific cuisine, looking to everything from Asian, Middle Eastern, Indian, European, and South American flavors to help complement the bounty they've received from local farmers. But at its foundation, Gilmore's food always has the flavor of home.

"I want the food I cook to be something I'd want to sit down to eat at my own dinner table," says Gilmore, who believes his customers have the same basic desire. "I think it's fair that a lot of people associate Texas with Tex-Mex and barbecue, but I love it when they're pleasantly surprised when they find out we're much more than that. I think it's fun for locals and visitors alike to experience something that's familiar but also exotic."

*When it comes to summers in the Southwest, few things are more refreshing than a cold watermelon salad laced with fresh herbs and a pinch of salt. Here, Bryce Gilmore introduces another great watermelon pairing: goat cheese. This delicious side salad won't fail to impress.*

# WATERMELON SALAD WITH GOAT CHEESE CREAM

*Serves 4     Hands-on 20 minutes     Total 45 minutes*

### SPICE MIX

½ teaspoon ground cumin

¼ teaspoon paprika

¼ teaspoon chili powder

⅛ teaspoon cayenne pepper

### WATERMELON SALAD

1 tablespoon sesame seeds

1 tablespoon roasted, salted pumpkin
  seed kernels (pepitas)

1 tablespoon roasted, salted sunflower
  seed kernels

4 cups (1-inch) cubed watermelon

2 tablespoons finely chopped red onion

1 tablespoon chopped fresh cilantro

1 tablespoon chopped fresh mint

1 tablespoon chopped fresh basil

2 tablespoons olive oil

1 tablespoon vegetable oil

4 fresh shishito peppers (about 1 ounce)

4 ounces goat cheese, crumbled

1 tablespoon white wine vinegar

1 teaspoon chile oil

½ teaspoon kosher salt

1 lime, quartered

**1.** Prepare the Spice Mix: Stir together all the Spice Mix ingredients in a small bowl.

**2.** Prepare the Watermelon Salad: Combine the sesame, pumpkin, and sunflower seeds in a skillet over medium-high; cook, stirring often, 1 minute. Add the Spice Mix, and cook, stirring constantly, until toasted and fragrant, 1 minute. Remove from the heat, and cool completely in the skillet, about 10 minutes.

**3.** Toss together the watermelon, onion, cilantro, mint, basil, and olive oil in a medium bowl. Cover and chill 15 to 20 minutes.

**4.** Heat the oil in a skillet over medium-high. Add the peppers. Cook, turning, until charred. Transfer to a bowl; cover with plastic. Steam 15 minutes. Peel, seed, and chop.

**5.** Process goat cheese, vinegar, chile oil, and ¼ teaspoon salt in a food processor until creamy, about 30 seconds. Divide mixture among 4 bowls; sprinkle with chopped peppers. Divide the watermelon mixture over peppers. Sprinkle with remaining ¼ teaspoon salt; top each with a squeeze of lime and ½ tablespoon seed mixture. Serve immediately.

*Smoking a brisket is a time- and labor-intensive process. The outcome can be magical but depends on many variables coming together well, from the quality of the meat purchased, to the patience and fire skills of the person managing the smoke, to the weather, the smoker, and the wood. The recipe below is one example of how to smoke a brisket. But it's worth spending time researching the traditions and science behind various brisket-smoking strategies such as smoking low at 225° versus 300°, wrapping or not wrapping, spritzing or mopping, fat cap up or down, and many other topics. This is how we do it in our backyard. For this recipe, you will need an offset smoker and oak or pecan logs (instead of wood chips); in Texas, it's the only way to go. As barbecue is all about "the feel," you're welcome to adapt the recipe to suit your own equipment.*

# TEXAS SMOKED BRISKET

*Serves 12     Hands-on 25 minutes     Total 24 hours, 25 minutes*

1 (10-pound) prime or Kobe beef
  brisket, untrimmed
5 tablespoons kosher salt
½ cup water
½ cup vegetable oil
½ cup apple cider vinegar

¾ cup piloncillo (Mexican unrefined
  cane sugar) or loosely packed brown
  sugar
½ cup black pepper
3 tablespoons garlic powder

**1.** The day before smoking: Trim the fat cap to ¼ inch across point and flat side of the brisket with a sharp knife. Turn over, and trim the fat and the silver skin. (It's normal to trim off 2 to 4 pounds of fat.) Rub the kosher salt all over the brisket, and place on a rack set in a rimmed baking sheet. Chill, uncovered, 8 to 24 hours. (The salt will absorb into the meat, enhancing the flavor and helping the meat retain moisture while smoking.)

**2.** Fill 2 charcoal chimneys with charcoal and paper so they are ready to light. Clean out the firebox. Clean out the drip bucket under the smoker. Fill the water pan, and place it close to the firebox-side of your smoke chamber. Place a long lighter or matches near the smoker. Check the grain of the meat, both in the flat and the point, and cut a notch off the flat, indicating the direction of the grain so it's easier to slice after smoking when the grain is less apparent.

**3.** Prepare the firewood, splitting about 8 quartered logs into thirds so you have enough to make it through 12 hours of smoking.

**4.** Combine the water, oil, and vinegar in a spray bottle. Stir together the piloncillo, black pepper, and garlic powder in a bowl, and transfer the mixture to an airtight container.

*continued on next page*

# Cattle Call

The Southwest has the Spanish to thank for making the introduction of cattle to the Texas plains in the late 1600s. By the 1730s, missionaries were managing cattle ranches near San Antonio. More than a century later, when the California gold rush began in 1849, the great cattle drives began to provide "forty-niners" with food. Drives left San Antonio and Fredericksburg for perilous journeys to San Diego and Los Angeles, a feat that could take as long as six months to complete. By the 1880s, the railroads had fully extended their reach into Texas. Refrigerated railcars also came around, meaning meat no longer needed to be transported on hoof. Thus, began a new era for the Texas cattle industry.

**5.** About 10 to 12 hours before serving: Remove the brisket from the refrigerator, and spray with the vinegar mixture. Rub the brisket liberally with the spice mixture.

**6.** Light the prepared charcoal chimneys. Transfer the hot charcoal to the firebox, and top with a few sticks of wood. Manage the fire, adding a few sticks at a time, until the internal temperature is between 225° and 275°F. Maintain the internal temperature for 15 to 20 minutes.

**7.** Place the brisket on the cooking grate so that the thicker brisket point is toward the firebox and the fat cap is positioned either up or down so it receives most of the heat, based on how the heat flows through your smoker. (Some smokers are hot on the top; some are hot on the bottom.) Keep the flat part of brisket as far away from the firebox as possible.

**8.** Smoke the brisket, covered with the smoker lid, until a meat thermometer inserted in the center of the brisket (where the point and flat meet) registers 150°F, squirting the vinegar mixture on the brisket every hour, about 6 hours. Quickly remove the brisket, and close the smoker lid to retain heat. Wrap the brisket in unwaxed butcher paper or aluminum foil. Return to the smoker, and smoke until a meat thermometer inserted in the brisket registers 190°F, 3 to 4 hours. (Check temperature each hour.) Quickly remove the brisket, and close the smoker. Unwrap the brisket, return the meat to the smoker, close the smoker. Smoke until the thermometer inserted in the brisket registers 200° to 205°F. Remove the brisket from the smoker, and wrap in foil and a towel. Place the wrapped brisket in a cooler; cover and let rest 1 to 2 hours. Unwrap and let rest on a work surface until a thermometer inserted in the brisket registers 140° to 150°F. Slice the brisket across the grain. Serve with the barbecue sauce, baked beans, potato salad, and coleslaw.

**NOTE:** When the brisket temperature registers around 150°F, the meat hits what pitmasters commonly refer to as "the stall." The stall is where excessive evaporation of moisture from the meat cools down the meat. Sometimes the temperature stalls out and can even decrease over a period of a few hours. Wrapping the brisket tightly at this point greatly decreases the evaporation and allows the temperature of the meat to remain elevated above the stall. This can save a couple of hours and hold in moisture. Wrapping is also a point of contention with purists, and it has other downsides such as making the crispy bark mushy.

*Recipes for classic macaroni and cheese are spread wide and far across the country, but not all of them are this good. Sometimes, it really does take a special grandmother to make the difference. In this case, a grandmother-in-law on my husband's side. A few caveats, this casserole works best with cheese shredded by hand, rather than preshredded cheese. (It just melts better.) You can make this ahead of time and refrigerate, but it takes a lot longer to get the casserole up to temperature if you do.*

# GRANDMA DOROTHY'S MAC 'N' CHEESE

*Serves 8 to 10     Hands-on 30 minutes     Total 1 hour, 10 minutes*

24 ounces uncooked elbow macaroni

4 ounces (½ cup) salted butter

1 large white onion, diced

4 garlic cloves, minced

5 cups whole milk

⅓ cup plus 1 tablespoon Worcestershire sauce

3 tablespoons yellow mustard

½ teaspoon table salt

½ teaspoon freshly ground black pepper

1 pound processed cheese (*such as Velveeta*), cubed

1 pound block Colby Jack cheese, shredded

1 pound block mild Cheddar cheese, shredded

1 ½ cups panko (Japanese-style bread crumbs) (optional)

**1.** Preheat the oven to 350°F. Grease a 13- x 9-inch baking dish. Prepare the macaroni in a large pot according to the package directions. Drain and return macaroni to the pot.

**2.** In a large saucepan, melt the butter over medium-high. Add the onion, and sauté until softened and translucent, about 4 to 5 minutes. (Do not brown.) Add the garlic and sauté 1 more minute or two, keeping it from browning.

**3.** Reduce the heat to medium-low. Add the milk, Worcestershire sauce, mustard, salt, and pepper, and stir. Heat until just warm enough to melt the cheese when added. Add the cubed processed cheese, half of the Colby Jack, and half of the Cheddar to the pan, and stir until the mixture is creamy.

**4.** Pour the contents of the saucepan into the pot with the macaroni, and stir. Pour the noodles and sauce into prepared baking dish and top with remaining cheese. Bake, uncovered, in the preheated oven until bubbly and the cheese is browned, about 35 minutes.

# CHICKEN FRIED STEAK WITH CREAMY PAN GRAVY

*Serves 6     Hands-on 30 minutes     Total 1 hour, 30 minutes*

The classic Chicken Fried Steak is one of the definitive dishes where the South and Texas resolutely embrace each other. Breaded and fried, as with many traditional Southern dishes such as fried chicken and fried okra, Chicken Fried Steak likely gained its crispy crust from the German immigrants in Texas who readily employed their methods for schnitzel to the available butchered cuts of the burgeoning beef industry of Texas. But it's the pan gravy and standard accompaniment of mashed potatoes that make it Southern indeed.

2 ¼ teaspoons kosher salt
2 ⅛ teaspoons black pepper
1 teaspoon garlic powder
2 pounds cubed round or sirloin steaks (about ¼ inch thick), cut into 4 equal portions
2 large eggs, lightly beaten
1 cup whole buttermilk
2 cups (about 8 ½ ounces) all-purpose flour

1 teaspoon seasoned salt
1 teaspoon ancho or New Mexico chile powder
½ cup vegetable oil
2 cups whole milk
2 tablespoons chopped fresh flat-leaf parsley (optional)

**1.** Combine 1 teaspoon kosher salt, 1 teaspoon pepper, and ½ teaspoon of the garlic powder in a bowl; sprinkle over both sides of the steaks. Place the steaks on a baking sheet lined with paper towels, and let stand at room temperature 15 minutes.

**2.** Whisk together the eggs and the buttermilk in a shallow baking dish or pie pan.

**3.** Combine 1 cup of the flour with ½ teaspoon of the seasoned salt, ½ teaspoon of the chile powder, ½ teaspoon of the kosher salt, ½ teaspoon of the black pepper, and ¼ teaspoon of the garlic powder in a second shallow baking dish or pie pan. Repeat with remaining 1 cup flour, ½ teaspoon seasoned salt, ½ teaspoon chile powder, and ¼ teaspoon garlic powder in a third shallow dish. Add ½ teaspoon each of the kosher salt and pepper. Reserve 2 tablespoons of flour mixture from 1 of the dishes to use in the gravy.

**4.** Dredge the steaks in 1 of the flour mixtures, dip in the buttermilk mixture, and dredge in the remaining flour mixture, shaking off excess. Place on a clean plate.

**5.** Heat the oil in a large cast-iron skillet over medium-high to 325°F. Fry the steaks, in batches, until golden, 2 to 3 minutes on each side. Transfer the steaks to a wire rack placed on a rimmed baking sheet lined with paper towels, reserving ¼ cup drippings in skillet. Discard the remaining drippings.

**6.** Gradually whisk the reserved 2 tablespoons flour mixture into the reserved ¼ cup drippings in the skillet over medium-high until smooth. Cook, whisking constantly, until bubbly and light brown, 1 to 2 minutes. Gradually whisk in the milk. Cook, whisking constantly, until the mixture is thickened, about 5 minutes. Stir in the remaining ¼ teaspoon kosher salt and ⅛ teaspoon pepper. Serve the steaks with the gravy, and top with the chopped parsley, if desired.

*This iconic dish made its way onto Tex-Mex menus in the early 1970s. Fajita literally means belt or sash, which is a pretty accurate description of what the skirt steak looks like before it's sliced into strips from the grill. These days, most beef fajitas are made with other cuts including flap, flank, or even sirloin, but if you can get your butcher to get you the outside cut of the skirt steak, you won't regret it. Because this marinade includes lime, it's important not to marinate it for more than six hours or you risk making the meat too tough.*

↠ ↞
## SOUTHERN STAPLE
↠ ↞

## German Chili Powder

Gebhardt's Chili Powder is probably one of the oldest on the market, and one of the Southwest's most prized as well. It was created by German-born William Gebhardt who would often venture from his home in New Braunfels to San Antonio to sample the fare of the famous Chili Queens who would gather in San Antonio's Military Plaza in the late 1800s through early 1900s. In 1896, he developed a formula of dried spices that brought to life the flavors of the storied San Antonio street vendors. His secret was a heavy dependence on dried ancho chiles backed by garlic and cumin. Today, when in need of a go-to chili powder mix, it's still the one to reach for.

# TEXAS FAJITAS

*Serves 7      Hands-on 45 minutes      Total 3 hours, 45 minutes*

½ cup soy sauce

½ cup fresh lime juice (from 6 to 8 limes)

½ cup fresh pineapple juice

½ cup vegetable oil

¼ cup packed light brown sugar

3 garlic cloves, minced (about 1 tablespoon)

1 tablespoon chili powder

2 teaspoons ground cumin seeds

1 teaspoon dried oregano

2 teaspoons black pepper

2 pounds trimmed skirt steak (about ¾ inch thick) (from outside cut, if possible)

1 small red bell pepper, stemmed, seeded, and cut into ½-inch-wide strips (from 1 bell pepper)

1 small yellow bell pepper, stemmed, seeded, and cut into ½-inch-wide strips (from 1 bell pepper)

1 small green bell pepper, stemmed, seeded, and cut into ½-inch-wide strips (from 1 bell pepper)

1 small white onion, cut into ½-inch-thick slices

21 (5-inch) fajita-size flour or yellow corn tortillas, warmed

Guacamole

Salsa

Sour cream

Shredded Cheddar cheese

Pico de gallo

**1.** Combine the soy sauce, lime juice, pineapple juice, vegetable oil, brown sugar, garlic, chili powder, cumin, oregano, and black pepper in a medium bowl. Transfer ½ cup soy sauce mixture to a large bowl, and reserve. Place the steak in a large ziplock plastic freezer bag, and add remaining soy sauce mixture. Seal bag, removing as much air as possible. Massage bag until meat is fully coated. Place bag flat on a rimmed baking sheet, and chill at least 3 hours and up to 6 hours, turning every couple of hours.

**2.** Toss together the peppers, onion, and reserved soy sauce mixture; cover and chill until ready to use, up to 6 hours.

**3.** Preheat the grill to high (450° to 500°F). Remove the steak from the marinade, discarding the marinade. Pat the steak dry with paper towels, and transfer to a large clean plate. Place the steak on the oiled grate; grill, covered, until the steak is well charred and a meat thermometer inserted in the center of the steak registers 115° to 120°F (medium-rare) or 125° to 130°F (medium), 3 to 5 minutes per side. Transfer the steak to a large plate, and cover loosely with aluminum foil. Let stand 10 minutes.

**4.** Meanwhile, transfer the peppers and the onion mixture to a metal grilling basket, and spread in an even layer; grill, stirring occasionally, until the vegetables are softened and beginning to char in spots, about 10 minutes.

**5.** Transfer the steak to a cutting board, and thinly slice the steak across the grain. Transfer the steak and vegetables to a large platter. Serve with the warm tortillas, guacamole, salsa, sour cream, shredded cheese, and pico de gallo.

# KING RANCH CHICKEN

*Serves 8     Hands-on 40 minutes     Total 1 hour, 20 minutes*

3 ounces (6 tablespoons) salted butter

1 cup chopped yellow onion
(from 1 onion)

1 cup chopped red bell pepper
(from 1 bell pepper)

1 cup chopped green bell pepper
(from 1 bell pepper)

1 jalapeño chile, seeded and chopped
(about 2 tablespoons)

3 garlic cloves, chopped (about
1 tablespoon)

1 tablespoon chili powder

1 tablespoon ground cumin

1 teaspoon dried Mexican oregano

½ teaspoon cayenne pepper

1 teaspoon kosher salt

1 teaspoon black pepper

¼ cup (about 1 ounce) all-purpose
flour

1 cup chicken broth

1 cup whole milk

1 (10-ounce) can diced tomatoes and
green chiles, undrained

1 (4.5-ounce) can chopped green
chiles, undrained

1½ cups sour cream

2 pounds cooked chicken breasts,
chopped

8 ounces Monterey Jack cheese,
shredded (about 2 cups)

8 ounces sharp Cheddar cheese,
shredded (about 2 cups)

18 (6-inch) white corn tortillas

½ cup chopped fresh cilantro

*The debate over where exactly King Ranch Chicken came from remains a mystery to this day. One thing that's clear is that the baked chicken lasagna-meets-Mexican-enchilada casserole has absolutely nothing to do with the legendary 825,000-acre King Ranch in South Texas, though it certainly hasn't complained about the added fame this dish has carried with it over the years. Skip the old recipes with canned cream of mushroom and chicken soups; this recipe is the real deal.*

**1.** Preheat the oven to 350°F. Lightly grease a 13- x 9-inch baking dish. Melt the butter in a large skillet over medium-high. Add the onion, red and green bell peppers, and jalapeño; cook, stirring occasionally, until tender and browning on the edges, 5 to 6 minutes. Add the garlic, chili powder, cumin, oregano, cayenne, salt, and black pepper; cook, stirring constantly, 1 minute.

**2.** Sprinkle the flour over the vegetable mixture; cook, stirring constantly, 1 minute. Stir in the broth and milk; bring to a boil, stirring constantly. Boil, stirring occasionally, until thickened, about 2 minutes. Remove from the heat, and stir in the tomatoes, green chiles, and sour cream. Stir in the chicken until well blended.

**3.** Combine the cheeses in a bowl. Heat the tortillas as directed on the package.

**4.** Line bottom of prepared baking dish with 6 tortillas, overlapping slightly, to cover the bottom of the dish. Top with half of the chicken mixture, one-third of the cheese, and 6 more tortillas. Top with the remaining chicken, one-third of the cheese, and remaining 6 tortillas. Sprinkle with remaining one-third cheese. Cover with lightly greased aluminum foil.

**5.** Bake in the preheated oven 20 minutes. Uncover and bake until the cheese is lightly browned and melted, 5 to 10 more minutes. Let stand 10 minutes before serving. Sprinkle with the cilantro.

# OKLAHOMA RESERVATION TACOS

Serves 8    Hands-on 35 minutes    Total 35 minutes

*These tacos have a lot of names including Navajo, Oklahoma, and Indian. They come from a time in the mid-1800s when many of the Native American tribes throughout the Southwest were relocated to reservations. Oftentimes different tribes, all of whom had various foodways, were placed to live together in certain camps. What connected them were the standard rations they were given for living, which included flour, baking powder, salt, sugar, lard, and powdered milk. Out of that came a flatbread that could be fried and served with meat brought in from hunting. Over time, the dish took on the flavors of the Southwest and evolved into a flat taco. You'll often see fry bread at state fairs in Oklahoma, Texas, and Arkansas. It's a fun alternative to your standard corn tortilla.*

2 tablespoons olive oil

1 cup chopped yellow onion (from 1 onion)

1 tablespoon minced (seeded, if desired) jalapeño

1 tablespoon minced garlic (from 1 garlic clove)

1 pound ground chuck

1 (14.5-ounce) can diced tomatoes

1 tablespoon chili powder

1 tablespoon ground cumin

1 teaspoon dried Mexican oregano

1 ½ teaspoons kosher salt

2 cups (about 8 ½ ounces) all-purpose flour

2 teaspoons baking powder

1 cup whole milk

Vegetable oil

2 cups shredded iceberg lettuce

4 ounces Cheddar cheese, shredded (about 1 cup)

2 plum tomatoes, diced

½ cup sour cream

**1.** Heat the olive oil in a large nonstick skillet over medium-high until shimmering. Add the onion, jalapeño, and garlic, and cook, stirring occasionally, until softened, 4 to 5 minutes. Add the ground chuck, and cook, stirring to crumble, until the meat is browned, 8 to 10 minutes; drain. Return the beef mixture to the skillet; add the diced tomatoes, chili powder, cumin, oregano, and 1 teaspoon of the salt; cook over medium, stirring occasionally, until slightly thickened, 4 to 5 minutes. Cover the meat mixture, and keep warm over low until ready to serve.

**2.** Sift together the flour, baking powder, and remaining ½ teaspoon salt in a medium bowl. Stir in the milk until just combined. (Do not overwork the dough.) Using floured hands, shape the dough into a ball. (The inside of the dough ball will still be sticky, while the outside will be well floured.) Cut the dough into 8 pieces. Using floured hands, shape, stretch, and pat each piece of the dough into a 5- to 7-inch disk.

**3.** Pour the vegetable oil to a depth of 2 inches into a Dutch oven; heat over medium-high to 350°F. Gently place the dough disks, 1 or 2 at a time, into the hot oil, being careful not to splatter the hot oil. Press the dough down so the top is submerged in the hot oil. Fry until browned on both sides, about 1 minute per side. Drain on a baking sheet lined with paper towels. Serve the fried bread with the meat mixture, lettuce, cheese, plum tomatoes, and a dollop of sour cream.

*In the Southwest, beef is king, and knowing how to deliver a good steak to the table is a necessity. Purists tout the simplicity of a basic salt and pepper rub on a good cut of meat. But when you want a little more punch, I like to add chipotle to the marinade. Be sure to let the steak stand for ten minutes before serving.*

# TEXAS RIB-EYE ASADO

*Serves 4     Hands-on 30 minutes     Total 1 hour, 30 minutes*

1½ tablespoons fennel seeds

1½ tablespoons coriander seeds

1½ tablespoons cumin seeds

1½ tablespoons mustard seeds

3 tablespoons ground oregano

2 tablespoons kosher salt

1½ tablespoons onion powder

1½ tablespoons black pepper

1 tablespoon paprika

4 garlic cloves, roughly chopped
  (about 4 teaspoons)

2 canned chipotle chiles (from
  1 [7-ounce] can chipotle chiles in
  adobo sauce)

¼ cup fresh lemon juice (from
  2 lemons)

½ cup olive oil

4 (1-inch-thick) rib-eye steaks
  (about 12 ounces each)

**1.** Cook the fennel seeds, coriander seeds, cumin seeds, and mustard seeds in a small skillet over medium-high until the seeds are toasted and the oils are released, 3 to 4 minutes. Transfer the toasted seeds to a blender or food processor, and add the oregano, salt, onion powder, black pepper, paprika, garlic, chipotle chiles, lemon juice, and olive oil. Process until well blended.

**2.** Rub the seed mixture evenly over both sides of the steaks, and place the steaks on a plate. Chill at least 30 minutes or up to 1 hour. Let the steaks stand at room temperature 20 to 30 minutes before grilling.

**3.** Preheat the grill to medium-high (400° to 450°F). Place the steaks on lightly greased grill grate, and grill the steaks, covered, to desired degree of doneness, 7 to 8 minutes on each side for medium-rare. Let stand 10 minutes before serving.

# CHICKEN SPAGHETTI WITH MUSHROOM CREAM

*Serves 8     Hands-on 1 hour     Total 2 hours, 30 minutes*

*It's unclear exactly where Chicken Spaghetti originated, but its presence in the myriad Junior League and community church cookbooks throughout Texas, Oklahoma, and Arkansas gives it firm seating in the Southwest. It's so important, in fact, that it was the first meal Arkansas native Amy Kelley Bell ever cooked for Chef Matt Bell of Little Rock's South on Main when she coaxed him to leave his home state of Montana for her. Most of the older recipes call for the standard can of condensed soup, but this dish is so much better when made from scratch.*

### MUSHROOM CREAM

20 ounces cremini mushrooms

1 quart water

½ teaspoon black peppercorns

4 thyme sprigs

2 tablespoons canola oil

1 ½ cups chopped yellow onion (from 2 onions)

1 cup (8 ounces) dry white wine

4 cups (32 ounces) chicken stock

1 quart heavy cream

2 teaspoons kosher salt

½ teaspoon black pepper

### CHICKEN SPAGHETTI

1 tablespoon canola oil

1 ½ cups chopped yellow onion (from 2 onions)

1 ½ cups diced green bell pepper (from 2 bell peppers)

1 ½ cups diced red bell pepper (from 2 bell peppers)

1 cup fresh or frozen sweet peas

1 pound spaghetti, cooked according to package directions for al dente

1 pound cooked chicken breasts, shredded

**1.** Prepare the Mushroom Cream: Remove and reserve mushroom stems. Slice the caps. Combine the reserved stems and 8 ounces of the sliced caps in a medium saucepan. Set remaining mushroom caps aside. Add 1 quart water, peppercorns, and 2 thyme sprigs to the saucepan. Bring to a boil over high; reduce to medium-low, and simmer until liquid is reduced to 2 ½ cups, 20 to 25 minutes. Pour the mixture through a strainer into a bowl, discarding solids. Reserve 2 cups of the mushroom stock.

**2.** Heat the oil in a saucepan over medium. Add the remaining sliced mushroom caps to the pan. Cook, stirring often, until mushrooms begin to brown, about 8 minutes. Add the onion to the pan; cook, stirring often, until soft and translucent and the mushrooms are caramelized, 8 to 10 minutes. Add the wine, stirring to loosen browned bits from the bottom of the pan. Simmer the mixture, stirring occasionally, until the liquid is reduced by two-thirds, 10 to 15 minutes.

**3.** Stir in the chicken stock, cream, reserved mushroom stock, and the remaining 2 thyme sprigs. Simmer, stirring occasionally, until reduced to about 5 cups, about 1 hour. Remove and discard the thyme. Stir in the salt and black pepper.

**4.** Prepare the Chicken Spaghetti: Heat the oil in a large saucepan over medium-high. Add the onion and bell peppers, and cook, stirring occasionally, until the vegetables are soft and slightly caramelized, about 4 minutes. Add the peas; cook, stirring often, 1 minute. Add the cooked spaghetti, chicken, and Mushroom Cream, stirring until blended. Remove from heat, and serve immediately.

# Matt Bell

## WHEN A MONTANA MAN SETTLES IN LITTLE ROCK

On any given weeknight, things are lively at Little Rock's South on Main. No, we're not talking about a crossroad but a laid-back restaurant and music venue managed in partnership with the *Oxford American* magazine and owned by Chef Matt Bell. While you'll find a compelling live music concert series throughout the year, regulars of South on Main return for the soulful comfort food.

Though it has drawn a steady stream of patrons since its opening in 2013, it isn't for the love of a Southern chef but rather for a chef who's originally from a place nearly 2,000 miles northwest of Little Rock. Bell hails from the mountains of Missoula, Montana.

While he still holds his mountain roots in high esteem, he was swayed to leave when his now-wife, Amy, convinced him to follow her to Austin, Texas. There he earned his culinary chops from the Texas Culinary Academy. He worked in local restaurants and as a personal chef. But Bell attributes the origin of his love of cooking to his Sicilian grandfather who taught him how to make a single dish before he went off to college: pasta with beans.

"It was a pretty simple recipe of canned white beans, tomatoes, and macaroni pasta. Nothing special," says Bell. "But his point was to teach me that even though I was young and didn't have a dime to my name, I could make my own food in the kitchen and sustain myself for days."

The two made their way to Amy's home state of Arkansas more than twelve years ago. For Bell, discovering a definition of Arkansas cuisine became a bit of a passion. He points to the state's substantial rice production, duck hunting, catfish farms, and unique ingredients such as pawpaw fruit, which is "like a weird Southern mango," says Bell.

He began working as a chef at Capital Hotel, one of Little Rock's most prestigious restaurants, alongside Chef Matthew McClure—now at The Hive at 21c Museum Hotel in Bentonville—

and then chef de cuisine Cassidee Dabney. Once Dabney left to run Blackberry Farm's fine dining restaurant, The Barn, in 2010, Bell and McClure also eventually moved on.

"At Capital, our main goal was finding a voice for Arkansas food, which first meant defining exactly what that meant to us," says Bell. "Matt and Cassidee were fortunate to have Arkansas roots; I had a bit more digging to do."

Bell found that in many ways Arkansas is best understood when divided into regions. The southeastern part of the state, which is near the Delta, naturally has a style very similar to northern Louisiana. Southwest Arkansas foods reflect a stronger South American influence, like Texas. Central Arkansas, with its strong agricultural industry, reflects more farm-to-table foodways, while the northwest side of the state, with its relationship to the Ozark Mountains, has an almost Appalachian food culture. This is also where influences from Missouri, Oklahoma, and Kansas have more of an impact with dishes such as German-inspired meat-and-cabbage pockets and bierocks showing up on menus.

"Being from Montana, a relatively young state with a small population, I didn't grow up with grandmothers passing down boxes of handwritten recipes. It's not like so many of the families in the South, and it's really drawn me to the region," says Bell. "My dad grew up in Savannah, and I did have some family from North Carolina, so I knew about things like grits and fish muddles, but there wasn't a social culture of food around me. My time at the Capital Hotel really drew me into Southern food, especially working with Cassidee and Matt who are from here. They both have a very soulful approach to cooking Southern food."

Bell recounts the first box of family recipes he ever received was from his wife's grandmother, who upon finding out that he was a cook, emptied her cupboard and handed him boxes and binders full of recipes to go through.

"Most were casseroles of some form, but they all had notes in the margins about different measurements and who liked the recipe a certain way. It was a treasure trove," says Bell.

At South on Main, Bell takes Southern dishes that people know and love, like Cajun jambalaya, Kentucky burgoo, and fried green tomatoes, and uses Arkansas-grown ingredients to offer the flavor of the state. You'll find everything on the menu from smothered pork chops to boiled peanuts and pimiento cheese, and most of it changes with the seasonal ingredients they procure from local farms. But one permanent item on the menu is a Southern favorite that has a stronghold in Arkansas: Chicken Spaghetti.

"It was the first dish my wife ever made for me," says Bell who was twenty-three at the time. "I watched her make it for the first time and was a little astonished by the ingredients. I never had Velveeta up until that point, and every vegetable in her recipe came from a can."

Rest assured, patrons at South on Main won't be dining on a recipe comprised of primarily canned ingredients. Bell took the humble casserole to its simplest ingredients and rebuilt it from there using a house-made mushroom cream sauce, fresh vegetables, and grilled chicken.

"And hopefully we do it in a way that is elevated and refined but still familiar and comfortable," says Bell. "I've spent a lot of time bent over plating things with tongs, and now I want people to feel like they're having a special night out but with food that they can identify with. That's what I've found to be the Arkansas way."

*A common pastime throughout the region is to sit on a dock and drop a line in from a fishing pole for bass or catfish. While a lot of people fry up the day's catch, sometimes it's nice to elevate the experience. This pan-sautéed version of bass from Chef Matt Bell at Little Rock's South on Main not only shows off the delicacy of the mild fish, but also the summer flavors of squash and tomato.*

# BASS IN GARLIC-FENNEL NAGE WITH GRANNY SQUASH

*Serves 4     Hands-on 45 minutes     Total 55 minutes*

**NAGE**

1 tablespoon olive oil

1 fennel bulb, thinly sliced

3 garlic cloves, thinly sliced (about
    2 tablespoons)

½ teaspoon kosher salt

1 ½ tablespoons (¾ ounce) anise liqueur
    (*such as Herbsaint*) or dry vermouth

1 ½ tablespoons (¾ ounce) dry white wine

1 cup heavy cream

**GRANNY SQUASH**

2 tablespoons canola oil

1 cup sliced yellow onion (from
    1 medium onion)

4 large yellow squash, cut into ¼-inch-
    thick slices (about 3 ½ to 4 cups sliced)

2 fresh thyme sprigs, stems removed

½ cup chicken or vegetable stock

¾ teaspoon kosher salt

¼ teaspoon black pepper

**BASS**

1 tablespoon unsalted butter

4 (6-ounce) skin-on bass fillets

¾ teaspoon kosher salt

½ teaspoon black pepper

Chopped fresh parsley

**1.** Prepare the Nage: Heat the oil in a medium saucepan over medium. Add the fennel, garlic, and salt. Reduce the heat to medium-low, and cook the fennel and garlic, stirring occasionally, until translucent and tender, 4 to 5 minutes. Add the liqueur and wine; cook, stirring occasionally, until almost all liquid has evaporated, 10 to 15 minutes. Increase the heat to medium, and add the cream. Bring to a boil, stirring occasionally. Reduce the heat to medium-low, and simmer, stirring occasionally, until reduced by half, 20 to 25 minutes.

**2.** Remove from the heat, and cool slightly, about 5 minutes. Transfer the mixture to a blender, and process until smooth, about 1 minute. Return the Nage to the saucepan over low, and cover with the lid to keep warm.

**3.** Prepare the Squash: Heat the oil in a large high-sided 12-inch sauté pan or skillet over

medium-high. Add the onion, and cook, stirring occasionally, until translucent, 2 minutes. Add the squash and thyme leaves, and cook, stirring occasionally, until the squash is caramelized, 10 to 15 minutes. Add the chicken stock, salt, and pepper, and simmer until the squash is overcooked (yes, like your granny used to cook it), 10 minutes.

**4.** Meanwhile, prepare the Bass: Melt the butter in a large nonstick skillet over medium-high. Pat the bass dry with a paper towel, and sprinkle with the salt and pepper. Add the bass to the skillet, skin-side down, and cook until the skin is crispy, 3 to 5 minutes. Turn the fillets over, and remove from the heat, leaving the fillets in the skillet until firm and flaky, 3 to 5 minutes.

**5.** Spoon the squash evenly among 4 plates, using a slotted spoon. Top each with a bass fillet, skin-side up. Drizzle each with 2 tablespoons Nage. Serve immediately with additional Nage. Garnish with the chopped fresh parsley, if desired.

*When it comes to pralines, there's more to dispute than just the simple pronunciation. In Louisiana, where the sugary melt-in-your-mouth confection originated, they're called "praw-leens," but in Texas, where Mexican immigrants quickly adopted them as part of standard Tex-Mex dessert offerings, they're called "pray-leens." In New Orleans, they tend to be thicker, chewy morsels of sugar and pecan, while their Texas counterparts tend to be thinner, flat disks that can sometimes be the size of a hand; and they have a little more crumble to them than chewiness. (For a chewier version, add a tablespoon of light corn syrup to this recipe.)*

# TEXAS-STYLE PRALINES

*Serves 24     Hands-on 20 minutes     Total 30 minutes*

1 cup packed light brown sugar

1 cup granulated sugar

1 cup whole milk

1 tablespoon unsalted butter

2 teaspoons vanilla extract

2 cups pecan halves, toasted

**1.** Line a baking sheet with wax paper or parchment paper. Fill a large bowl with ice; set the ice bath aside. Combine the sugars and the milk in a medium-size heavy saucepan over medium. Cook, stirring often and washing down any sugar that clings to sides of pan with a pastry brush dipped in cold water, until the sugars dissolve, about 7 minutes.

**2.** Bring the mixture to a boil over high. (Do not stir.) Boil until a candy thermometer registers 238°F (soft ball stage), about 9 minutes.

**3.** Remove the pan from the heat, and place in the prepared ice bath until the temperature reduces to 175°F, about 2 minutes. Immediately stir in the butter, vanilla, and pecans, stirring just until the mixture begins to lose its gloss, about 2 minutes. (Mixture will become thicker in texture.)

**4.** Working quickly, spoon the pecan mixture by tablespoonfuls onto the prepared baking sheet. Let the candy spread into flat disks. Let the pralines stand at room temperature until firm, about 10 minutes. Store sealed in an airtight container at room temperature for up to 1 week.

# CANE SYRUP PECAN PIE

*Serves 8    Hands-on 15 minutes    Total 3 hours*

*Pecan pie has its origins in New Orleans but has long been a welcomed holiday dessert throughout the South. This version from pastry chef Jessica Maher of Austin's Lenoir has a nutty character from the use of cane syrup. Cane syrup is a by-product of sugar production and made by simply reducing cane juice in open kettles. It is dark with a slightly bitter tang.*

Chilled dough from Crust (page 114)
All-purpose flour for work surface
1 cup packed dark brown sugar
⅔ cup cane syrup (*such as Steen's*)
¼ cup (2 ounces) unsalted butter, melted
1 tablespoon (½ ounce) bourbon
¼ teaspoon table salt
3 large eggs, lightly beaten
1 ½ cups pecan halves, toasted and coarsely chopped
50 pecan halves

**1.** Preheat the oven to 350°F. Roll the Crust dough into a 12-inch circle on a lightly floured surface. Fit into a 9-inch pie pan; crimp the edges. Chill the Crust until ready to fill.

**2.** Whisk together the brown sugar, cane syrup, butter, bourbon, and salt in a medium bowl until well blended. Whisk in the eggs just until blended.

**3.** Fold the toasted chopped pecans into the sugar mixture. Pour the mixture into the chilled Crust; arrange 50 pecan halves decoratively on top of filling.

**4.** Bake in the preheated oven until golden brown and set, about 40 to 45 minutes; cover the pie with aluminum foil after 25 minutes to prevent overbrowning. Cool completely on a wire rack, about 2 hours.

**SOUTHERN STAPLE**

## Pecans

A true American native, the pecan tree grows almost exclusively along the coastal stretches of Georgia all the way west to Texas. Though the leading pecan-producing state in the U.S. is Georgia, the first recorded discovery of the pecan was by Spanish explorers as they moved their way up from Mexico into Texas and later Louisiana. Many of the native Texas tribes that lived along the coast, including the Karankawa and the Coahuiltecans, would migrate up to Central Texas rivers to feast on pecans for the fall when the nuts were falling from the trees.

In 1919, the humble pecan tree was officially recognized as the state tree of Texas, and in 2009, Arkansas adopted the pecan as its official state nut.

# ARKANSAS POSSUM PIE

*Serves 8     Hands-on 30 minutes*
*Total 4 hours, 30 minutes, including 4 hours chilling*

**CHOCOLATE FILLING**

1 ½ cups whole milk

½ cup granulated sugar

3 ½ tablespoons cornstarch

5 large egg yolks

6 ounces milk chocolate chips

1 tablespoon salted butter

1 teaspoon vanilla extract

**CRUST**

1 ½ cups graham cracker crumbs

⅓ cup packed light brown sugar

2 ⅔ ounces (⅓ cup) salted butter, melted

**CREAM CHEESE FILLING**

6 ounces cream cheese, softened

¾ cup powdered sugar

¼ cup chopped pecans, toasted

**TOPPING**

¾ cup whipping cream, whipped

**1.** Prepare the Chocolate Filling: Bring the milk to a simmer in a medium-size heavy saucepan over medium. Remove from heat. Combine the granulated sugar and cornstarch in a large bowl. Add the egg yolks to the sugar mixture, and whisk vigorously. Gradually whisk the hot milk into the yolk mixture, whisking constantly. Return the egg mixture to the saucepan, and cook over medium, whisking constantly, until the mixture just begins to boil and thicken, 6 to 7 minutes. Boil, whisking constantly, 1 minute. Remove from the heat, and whisk in the chocolate chips, butter, and vanilla until melted and smooth. Pour into a bowl, and cool, stirring occasionally, about 3 minutes. Press plastic wrap directly onto the surface of the Chocolate Filling (to prevent a film from forming), and chill 3 hours.

**2.** Prepare the Crust: Preheat oven to 350°F. Stir together the graham cracker crumbs, brown sugar, and butter until blended; press into the bottom and up the sides of a 9-inch pie pan. Bake the crust in the preheated oven until golden brown and fragrant, 12 to 15 minutes. Transfer to a wire rack, and cool completely, about 30 minutes.

**3.** Prepare the Cream Cheese Filling: Beat the cream cheese and the powdered sugar in a medium bowl with an electric mixer on medium speed until smooth.

**4.** Spread the cream cheese mixture evenly in the cooled crust, and sprinkle with the chopped pecans. Spoon the chilled Chocolate Filling over the pecans, and spread evenly. Chill 1 hour before serving. Top with the whipped cream just before serving.

*Only in certain parts of the South do you mention a dessert like this and not get a quizzical grimace from dinner guests. But in Arkansas, Possum Pie is as normal as New York Cheesecake in New York or chocolate chip cookies anywhere. In other parts of the South, such as Mississippi, this same pie is more commonly referred to as "Husband's Delight," which is perhaps a bit more appetizing. Both are traditionally a quick recipe of boxed vanilla and chocolate puddings poured over a graham cracker crust layered with a sweet cream cheese filling. This recipe is a little more involved but well worth the extra steps.*

*This recipe combines two of my favorite childhood desserts: banana pudding and strawberry shortcake. Sometimes banana pudding can be a little too dense, but using angel food cake as an alternative to vanilla wafers and adding the brightness of fresh strawberries lightens up this classic Southern treat. It's certainly not the way my great-grandmother used to make it, but it stays true to her French custard recipe, which is always preferred to those fake, boxed banana-flavored puddings.*

# STRAWBERRY-BANANA PUDDING TRIFLE

*Serves 8     Hands-on 25 minutes     Total 3 hours, 25 minutes*

1 pint fresh strawberries, sliced

½ cup granulated sugar

2 tablespoons cornstarch

¼ teaspoon table salt

2 cups whole milk

2 large egg yolks, lightly beaten

1 tablespoon unsalted butter

1 teaspoon vanilla extract

3 cups cubed angel food cake (from
   1 [12-ounce] cake)

4 ripe small bananas, sliced
   (about 3 ½ cups)

2 teaspoons fresh lemon juice
   (from 1 lemon)

**1.** Toss the strawberries with 1 tablespoon of the sugar in a large bowl. Whisk together the cornstarch, salt, and remaining 7 tablespoons sugar in a medium saucepan; gradually whisk in the milk until well blended. Cook over medium, whisking constantly, until the mixture thickens and boils, about 9 minutes. (Be careful not to scorch.) Remove from the heat. Place the egg yolks in a small bowl; gradually whisk ¼ cup of the hot milk mixture into the egg yolks, whisking constantly. Gradually whisk the egg mixture into the warm milk mixture. Bring to a boil over medium, whisking constantly, until thickened, about 1 minute. Remove from the heat, and stir in the butter and vanilla. Transfer to a medium bowl, and press plastic wrap directly on the surface of the pudding (to prevent a film from forming). Refrigerate until completely cooled, about 2 hours.

**2.** Place half of the cubed angel food cake in the bottom of a small trifle dish or deep glass serving bowl. Toss the banana slices with the lemon juice in a bowl to prevent browning. Top the cake with half of the banana slices, and spoon half of the pudding over the bananas, and top with half of the strawberries. Repeat the layers once. Cover and chill at least 1 hour before serving.

# SOUTHERN GATHERINGS

# Southern Gatherings

**IN THE SOUTH,** soulful food and warm hospitality are two key traits that go hand in hand. Though people hardly need much of an excuse to whip up a quick batch of pimiento cheese and some homemade lemonade when friends stop by to visit, Southerners get downright giddy when there's something special to celebrate. Whether a seasonal holiday, a special anniversary, or simply a football tailgate, there's always a good reason to pull out all the stops and put on a bountiful feast for family and friends.

## BAR STOPS

The Atomic Lounge, Birmingham, AL

Ticonderoga Club, Atlanta, GA

Rocks on the Roof, Savannah, GA

The Silver Dollar, Louisville, KY

The Brown Hotel, Louisville, KY

Carousel Bar, New Orleans, LA

The Sazerac Bar, New Orleans, LA

The Coop, Oxford, MS

The Crunkleton, Chapel Hill, NC

The Ordinary, Charleston, SC

The Bar at Husk, Charleston, SC

Bastion, Nashville, TN

Eight Row Flint, Houston, TX

Julep, Houston, TX

Mario's Fishbowl, Morgantown, WV

# COCKTAILS

Southerners have long held a love affair with spirits. In its early, Colonial history, rum and Madeira were two of the most valuable imported goods. In addition, apples and peaches were often used to make ciders and brandy. Today, it's bourbon that most people associate as the consummate Southern spirit. When it comes to cocktails, the South has New Orleans, Kentucky, and Texas to thank for leading the country in the invention of what we now consider "classic cocktails." From the Mint Julep and Sazerac to the Ramos Gin Fizz and Margarita, the South has had a dynamic impact on the history of American cocktail culture.

*The first thing I ever learned about a Mint Julep had nothing to do with its popularity at the Kentucky Derby. Instead, it was about how not to screw it up. For one, you have to use really good bourbon—don't skimp on the bottom shelf stuff. Second, there is no such thing as too much mint. Third, don't make the mistake of adding too much sugar, it should only be enough to just take the edge off the spirit. Fourth, a classic metal cup is essential as it conducts the temperature in just the right way to enhance the experience of the drink—ditto with a metal straw. Finally, the beauty of the Mint Julep is how it changes over time in the glass. It starts out stiff, and as the ice melts the drink evolves with intrigue.*

# A PROPER MINT JULEP

*Serves 1    Hands-on 10 minutes    Total 10 minutes*

⅓ cup fresh mint leaves, plus 3 mint sprigs

1 teaspoon Rich Cane Syrup (page 316)

1¼ cups crushed ice

6 tablespoons (3 ounces) high-proof, good-quality bourbon (*such as Old Weller Antique Original 107 or Four Roses Single Barrel*)

Powdered sugar

**1.** Place ⅓ cup mint leaves in bottom of a metal julep cup. Gently muddle leaves in cup. Add ½ teaspoon Rich Cane Syrup. Fill cup to top with crushed ice, and pack firmly. Pour 4 tablespoons bourbon over ice, packing in more of the remaining crushed ice as bourbon melts ice in the cup. Pour remaining ½ teaspoon Rich Cane Syrup over ice.

**2.** Mound remaining crushed ice over top of cup like a snow cone. Slap tops of 3 mint sprigs on the back of your hand. Gather sprigs into a bouquet, and stuff between rim of cup and crushed ice. Insert a straw next to mint bouquet. Slowly pour remaining 2 tablespoons bourbon over ice. Garnish with powdered sugar over top of ice.

# KENTUCKY PORCH TEA

*Serves 8    Hands-on 30 minutes    Total 3 hours, including syrup and tea*

1¼ cups (10 ounces) bourbon (*such as Buffalo Trace*)
Honey Syrup (recipe follows)
½ cup fresh lemon juice (from 2 lemons)

Strong-Brew Mint and Verbena Tea (recipe follows), chilled
6 dashes of Angostura bitters
Lemon slices (optional)
Fresh mint sprigs (optional)

Chill bourbon, Honey Syrup, lemon juice, tea, and bitters at least 1½ hours before preparing recipe. Stir together bourbon, syrup, lemon juice, Strong-Brew Mint and Verbena Tea, and bitters in a frosted pitcher until well blended. Pour into ice-filled Mason jars, and garnish with lemon slices and mint sprigs, if desired.

**HONEY SYRUP** Stir together 2 tablespoons honey and ⅓ cup boiling water in a small bowl until honey dissolves and mixture is blended. Makes about ⅓ cup

**STRONG-BREW MINT AND VERBENA TEA** Prepare 16 ounces double-strength lemon verbena tea according to tea maker's brewing instructions, adding 30 fresh mint leaves. Remove tea bags, and pour through a fine mesh strainer; discard solids. Chill at least 1 hour before using. Makes 2 cups

*There's no question sweet tea has a stronghold in the South. When you add bourbon to it, it only strengthens its appeal. This recipe from Jason Stevens of La Corsha Hospitality Group in Texas is a nod to the porch-sipping culture of Kentucky.*

---

# SEELBACH

*Serves 1    Hands-on 5 minutes    Total 1 hour, 5 minutes*

3 tablespoons (1½ ounces) good-quality bourbon (*such as Bulleit or Booker's*)
1½ tablespoons (¾ ounce) orange liqueur (*such as Cointreau*)

5 dashes of Angostura bitters
5 dashes of Peychaud's bitters
6 to 8 tablespoons (3 to 4 ounces) dry sparkling wine
Wide orange peel strip

Freeze a large coupe glass. Chill the bourbon, orange liqueur, Angostura and Peychaud's bitters, and sparkling wine at least 1 hour before preparing recipe. Fill a mixing glass with ice; add the bourbon, orange liqueur, and Angostura and Peychaud's bitters. Stir until well chilled, about 1 minute; strain into prepared coupe glass, and top with the sparkling wine. Twist the orange peel strip over glass, expressing oil into drink; garnish with the orange peel strip, if desired.

*A signature Kentucky Bourbon Trail drink from the historic Seelbach Hotel in Louisville that dates back to before Prohibition, there's a reason this elegant cocktail is a classic. Though the original was made with Old Forester, you can play around with the bourbon of your choice.*

# ATLANTIC 75

*Serves 1    Hands-on 8 minutes    Total 8 minutes*

The French 75—named for a World War I artillery weapon—may be known for its powerful punch, but its contents make a pretty great pairing for oysters on the half shell. I'm partial to the fruitiness of a dry sparkling rosé and like to add a little bit of salt tincture to this to elicit the salty air of coastal sea breezes.

3 tablespoons (1 ½ ounces) dry gin (*such as Nolet's or No. 3 London*)

1 ½ tablespoons fresh lemon juice (from 1 lemon)

1 tablespoon simple syrup or agave nectar

3 drops of Salt Tincture (recipe follows)

6 tablespoons (3 ounces) dry sparkling rosé

Combine gin, lemon juice, and simple syrup in a mixing glass. Fill with ice, and stir. Strain into a chilled flute, add salt tincture, and top with sparkling rosé.

**SALT TINCTURE** Combine 1 teaspoon table salt and 1 teaspoon warm water in a small bowl. Let stand, stirring occasionally, until salt dissolves, about 2 minutes. Makes 1 teaspoon

---

# MILK PUNCH

*Serves 1    Hands-on 5 minutes    Total 5 minutes*

This soul-comforting sipper has long been a holiday treat dating as far back as the seventeenth century. Traditionally made with brandy and/or rum, bourbon also makes a great substitute. The key ingredient is the velvety texture from the milk. Some enjoy this punch served over ice, but I think you get more out of the flavors by serving it strained.

1 tablespoon ( ½ ounce) Rich Cane Syrup (page 316)

1 tablespoon ( ½ ounce) brandy

2 tablespoons (1 ounce) dark rum (such as Myers's Rum)

½ cup whole milk

1 teaspoon vanilla extract

Freshly grated nutmeg

Fill a metal cocktail shaker three-fourths full with ice. Add the Rich Cane Syrup, brandy, rum, milk, and vanilla; shake vigorously until well chilled, about 30 seconds. Strain into a rocks glass, and garnish with freshly grated nutmeg.

# THE PREAKNESS COCKTAIL

*Serves 1     Hands-on 5 minutes     Total 5 minutes*

3 tablespoons (1 ½ ounces) rye whiskey

1 tablespoon (½ ounce) sweet dry vermouth

¼ ounce Bénédictine D.O.M. liqueur

1 tablespoon (½ ounce) grapefruit liqueur (*such as Bittermens Citron Sauvage*)

Dash of Angostura bitters

Grapefruit peel strip

Freeze a coupe glass. Fill a mixing glass with ice, and add the whiskey, vermouth, Bénédictine, grapefruit liqueur, and bitters, stirring until chilled, about 30 seconds. Strain into prepared glass. Twist the grapefruit peel strip over glass, expressing oil into drink, and garnish with the grapefruit peel strip, if desired.

*This highlight of the first Preakness Ball in 1936 is a rather boozy libation. The event at Baltimore's Fifth Regiment Armory is part of the celebration of the Preakness Stakes, the second leg of the Triple Crown. The drink never quite held the thirst-quenching prowess that the Kentucky Derby's Mint Julep did, but with a bit of renewed spirit from a hit of grapefruit liqueur, it makes for a perfect evening sipper.*

---

# LIGHT DRAGOON PUNCH

*Serves 24     Hands-on 10 minutes     Total  9 hours, 10 minutes*

2 cups granulated sugar

12 (1- x 2-inch) lemon peel strips (from 3 lemons)

2 cups (16 ounces) Jamaican pot still dark rum (*such as Myers's*)

8 cups (64 ounces) cognac (*such as Pierre Ferrand 1840 Original Formula Cognac*)

½ cup (4 ounces) peach liqueur (*such as Rothman & Winter Orchard Peach Liqueur*)

8 cups brewed black tea (*such as Earl Grey*)

3 cups sparkling mineral water (*such as Topo Chico*)

**1.** Combine the sugar and the lemon peel strips in a bowl; cover and let stand at room temperature 8 hours or overnight.

**2.** Stir together the rum, cognac, liqueur, tea, and lemon peel mixture in a large bowl until the sugar dissolves. Cover and chill at least 1 hour or overnight. Transfer the mixture to a punch bowl with 1 large ice cube. Serve the punch in Collins glasses filled with ice, and top each with 2 tablespoons mineral water.

*Rooted in Civil War history, the Light Dragoons were an elite cavalry unit made up of some of Charleston, South Carolina's, wealthiest residents. As part of Company K of the Fourth Regiment South Carolina Cavalry, the men had seen considerable action in the field. This recipe is inspired by the potent punch that became a signature of their gatherings following the war.*

*When it comes to bitters, this drink isn't fit without Peychaud's, which was originally marketed as a medicinal tonic by Antoine Peychaud at a New Orleans apothecary in the 1830s. It later found its way to the Sazerac Coffee House where it was mixed with cognac into a cocktail aptly named Sazerac. Though the original included cognac, rye whiskey later replaced it.*

# SAZERAC

*Serves 1    Hands-on 15 minutes    Total 15 minutes, including syrup*

4 tablespoons (2 ounces) good-quality rye whiskey (*such as WhistlePig 10 Year Old Straight Rye Whiskey*)
1 ½ teaspoons (¼ ounce) Rich Cane Syrup (recipe follows)

6 dashes of Peychaud's bitters
1 ½ teaspoons (¼ ounce) absinthe
Lemon twist

Freeze a rocks glass. Fill a mixing glass with ice; add rye whiskey, Rich Cane Syrup, and bitters, and stir until well chilled, about 1 minute. Pour absinthe into prepared rocks glass, and swirl to coat walls of glass; discard excess absinthe. Strain whiskey mixture from mixing glass into rocks glass. Garnish with a lemon twist, if desired.

**RICH CANE SYRUP** Bring 2 cups cane sugar and 1 cup water to a boil in a small saucepan over medium-high, stirring often, until sugar is dissolved. Remove from heat, and stir in 1 tablespoon (½ ounce) Everclear grain alcohol. Store in an airtight container in refrigerator indefinitely. Makes about 2 cups

*The first gin fizz recorded was by Jerry Thomas in the late 1870s. Since then, this refreshing mixture of gin, lemon juice, sugar and carbonated water experienced a varied evolution over the next decade that achieved a level of immortality when Henry Carl Ramos added a bit of orange flower water to the cocktail at his Imperial Cabinet Saloon in New Orleans in 1887. Later came the Diamond Fizz substituting Champagne for sparkling water, and just after Prohibition, a spin-off with Champagne, orange juice, and grenadine came to be known as the Texas Gin Fizz—though connections to anything remotely Texan about the drink have yet to be confirmed. This is the Texas Fizz, which would be nothing if not for Ramos.*

# SPARKLING TEXAS RAMOS GIN FIZZ

*Serves 1     Hands-on 10 minutes*
*Total 10 minutes*

3 tablespoons (1½ ounces) dry gin

2 tablespoons (1 ounce) Hibiscus Grenadine (recipe follows)

1½ teaspoons fresh lime juice (from 1 lime)

2 tablespoons fresh orange juice (from 1 orange)

1 large egg white

2 tablespoons heavy cream

⅛ teaspoon vanilla extract

2 tablespoons (1 ounce) dry sparkling wine or Champagne

⅛ teaspoon orange flower water (optional)

Freeze a Collins glass. Combine the gin, Hibiscus Grenadine, lime juice, orange juice, egg white, heavy cream, and vanilla in a metal cocktail shaker. Do not add ice. Shake vigorously until well blended, about 1 minute. Add ice until filled, and shake until well chilled, about 2 minutes. Strain into prepared Collins glass, and freeze 3 to 4 minutes. Remove from freezer, and top with sparkling wine and, if desired, flower water.

**HIBISCUS GRENADINE** Prepare 1 cup strong hibiscus flower tea (*such as Organically Hip Hibiscus Tea*) according to package directions. Stir 2 cups granulated sugar into hot tea until sugar dissolves. Stir in 1 tablespoon (½ ounce) Everclear grain alcohol, and store in an airtight container in refrigerator indefinitely. Makes 2 cups

# OVERPROOF MARGARITA

*Serves 1     Hands-on 5 minutes     Total 5 minutes*

Considering a basic margarita is a simple three-ingredient cocktail, it's not hard to imagine that it was probably cooked up by a number of different people before it ever became famous. In all likelihood, the Margarita was probably created sometime during Prohibition, when many affluent Americans along the Southwest Border States would head over to Mexico for guilt-free libations along a string of border towns. This elevated version packs quite a punch, but it redefines what a good margarita should be.

3 tablespoons (1½ ounces) overproof tequila (*such as Siembra Valles High Proof or Tapatio Blanco 110*)

1 tablespoon (½ ounce) orange liqueur (*such as Cointreau or Pura Vida Naranja*)

2 tablespoons fresh lime juice (from 1 lime)

1½ teaspoons (¼ ounce) Lime Oleo-Saccharum (recipe follows)

1 large egg white

Combine tequila, orange liqueur, lime juice, and Lime Oleo-Saccharum in a metal cocktail shaker. Lightly whisk egg white until frothy; add half of egg white to metal cocktail shaker, and fill completely with ice. Shake until well chilled, about 1 minute. Do not strain. Pour all contents, including ice, into a rocks glass.

**LIME OLEO-SACCHARUM** *An oleo-saccharum is essentially citrus-oiled sugar that is then used in a simple syrup. It's typically used to provide an elegant, citrusy flavor and aroma to cocktails. It's a great tool to have on hand. Makes about 4 cups*

Zest 12 limes with a Microplane grater to equal ¼ cup; place in a ziplock plastic bag. Add 2 cups granulated sugar to bag; seal and let stand at room temperature 12 hours or overnight. Transfer lime zest mixture to a medium saucepan, and stir in 1 cup water. Cook over medium-high, stirring often, until sugar is fully dissolved, 8 to 10 minutes. Bring to a boil, and remove from heat. Immediately pour through a fine mesh strainer, discarding solids. Let liquid cool 30 minutes. Stir in 1 tablespoon (½ ounce) Everclear grain alcohol, and store in an airtight container in refrigerator indefinitely.

# WEST TEXAS RANCH WATER

*Serves 1     Hands-on 5 minutes     Total 1 hour, 5 minutes*

3 tablespoons (1½ ounces) overproof tequila (*such as Tapatio Blanco 110*)

2 tablespoons fresh lime juice

1 tablespoon (½ ounce) Lime Oleo-Saccharum (page 318)

Sparkling mineral water

Wide grapefruit peel strip

Freeze tequila, and refrigerate lime juice, Lime Oleo-Saccharum, and mineral water at least 1 hour before preparing recipe. Combine tequila, lime juice, and Lime Oleo-Saccharum in a Collins glass, and add ice to fill glass. Gently top with mineral water. Twist grapefruit peel strip over glass, expressing oil into drink; garnish drink with grapefruit peel strip, if desired.

*This unofficial drink of West Texas dive bars and house parties carries a lot of weight in this region of the Lone Star State—particularly for its thirst-quenching abilities in the extreme summer heat. With just the simple flavors of tequila, lime, and orange, this drink makes its splash with the addition of an über-bubbly mineral water like Topo Chico.*

# YOAKUM EGGNOG

*Serves 4 to 6     Hands-on 35 minutes*
*Total 2 hours, 10 minutes, including syrups*

5 large eggs

1 cup (8 ounces) bourbon

½ cup whole buttermilk

1½ cups heavy cream

4 tablespoons Sorghum Vinegar (recipe follows)

4 tablespoons (2 ounces) Corn Husk Simple Syrup (recipe follows)

Ground nutmeg

Chill the first 6 ingredients before preparing recipe. Beat the eggs in a bowl with an electric mixer on medium-high speed 5 minutes. Whisk in the bourbon, buttermilk, cream, vinegar, and simple syrup. Serve with a sprinkle of nutmeg.

**SORGHUM VINEGAR** Combine 4 tablespoons sorghum syrup (*such as Muddy Pond*) and 2 tablespoons cane vinegar (*such as Steen's*) in a small bowl. Store in an airtight container in refrigerator indefinitely. Makes 6 tablespoons

**CORN HUSK SIMPLE SYRUP** Bring 2 cups granulated sugar and 1 cup water to a simmer in a saucepan over medium. Cook, stirring often, until the sugar is dissolved, about 5 minutes. Remove from the heat. Halve 6 dried corn husks, and place in sugar mixture; let steep 30 minutes. Remove husks, squeezing liquid into pan; discard husks. Stir 1 tablespoon (½ ounce) Everclear grain alcohol into sugar mixture, if desired. Store in an airtight container in refrigerator indefinitely. Makes 1½ cups

*Eggnog itself doesn't exactly belong to one region—its origins date back to medieval England. But when it comes to what exactly to put in eggnog, that's where the regionality begins to take hold. Rum was the front-runner for the Atlantic Coast, particularly before the Revolution. But brandy and rye also took a particular stronghold until bourbon entered the scene in the late 1870s. When it comes to modern times, the preference is really up to you. This is an adaptation of a family recipe served in South Central Texas from Houston-based Morgan Weber, restaurateur and beverage director of Agricole Hospitality.*

# DEEP SOUTH PIG PICKIN'

### Deviled Eggs

*(page 90)*

A lunch plate favorite and go-to happy hour nosh, the deviled egg is divine.

### Country Cornbread

*(page 86)*

Born of necessity and a few ingredients, this humble staple has evolved into countless renditions worth taste-driving.

### Rodney Scott's Potato Salad

*(page 107)*

The award-winning pitmaster's stick-to-your ribs side dish deserves star status.

### Grandma Dorothy's Mac 'n' Cheese

*(page 281)*

Comfort food from my husband's grandma's kitchen to yours.

### Wilted Collard Greens

*(page 108)*

The South's favorite cooking green comes with a flavorful potlikker prize.

### Mango-Key Lime Pie

*(page 152)*

Tart Key limes collide with juicy mango in a grand finale that's the ideal tart-sweet palate cleanser.

# DERBY DINNER

## A Proper Mint Julep
*(page 312)*

No Derby party would be complete without Kentucky's iconic sip.

## Kentucky Porch Tea
*(page 313)*

Don't be fooled, this front porch refresher packs a spirited punch.

## Louisville Benedictine
*(page 19)*

This creamy cucumber spread is delicious as a dip or sandwich filler.

## Classic Hot Brown
*(page 54)*

The Brown Hotel's famous sandwich is company-worthy.

## Kentucky Green Beans and Potlikker
*(page 34)*

A low and slow simmer with bacon gives this favorite Southern side the kiss of smoke.

## Kentucky Bourbon Butter Cake
*(page 68)*

Bourbon gives this decadent butter cake a delicious depth of flavor.

# TAILGATE

### Light Dragoon Punch

*(page 315)*

Truth be told, there's nothing
light about this potent punch.
Drinker beware!

### Boiled Peanuts

*(page 94)*

Green goobers, simmered for hours,
remain a revered Southern snack.

### Slow-Cooker Pulled Pork
### on slider buns

*(page 57)*

A bit of the pig, sauced and sandwiched, is
an enduring game day crowd-pleaser.

### Memphis Barbecue Sauce

*(page 100)*

Tomato-meets-vinegar zing
makes this classic 'cue sauce
pork's best friend.

### Creamy Coleslaw

*(page 61)*

Tangy and cool, coleslaw provides
balance to any barbecue plate.

### Moon Pies

*(page 242)*

This iconic Chattanooga
sweet is a Southern favorite
that's easy to make.

# MIXED FRY

### Crispy Fried Pickles with ranch dressing

*(page 259)*

If you've ever heard that if it tastes good, it'll taste better fried...
well, the proof's in this pickle.

### Skillet Fried Okra

*(page 33)*

Crunchy, crispy, and addictive, this is a winning way to serve the South's favorite pod.

### Texas Coleslaw

*(page 61)*

The heat of a fresh chile, brightness of lime, and cilantro's distinctive flavor note leave no doubt where this slaw was born.

### Summer Squash-Rice Gratin

*(page 115)*

Casseroles are king when it comes to feeding a crowd and this hearty bake spotlights a summer bumper crop.

### Fried Catfish with Mississippi Comeback Sauce

*(pages 226–227)*

Consider this sauce a marriage of tartar sauce and rémoulade guaranteed to make guests come back for seconds.

### Hush Puppies and Tartar Sauce

*(page 128)*

No fish fry is complete without these bready bite-size fritters hot from the fryer.

# METRIC EQUIVALENTS

The information in the following chart is provided to help cooks outside the United States successfully use the recipes in this book. All equivalents are approximate.

## COOKING/OVEN TEMPERATURES

|  | Fahrenheit | Celsius | Gas Mark |
|---|---|---|---|
| Freeze Water | 32° F | 0° C | |
| Room Temp. | 68° F | 20° C | |
| Boil Water | 212° F | 100° C | |
| Bake | 325° F | 160° C | 3 |
| | 350° F | 180° C | 4 |
| | 375° F | 190° C | 5 |
| | 400° F | 200° C | 6 |
| | 425° F | 220° C | 7 |
| | 450° F | 230° C | 8 |
| Broil | | | Grill |

## LIQUID INGREDIENTS BY VOLUME

| | | | | | |
|---|---|---|---|---|---|
| ¼ tsp | | | | = | 1 ml |
| ½ tsp | | | | = | 2 ml |
| 1 tsp | | | | = | 5 ml |
| 3 tsp | = | 1 Tbsp | = ½ fl oz | = | 15 ml |
| 2 Tbsp | = | ⅛ cup | = 1 fl oz | = | 30 ml |
| 4 Tbsp | = | ¼ cup | = 2 fl oz | = | 60 ml |
| 5⅓ Tbsp | = | ⅓ cup | = 3 fl oz | = | 80 ml |
| 8 Tbsp | = | ½ cup | = 4 fl oz | = | 120 ml |
| 10⅔ Tbsp | = | ⅔ cup | = 5 fl oz | = | 160 ml |
| 12 Tbsp | = | ¾ cup | = 6 fl oz | = | 180 ml |
| 16 Tbsp | = | 1 cup | = 8 fl oz | = | 240 ml |
| 1 pt | = | 2 cups | = 16 fl oz | = | 480 ml |
| 1 qt | = | 4 cups | = 32 fl oz | = | 960 ml |
| | | | 33 fl oz | = | 1000 ml = 1 l |

## DRY INGREDIENTS BY WEIGHT

(To convert ounces to grams, multiply the number of ounces by 30.)

| | | | | |
|---|---|---|---|---|
| 1 oz | = | 1/16 lb | = | 30 g |
| 4 oz | = | ¼ lb | = | 120 g |
| 8 oz | - | ½ lb | - | 240 g |
| 12 oz | = | ¾ lb | = | 360 g |
| 16 oz | = | 1 lb | = | 480 g |

## LENGTH

(To convert inches to centimeters, multiply inches by 2.5.)

| | | | | | | |
|---|---|---|---|---|---|---|
| 1 in | | | | = | 2.5 cm | |
| 12 in | = | 1 ft | | = | 30 cm | |
| 36 in | = | 3 ft | = 1 yd | = | 90 cm | |
| 40 in | = | | | | 100 cm | = 1 m |

## EQUIVALENTS FOR DIFFERENT TYPES OF INGREDIENTS

| Standard Cup | Fine Powder (ex. flour) | Grain (ex. rice) | Granular (ex. sugar) | Liquid Solids (ex. butter) | Liquid (ex. milk) |
|---|---|---|---|---|---|
| 1 | 140 g | 150 g | 190 g | 200 g | 240 ml |
| ¾ | 105 g | 113 g | 143 g | 150 g | 180 ml |
| ⅔ | 93 g | 100 g | 125 g | 133 g | 160 ml |
| ½ | 70 g | 75 g | 95 g | 100 g | 120 ml |
| ⅓ | 47 g | 50 g | 63 g | 67 g | 80 ml |
| ¼ | 35 g | 38 g | 48 g | 50 g | 60 ml |
| ⅛ | 18 g | 19 g | 24 g | 25 g | 30 ml |

## ACKNOWLEDGMENTS

If it weren't for God and his divine providence in letting me be born in a part of the South, I'm not sure I could have done this book proper justice, so I'll begin my deepest thanks with Him.

I'd like to thank my editor, Katherine Cobbs, who championed this project from its infancy and who is easily one of my favorite people to work with. May there be many more collaborations in our future. I'm deeply grateful for the many chefs who you'll find spotlighted in this book along with others including Sean Brock, Matt and Ted Lee, John T. Edge, Morgan Weber, Jack Gilmore, and the late Bill Neal, John Egerton, and Helen Corbitt for carrying the torch for Southern food and the rich history behind its flavors.

Many thanks to my team of recipe testers who were willing to take on a few new challenges, including my mom, Janice Stewart; my husband, Myers Dupuy; my kids, Gus and Ashlyn Dupuy; Sibby Barrett; Brenda Metro; Lisa Baker; Dana Stewart; and Stacy Hollister. Your tasting notes helped make this book a reality.

To my dad, for teaching me that you don't have to be a chef to be a great cook.

To my grandmothers, Joyce Stewart and Marian Norman, for giving me that little taste of the South from their mothers and grandmothers.

To the many friends and family with roots spread deep throughout the various regions of the South for recipes and insight on what matters most, including Fritzi Dupuy, Dane Dupuy, Jamie Hancock, Bridget Buck, Johnny Fred, Elizabeth Hogue, Michael Clarke, Dana and Craig Doerksen, Dee and John Clarke, Denise Clarke, Joshua Thomas, Jan Heaton, Martha Lynn Kale, and Kat Todd.

To my agent, David Hale Smith, for his wisdom and support, and to Martha Hopkins, who got this ball rolling for me and deserves a long overdue note of thanks.

## WORKS CONSULTED

Alfred A. Knopf, Inc.: *Biscuits, Spoonbread, and Sweet Potato Pie* by Bill Neal. Copyright ©1990 Alfred A. Knopf, Inc.

Artisan: *Frank Stitt's Southern Table* by Frank Stitt. Copyright ©2004 Artisan.

Gibbs-Smith Books: *Mastering the Art of Southern Cooking* by Nathalie Dupree and Cynthia Graubart. Copyright ©2012 Gibbs-Smith Books.

Little, Brown and Company: *Deep Run Roots* by Vivian Howard. Copyright ©2016 Little, Brown and Company.

Peachtree Publishers, LTD.: *Side Orders: Small Helpings of Southern Cookery & Culture* by John Egerton. Copyright ©1990 Peachtree Publishers, LTD.

Ten Speed Press: *Big Bad Breakfast* by John Currence. Copyright ©2016 Ten Speed Press.

Ten Speed Press: *The Tex-Mex Cookbook* by Robb Walsh. Copyright ©2004 Ten Speed Press.

Ten Speed Press: *Southern Spirits* by Robert Moss. Copyright ©2016 Ten Speed Press.

University of North Carolina Press: *Southern Food At Home, On the Road, In History* by John Egerton. Copyright ©1993 University of North Carolina Press.

University of North Carolina Press: *Bill Neal's Southern Cooking* by Bill Neal. Copyright ©1985 University of North Carolina Press.

University of North Carolina Press: *The New Southern Garden Cookbook: Enjoying the Best from Homegrown Gardens, Farmers' Markets, Roadside Stands, and CSA Farm Boxes* by Sheri Castle. Copyright © 2011 University of North Carolina Press.

University of South Carolina Press: *The Carolina Housewife* by Sarah Rutledge. (A Facsimile of the 1847 Edition, With an Introduction and a Preliminary Checklist of South Carolina Cookbooks Published before 1935 by Anna Wells Rutledge.) Copyright ©1979 University of South Carolina Press.

BLACKBOTTOM
BUTTERMILK PIE,
PG 69

"*One place understood helps us understand all places better.*"

**—EUDORA WELTY**